THE REIGN OF
EDWARD IV

ERIC N. SIMONS

BARNES & NOBLE, Inc.
NEW YORK
PUBLISHERS & BOOKSELLERS SINCE 1873

First published in Great Britain 1966 by
Frederick Muller Limited
First published in the United States 1966 by
Barnes & Noble, Inc., New York, N.Y.

Manufactured in Great Britain

Dedicated once again to
Lily, Wife and Comrade

CONTENTS

LIST OF ILLUSTRATIONS

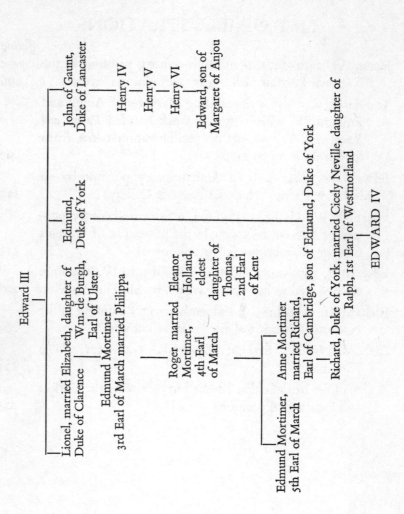

Edward III

Lionel, married Elizabeth, daughter of Wm. de Burgh, Earl of Ulster

Edmund Mortimer 3rd Earl of March married Philippa

Roger married Eleanor Holland, eldest daughter of Thomas, 2nd Earl of Kent
Mortimer, 4th Earl of March

Edmund Mortimer, 5th Earl of March

Anne Mortimer married Richard, Earl of Cambridge, son of Edmund, Duke of York

Edmund, Duke of York

Richard, Duke of York, married Cicely Neville, daughter of Ralph, 1st Earl of Westmorland

EDWARD IV

John of Gaunt, Duke of Lancaster

Henry IV

Henry V

Henry VI

Edward, son of Margaret of Anjou

PREFACE

EDWARD IV was a remarkable king, much more so in my view than many who have been more frequently studied. In this book I have presented him and his deeds as I see them. It is nearly fifty years since he was extensively treated, and much has happened since then to change our outlook on him and his period. If my assessment of his character and reign reflect to some extent a modern view, this is no indication of perversity or aberration.

I have tried to tell his story simply and clearly, but I must make it clear that my aim has been not primarily to satisfy or appease the erudite, but to paint a broad, convincing and, I hope, readable picture of a somewhat neglected royal personage. At times, therefore, I have used the brush rather than the slide rule. However, the reader plunged suddenly and unprepared into the struggles and events of the reign of Edward IV must feel much as a latecomer to a play, who, having missed the first act, is hampered by not knowing what has gone before. I have therefore opened this book with a Prologue which briefly condenses the history of England during the hundred years or so before Edward was born. This can be skipped if desired, or may be used merely as a reference should any point in the story seem obscure.

My geographer son, Martin Simons, B.Sc., has put me in his debt by supplying the sketch maps of the battle of Barnet, and making perspicuous comments on the topography of the battlefield. I have myself visited most of the principal battlefields mentioned in this account.

I am indebted also to Miss Aileen Carpenter for so clearly indicating the relation between the modern roads around Barnet and those of Edward's day. Miss L. V. Paulin is responsible for useful information concerning the obelisk commemorating the supposed site of the Barnet affray, for which I thank her. Mme. la Directrice of the Library of Rouen has furnished notes on the celebrated castle of that city and bibliographical references to it, which I here acknowledge. Lastly, I must once again thank my wife for her intelligent study of the text, and for her comments and criticisms, as well as for reading the proofs.

Eric N. Simons.

Westham, Sussex, 1965.

PROLOGUE: 1337-1452

THE PERIOD preceding the advent of Edward IV may be regarded as beginning with the Hundred Years War between England and France. Essentially this was a struggle of ambitious, greedy and small-minded English monarchs for territory that did not belong to them. It fluctuated according to the characters, resources and fortunes of the particular kings, and began roughly about the year 1337.

War had been going on intermittently between these two powers or groups of powers ever since the Norman Conquest. Great slabs of France had been temporarily conquered and held by the English, one of them being the province of Guienne, an old duchy in the region of Bordeaux. Another was Bayonne. While the rule of the Kings of England penetrated deep into the neighbouring river valleys, the French King of the period, Philip VI, resented these foreign enclaves as our own kings would have resented a permanent French occupation of, for example, Devon, Hereford, Monmouth and areas on the banks of the Severn.

The French attempted to break the hold of their rivals either by armed conflict, or, where this was inadvisable, by the subtler process of infiltration. Areas held by the English were quietly reoccupied by unauthorized settlers, and when disputes over ownership flared up as these infiltrations were discovered, the rival contenders, who had often come to blows, were called to the capital, Paris, where the law was often twisted and bent to the advantage of the native claimants.

Nevertheless, apart from these minor annexations, the English grip remained largely secure because the people of the conquered districts were not French, but Gascons, and were as hostile to French rule as the Welsh to the English. This was particularly true of Guienne, whose Duke, owing allegiance to the King of England,

13

knew the feelings of his subjects and made no effort to free himself from alien dominion.

The explanation was not merely the difference of race. It rarely is. There was marked advantage in being governed by England, for trade between the English and their lands in France was extensive and profitable to both parties. Moreover, the English were easier-going, less autocratic, interfered less with private lives, and above all, taxed the Guiennese less heavily, than the French had been accustomed to do.

This does not mean that the French found no support at all in their former territories. Some of the Guiennese nobles had reasons of their own for siding with them, and did what they could in a quiet way to prise up the royal English fingers grasping their corners of France.

Away to the north of Britain was another troublesome nation, the Scots, whose leader, David Bruce, expelled by the English King, had been greatly assisted by Philip VI, so that Edward III, annoyed, retaliated by offering hospitality and a generous welcome to Robert, Count of Artois, whom Philip had forced to leave France. At the same time, Edward solicited and found friends and allies in the border regions of France as the first stage in preparing a revenge. For example, provincial potentates in the Low Countries as well as the Emperor of Bavaria united with him in a pact designed to threaten the French should they attempt to cause trouble.

Whether Edward meant to make war is uncertain. At all events it was not he who struck the first blow, which was entirely the doing of Philip, who without warning suddenly claimed all the English possessions in his country, and particularly Guienne. He followed up this audacious claim by sending raiding parties to sack southern English seacoast towns and villages. The date of these attacks was 1337, and they marked the beginning of desperate struggles extending over a century and more.

The one obvious reply for the English was a counterclaim, Edward III's was a bold one. He declared himself King of France, supporting this by the argument that Isabella, his mother, was closer in kinship to the last Capet king (the Capets were the main royal stock) than the Valois, Philip. Isabella was the previous French king's sister, whereas Philip was but his cousin. The claim had no genuine basis, for there were strong legal arguments to the contrary, into which it would be tedious to enter. However, the claim infuriated Philip, as it was meant to do.

This is not to say that Edward derived no advantages from putting forward his claim. All those subject peoples under the French crown could now, with some justification, however doubtful in law, transfer their allegiance to Edward. The Flemings, for example, were already united by strong commercial ties to this island, and went over without hesitation to the English, providing henceforward a stout body of supporters for Edward III in the Low Countries.

Again, those minor princes who resented having to pay homage to Philip could break their feudal ties at last on the pretence that they no longer owed loyalty to him, but to the true King, Edward III. It was also possible for Edward to regard those inhabitants of France who remained faithful to Philip as "traitors", and on occasion he did in fact take advantage of this. Yet he did not genuinely believe in his own claim, for during the years that followed he more than once offered to abandon it for more land or cash. The claim, however, became an established factor in English politics, and was handed on to successive rulers, with the result that bloodshed, hatred and misery lasting for decades ruined the relations of these two great peoples.

For Edward and Philip, however, the inevitable upshot was war, whose course space does not allow us to follow in any detail. In its early stages it brought no great credit to English generalship. Aided by their allies in the Low Countries the English sought to penetrate the northern areas of France, but though the Netherlands princes were willing, the flesh of their subjects was weak, and presently they marched off home, leaving Edward's men stranded. The campaigns were extremely costly, and although a big naval battle at Sluys was won in 1340, no military advantage could be taken of it. Indeed, the King had to bring his army home because, in homely language, he was "broke".

In the vain endeavour to extract from Parliament the money with which to resume the fight, he quarrelled with his ministers, and in 1345 became a financial defaulter, repudiating his debts and ruining the Italian bankers who had lent him money. The friendly Flemings also suffered heavy financial loss.

The retreat of the English army brought no great relief to Philip. Trouble came to him now from a different quarter. John of Montfort, claiming the French throne in his turn, began an armed insurrection in Brittany, and Edward with curious inconsistency supported him, landing men in Brittany and being allowed to occupy some of its most powerful strongholds.

However, his military efforts failed, largely because he again relied too greatly on his allies.

No English king could afford continuous failure, and therefore in the following year he set foot once more on the European continent, landing this time in Normandy. It was not a true invasion but rather a raid in force, but it took the French by surprise. Laying the country waste as they went, this purely English army almost took Paris, but like hornets whose nest is assailed, the French recovered their nerve and swarmed to the attack. Taking fright, Edward retreated, hoping to elude them and escape to the Low Countries, but having crossed the Somme, he changed his mind, and at Crécy awaited the onslaught of an army four times as great as his own.

The result was a magnificent victory. Moving back towards the coast unhindered, the English besieged Calais, which, after nearly a year of resistance, surrendered, having been left by the frightened Philip to its fate. It was to remain in English hands for 200 years, and gave Edward his first permanent harbour and jumping-off ground in northern France, one moreover directly and conveniently opposite to his own port of Dover.

After further land victories and a defeat of the Scots, a truce followed, largely imposed on the English by the depletion of their exchequer and a terrible outbreak of bubonic plague known as "the Black Death", which also ravaged the populations of Asia and Europe, and persisted till 1350. Its effect in England was a vast decline in the number of agricultural labourers. Bitter disputes broke out between the landlords or lords of the manor and the villeins or landless men. The shortage of farmhands enabled them to claim higher wages, and when the lords refused to pay these, violent conflicts occurred, lasting intermittently for thirty years.

During 1351 Parliament passed a Statute of Labourers which sought to peg the wages of hired men to what they had been before the plague, but however hard they tried, the Government could not enforce the law, which the labourers circumvented by leaving their native districts and selling their services wherever they could command a higher wage.

Gradually the manorial system whereby farms were cultivated by forced labour was abandoned. Instead, the land was parcelled out into small holdings rented by "farmers". This new system was not introduced by a stroke of the pen, but slowly made its way into general acceptance. For decades peasants and landlords disputed, until in the end there came into being as a permanent feature of English life the yeoman farmer class, whose sterling qualities were to benefit the country for many generations.

The truce between England and France lasted for eight years, with occasional skirmishes to relieve the monotony. In 1350, John succeeding Philip VI, occupied the throne of France, and the war came to life again. The young Black Prince, son of Edward III, conquered great areas of France, and in 1356 came the battle of Poitiers, where the superiority of the English long-bowmen, combined with strategic opportunism, resulted in the French King being captured. After further English successes, which brought them to the gates of Paris, the French, under John's son, the Dauphin, gave in, and a peace treaty was signed in October, 1360.

John's ransom was fixed at three million gold crowns, huge slices of France were handed over to the English, to be held "in perpetuity and in the manner in which the Kings of France had held them". In return for these acquisitions, Edward III forfeited his claim to the kingship of France. At about the same period he made a satisfactory treaty of peace with the Scots.

The French peace lasted a mere nine years. The young Black Prince, virtually King of all France south of the Loire, made the mistake of marching into Spain with an army designed to restore the exiled King Peter of Castile to his throne. He won his battle, but the restored monarch, a monster of ingratitude, left him to meet the entire cost of the campaign. To pay his grumbling soldiers the Prince had to impose new taxes on his French subjects, who

2

rebelling, appealed to the new King, Charles V (John having died in 1364). Charles took advantage of this discontent to tear up his treaty with the English on a feeble pretext. In consequence war was renewed.

During the intervening period England had greatly benefited by the cessation of armed conflict. Her manufacturing industry increased in importance, her towns enlarged, subtracting masses of new "hands" for their looms and benches from the underpaid rural communities. The Flemings, invited to England by Edward, had already established a valuable weaving industry, and were using the ample wool of the country to produce a magnificent cloth. Shipbuilding had recovered, and English vessels were taking cargoes into many foreign ports. In 1343 a gold currency based on the "noble" was introduced for the first time, replacing silver, and gold coinage came into general use throughout Europe. Merchant traders were rising slowly to fortune, and a middle class of manufacturers and merchants was developing at the expense of the landowners.

Charles's denunciation of the peace treaty enabled Edward to reassert his claim to the throne of France, but Charles retaliated by announcing his sovereignty over all the lands occupied by the English in his country.

During the treaty period Edward had become what was, for that day, an old man of 57. The Black Prince, disease-ridden, could no longer lead an army in the field. The English forces were therefore entrusted to John of Gaunt, Duke of Lancaster, a general rash, stubborn and lacking in foresight, with singularly poor judgment of men. He had as his opponent one of the greater military commanders of all time, the celebrated Bertrand du Guesclin, who allowed the Englishman to cart his footsore men around the country destroying much but achieving nothing, while du Guesclin harassed them from the rear, cutting off and killing laggards, slaying isolated parties and encouraging the inhabitants of the conquered provinces to rise.

In desperation the Black Prince rose from his sick bed, took the field, and in 1370 recaptured Limoges, which he so savagely pillaged that the surrounding areas flamed with rage. It was the Prince's last battle, and soon afterwards he returned to England.

Two years later the French found invaluable allies in the Spaniards. Peter of Castile had been killed by his rival, who had never forgotten his defeat by the Black Prince and remained his undying enemy. The combined fleets of these two countries smashed an English convoy bringing reinforcements of all kinds, regained control of the narrow seas, and tormented the southern shores of England by constant and destructive raids. Du Guesclin threw John de Montfort out of Brittany, and by 1374 England was left with only Calais and a thin stretch of the Atlantic coast between Bordeaux and Bayonne. In 1375 Edward sought peace, but all he got was a truce.

The terrible disasters which had befallen English arms were attributed entirely to John of Gaunt, Duke of Lancaster, and none were more critical of him than Edmund Mortimer, Earl of March. (The March was the border area between England and Wales.) Space allows of only a brief mention of the Wycliffe agitation against the Papacy, but because among the leading opponents of John of Gaunt were many of the established clergy, it was not surprising that for a time Gaunt and Wycliffe became uneasy allies.

In 1376 John of Gaunt exiled the Earl of March and dismissed his opponents, taking over supreme control. In that same year the Black Prince died, his father dying shortly after him. It was feared that John would seize the throne for himself, but he acknowledged the Black Prince's son, Richard, as King Richard II. Just before Edward III died, the Hundred Years War was resumed, the French landed in Sussex, and putting Rye and Hastings to sack, burned many houses and defeated the scratch force sent to resist them.

Throughout the reign of Richard II one military disaster followed another, armies landing in France but achieving enormous expenditure for no result but defeat. Consequently, taxes once more weighed heavily on the people, and in 1381 they rose in revolt under Wat Tyler, who for a time threatened the land, but was assassinated by the Mayor of London, William Walworth.

In 1380 Charles V and his great commander, du Guesclin, died. Richard II was no longer a boy under the thumb of elder statesmen and began to take the reins into his own hands. He made many errors of judgment, and in 1387 civil strife broke out, the King being placed under the control of a council of lords. His favourite ministers were either executed or forced to fly the country.

The years passed. Richard, outwardly submissive, secretly planned revenge, which he took in 1397, executing one great noble, imprisoning another and banishing two more, one of them being Henry of Bolingbroke, son of John of Gaunt.

Now unchallenged in authority, and drunk, if not maddened, with power, Richard fined heavily all who had aided his enemies, borrowed and recklessly wasted great sums of money, threw people into jail, kept them there without trial, and bullied Parliament into handing over its authority to a junta of ten lickspittles of his own choice. The traditional freedoms of the English were thus at a blow filched from them.

His cousin, the 4th Earl of March, son of the House of Mortimer, was an ancestor of Edward IV. Heir-presumptive to the throne, he was made Lord Lieutenant of Ireland, but achieved little against that turbulent, ever-rebellious people, and was killed in battle. In 1399 to avenge him Richard himself invaded Ireland with a large army.

It was always dangerous for an English king, especially a tyrannical one, to leave his own country. Seizing his opportunity the exiled Henry of Bolingbroke, John of Gaunt having died, set an example for Edward IV by coming ashore at Ravenspur on the east coast, bringing with him a body of supporters, many of whom had been, like himself, unjustly exiled. He brought also a band of professional soldiers hired to fight for him. Again affording an example followed later by Edward IV, he declared that he had come only to resume the possessions, lands and title of his dead father.

This army, led by a man against whom they had no enmity, was just what the bitter, humiliated, rageful victims of Richard II needed. They flocked to Bolingbroke's standard. Troops sent to oppose went over to him as a man, and by July he controlled the entire kingdom. Richard came racing back with his army, but the news he received on landing so terrified him that instead of marching bravely on London, he stole away from his own soldiers in the darkness like a guilty man, and took refuge in the hills of Wales. After three weeks of this he had had enough, giving himself up on condition that he should be allowed to live, be pensioned, and his friends be granted pardon.

Promptly Bolingbroke picked up and put on Richard's abandoned crown. None gainsaying him, he was crowned in October, 1399, as Henry IV. Richard's folly in trusting him was soon exposed, for he was thrown into prison without even reasonable treatment, and his friends were attainted, though allowed to live.

Legally Henry's right to the throne was invalid. Edmund, the young son of the 4th Earl of March, had the better title, and in consequence a considerable body of Englishmen whose estates had been forfeited opposed the new King. The reprieved friends of the captive Richard (who died in February, 1400, from deliberate deprivation of the necessities of life) rose prematurely in revolt, proclaiming him King. They seized Windsor Castle, where Henry was living, but escaping, he quickly mustered his supporters and defeated the rebels at Cirencester. The death of Richard following upon this meant that his prisoner could no longer serve as a focus of rebellion.

The Welsh had always favoured the dead monarch, and under Owen Glendower, a chieftain of the old royal blood of Wales, they rose to claim their independence, hailing Glendower as their Prince. Henry twice led a force against them, but the Welshmen and their leader, refusing to meet him in pitched battle, harried him mercilessly from their strongholds in the mountains and led him on a wild goose chase up and down the valleys, until he had to abandon the campaign for lack of supplies.

The King's difficulties were the signal for his enemies to stir again. The country, groaning under taxes heavier than ever, was weary of bloodshed. The Scots decided their chance had come, and attacked, but even more serious than this was the great ambush in which Glendower trapped the border knights and their troops, many of whom were killed, while young Edmund March's uncle and guardian, Sir Edmund Mortimer, was captured.

Harry Hotspur and the Earl of Northumberland, his father, smashed the Scottish army at Homildon Hill, but quarrelled with the King over who had the better right to the ransom of the captured Scottish nobles. The outcome was a new rising in 1403, when Glendower thrust deep into South Wales. Northumberland

brought out the north, while Hotspur and Earl Douglas of Scotland moved into Cheshire, which supported them, aiming to link
up with the Welsh, and were joined there by the Earl of Worcester.
The designed union with Glendower was, however, prevented
by Henry's prompt countermeasures. He and his son, Harry of
Monmouth, caught the advancing forces of Hotspur outside
Shrewsbury and overcame them after a fierce contest marked by
the great valour and initiative of the young Prince. Hotspur was
killed, Worcester captured and Douglas badly wounded. Northumberland at once begged for mercy, which was granted, but he
was compelled to pay a heavy fine and give up all his fortresses.

The French profited by the obvious weakness of the new English régime. One of their land forces penetrated into Guienne,
while their navy raided the south-west coast of England, setting
Plymouth on fire. Another convoy arrived in Welsh harbours
with munitions and supplies for Glendower, who now controlled
virtually the whole of Wales.

Badly in need of money to pay for his defence of the country,
Henry found Parliament and his ministers ill-disposed to grant it
to him. He quarrelled with the ministers, and lost his argument
with the Parliament. Eventually he was constrained to knuckle
under. The taxes for continuation of the war no longer poured
direct into his gaping pockets, but were collected by a special
commission of finance appointed by the Parliament, and in
addition his own private expenses had to be considerably reduced.

Even this did not bring internal peace because the treacherous
Northumberland rose again in 1405, aided by the Earl Marshal,
Thomas Mowbray, and Scrope, Archbishop of York. This rising
was broken when the two accomplices were dishonourably captured by the Earl of Westmorland, who had invited them to a
meeting. Westmorland sent the captives on to the King, who had
them executed without trial outside York. Northumberland took
refuge in Scotland, but in 1408 was killed in a final struggle at
Bramham Moor.

Meantime Harry of Monmouth was proving himself a brilliant
soldier. Slowly but surely he broke Glendower's grip on Wales
until, by 1408, he had taken Harlech, the last great hostile fortress,
manned by the Welsh, but defended by Sir Edmund Mortimer,

who had married Glendower's daughter, and died of starvation as a result of the siege. Glendower was driven back into his mountains, whence he kept up a hostility that achieved little, but lasted till his death in 1416.

In France also the position improved. The French themselves were afflicted by ferocious civil wars, losing interest for the time being in England and her possessions inside their borders. The Scots were quiet, too, the heir to their throne having been seized in 1406 by English ships and kept as a prisoner guest at Windsor. For five years Henry knew peace, but a worse enemy than even civil strife robbed him of joy. After 1409 it became manifest that the dread disease of leprosy was permanently disabling him so that he could no longer play an active part in the administration of his kingdom.

His feebleness plunged England once more into civil dissension, which arose between the Prince of Wales (Harry of Monmouth) and Archbishop Arundel, the Chancellor. Both had strong supporters. The Prince, though admirable in the field, was not esteemed as a statesman at Court, where he offended many by his pride, quarrelsome character and riotous conduct, which gave Shakespeare the opportunity to write a magnificent play. Indeed, it was widely believed, and probably true, that he wished and urged his father to abdicate in his favour, but the sick Henry would have none of this.

Harry's thirst for glory caused him, therefore, to turn an aggressive eye on France, and in this he and the Chancellor were for once in agreement. He sent a detachment to help the Burgundians, who were undergoing siege in Paris, and with this assistance they broke the ring around them and relieved the capital. In the following year he and the Chancellor sent another army under the Duke of Clarence to help the Duke of Orleans, but the French bribed the English Duke with 210,000 gold crowns to leave without fighting, and he came home.

Henry IV died in 1413, and the new King, Henry V, came to the throne on a rising tide of popularity and with no immediate rival to worry him. During these years the young Earl of March had grown up, but seemed to cherish no aspiration towards the crown. On assuming power, Henry V was quick to appreciate his new responsibilities, abandoning with surprising determination the loose living and arrogance that had earlier tainted his behaviour. He governed wisely and well, but his devotion to the religion of his fathers caused him to persecute the Lollards, who at one time planned to murder him, but were prevented.

As the French had not hesitated to take advantage of England's internal troubles, Henry now took advantage of theirs. The faction and strife across the Channel made a rich and healthy soil in which to plant a new claim to all the territory wrested from Edward III. If these lands were not restored, he declared, he would invade. The French rejected this open blackmail, but instead offered him Katharine, the daughter of Charles VI, as a wife, and promised she should bring him a "dot" of 800,000 crowns as well as a couple of rich provinces.

Henry, however, had his mind firmly fixed on war, and refusing all bribes, prepared in 1415 to sail with a small body of hardy warriors. Just before they sailed, however, the unadventurous Earl of March revealed to him that he had been approached by dissidents and invited to head a rising in Wales and the north, but had refused. This conspiracy was quickly crushed.

The King's new military venture was rash and invited disaster, but he was saved by a remarkable victory against great odds won at Agincourt. In appearance the contest was one-sided and hopeless, for the English were vastly outnumbered and badly weakened by disease. Their victory was essentially a triumph for their weapons and tactics. The light English archers mowed down the horsemen of the French, who weighed down by their armour were pinned in the mud of the soft marshy land on which the battle was fought. Nevertheless, being too weak, Henry could do nothing with his victory, and had to withdraw to England with the port of Harfleur as the only substantial reward for his pains. The Burgundians, who had previously undertaken not to oppose him, were, however, confirmed in their opinion that they had been wise, which was one advantage afforded by his triumph.

In 1417 the King returned to France, this time at the head of a much stronger force, and slowly but methodically won and consolidated position after position, until in 1418 he sat down before the fine old city of Rouen, which after brave resistance capitulated in January, 1419. The Burgundians asked Henry to ally with them against the Dauphin, Charles, but their efforts were unsuccessful, the terms Henry asked being too high. In September, however, the Duke of Burgundy was murdered in cold blood by the Dauphin. The enraged Burgundians not only offered a lasting peace to the English King, but also consented to admit his right to the crown of France if he would strengthen his claim by marrying Katharine, and agree to preserve their freedoms. Charles VI who had lost his reason, was to remain King while ever he lived, Henry, however, being acknowledged as his heir.

These terms were to the liking of the English King, who accordingly married Katharine and carried on the fight against the Dauphin. In August, 1422, however, he died of dysentery caught while besieging a French stronghold, and his infant son, Henry, aged two, became King as Henry VI.

These years of fighting had crippled France, bankrupted England, and led to the moral disintegration of her governing class. Two nobles, the Dukes of Bedford and Gloucester, assumed power as the infant King's guardians. Bedford was appointed Regent, and joined with Burgundy in prosecuting the French war, he having married the sister of the young Duke Philip of Burgundy. As Charles VI had died shortly after Henry V, Henry VI, the successor to the English throne, became nominally King of France also, and Bedford claimed the French throne on his behalf. Gloucester had charge of the child himself.

For the next twenty years these two peers and other statesmen bickered with one another. Bedford fought well in France, but Gloucester alienated the Burgundians by supporting his wife's claim to estates in the Duchy. She was a cousin of the Burgundian Duke. The Burgundians in consequence deserted Bedford, but he won back their regard and support by proving his innocence of the Gloucester intrigue.

The war went on, and Bedford came at length to the very gates of Orleans. Everywhere defeated and driven back, Charles VII, the former Dauphin, lost heart and would have fled the country but for the astounding feats of Jeanne d'Arc, who breathed new fire into the hearts of the French soldiers, and first relieving Orleans, inspired both generals and men, who believed her heaven-sent.

They beat back the English. In vain Bedford brought Henry VI to Paris and had him crowned there, for in 1435 the Burgundians, war-weary, rejoined the French, who offered England their friendship in exchange for the departure of their armies. Bedford died, but the English refused this offer. No longer led by a general so able as the dead Duke, however, they lost Paris and part of Normandy, and the Burgundians besieged Calais.

A new figure now appeared on the scene—Richard, Duke of York, heir of the House of Mortimer, born in 1411, who saved the port and regained much of the lost Norman territory. He held on firmly to what remained of the English possessions in France till at last, in 1444, a two-year truce was signed. Henry VI was formally betrothed to Margaret of Anjou, niece of Charles VI, but the signing of a firm peace was deferred till he formally abandoned his claim to the French crown.

Though Henry VI presently married Margaret, he gave no sign of possessing will, intelligence or anything other than piety. He was now 23. England resented the uneasy truce, and the King's two ministers, the Dukes of Suffolk and Somerset, were openly censured by the Duke of Gloucester. This brought down upon him the anger of the Queen, who relied upon her two advisers. Gloucester was imprisoned and probably put to death, though it was pretended that he had died of apoplexy.

The two countries flew at one another's throats again in 1449, both sides being guilty of breaches of the peace. France attacked Normandy, defeated the incompetent Duke of Somerset, who had now taken over command of the English in France, and also smashed an expedition sent to reinforce him in 1450. In the general consternation and dismay Suffolk was impeached and banished, being murdered at sea on his way over. Jack Cade, said by some to be a Mortimer and to have been instigated by the Duke of York, headed a rebellion in Kent which took London for three days and almost succeeded, but he was caught and killed.

Presently the discontent prevalent throughout the country was brought to a head by York, first prince of the blood royal, and a great grandson of Edward III, who had a legitimate claim to the throne, as is shown by the previous genealogical table. On the death of his uncle, Earl of March, in 1424, he became heir to his mother's enormous wealth and estates, and acquired great influence.

From his arrival on the political scene the events related in the main text and also the Wars of the Roses followed. At the outset, however, York does not appear to have coveted the crown, and his first insubordination was primarily caused by his conviction that the removal of the incompetent, blundering Somerset was essential. He was forced into self-assertion also largely by the hostility to him of the childless Queen and an injudicious advocacy of his claims by over-enthusiastic partisans, who detested Somerset and feared his known cruelty. Indeed, so little was York responsible for these machinations that for several years he did not formally claim the succession.

It will be seen, however, that as a direct descendant of an elder son of Edward III, his claim to the crown was superior to that of Henry VI and his future descendant. The above table does not, of course, include Lionel's elder brothers, the Black Prince, father of Richard II, and William of Hatfield, who died young.

So we take up the story in the year 1442 with the birth of his second son in the ancient castle of Rouen.

ONE

1442 - 1460

[1]

IN THE CASTLE of Rouen, which was to be destroyed by gunfire in 1590, a woman lay in her bed—Cicely Neville, wife of Richard, Duke of York, daughter of Ralph Neville, first Earl of Westmorland, and sister of the Earl of Salisbury. She was the youngest of twenty-three children, her mother being Joan Beaufort, and she had married at the age of nineteen, her husband being then 26.

A huge log fire burned in the hearth, and before it, a new-born child lay sleeping in the cradle of the period, an oval wicker basket, but not so near as to risk scorching or spark. Cicely's bed was unusually large, and to mark her high position the mattress was stuffed with feathers instead of straw or dried pea pods. The room was floored with strewn rushes, while on the stone walls hung freshly-cut boughs, giving out an odour of rising sap and bringing in an agreeable coolness. Spring was peering through the decorative, coloured window panes, each of which told part of some old story. The child's nurse, Anne de Caux, was already exercising a benevolent supervision over mother, child and visitors.

Cicely's babe had been born at approximately 2 a.m. on Saturday, the 28th April, 1442, and one glance had assured his mother that he was worth what he had cost her in pain and effort, for he was big, bonny, a lusty, howling infant who, she was sure, would thrive and flourish, not like her first-born son, Henry, prove weakly and delicate. The new infant, nearly three years younger than his sister, Anne, had been conceived in a happy hour, when her young and valiant husband made love to her in the room adjoining the Palace Chapel at Hatfield House. Perhaps this child's sturdiness sprang from that. Now she could love, hope and be young again, for with her in this room reposed a son who did credit to the womb that had carried him. He should be christened Edward, and baptized in the Castle Chapel.

She had been a wife now for nearly four years, during more than two of which the Duke had been Lieutenant-General of English France, which included the fine city of Rouen, but they had not taken up residence in the Castle until the previous May. It is doubtful if her life here had been happy, for whenever she ventured outside the castle, she was met by indifferent or sullen glances from the Rouennese, to whom she and her husband were interlopers, occupants of a soil and a city not their own.

She was already longing to return to her home at Ludlow Castle. Popularly known as "the Rose of Raby", from her birthplace in Raby, Northumberland, Cicely was said by salacious nobles of the French Court to have misconducted herself with Blackburn, a bowman of her guard. This new child, they declared—with little cause—was his son. Hence, later in life he was called by both Louis of France and Duke Charles of Burgundy "le fils d'archier"—the archer's son. Some English historians also have accused Cicely of not being a faithful wife, but have produced no evidence.

Over a period of sixteen years she was to give birth to eight sons —four dying in childhood—and three daughters, so perhaps her primary claim to remembrance lies in her frequent gestations and in the bereavements she suffered, for during the events to be related she lost a brother, son, son-in-law, brother-in-law and six nephews, while her niece's husband, Lord Hastings, was beheaded in the reign of Richard III. She had brought to the Duke of York alliance with a rising family of great wealth and influence—the Nevilles, potentates of the north—enhancing his already considerable fortune and power.

Four years were to elapse before the Duke returned to England, and by the time of his return, the young Edward, made Earl of March by royal decree in either 1445 or 1446, had acquired a younger brother, Edmund, named Earl of Rutland in the same decree.

[2]

Cicely and her growing family lived for the next few years, in between visits to Fotheringay Castle in 1446–47, at Ludlow Castle on the border of Wales, gloriously situated and forming the central point of the great Mortimer estates. It stood on the crest of a well-wooded eminence, overlooking twin rivers, gleaming and clear. From the battlements the inmates could see dark, shaggy forests, upthrusting church spires and towers, and the stone walls of a Benedictine monastery. In the town at the foot of the hill tanners and millers laboured and sweated, avaricious citizens chaffered at market stalls, scholars streamed into and out of the grammar school, and semi-somnolent burgesses debated in the Guildhall. The recurring plots, hatred and ambitions of England's rapacious and insolent barons, their bloody conflicts, which the weak and ailing Henry VI could not prevent, had so far left this castle undisturbed. Tranquil and sightly it stood, being dominant and well-defended.

In between prescribed periods with their nurse, the faithful Anne, and their stern dignified tutor, Sir Richard Croft of Croft Castle, probably a Herefordshire squire, the two young Earls played and worked amicably together. Little is known of this formative period of their life, but a couple of letters jointly written by the brothers have come down to us. The handwriting was Italianate, perpendicular, legible and boyish, and the letters themselves were signed "E. March" and "E. Rutland".

One was dated the 3rd June, Saturday, in Whit-week. After declaring themselves "in as lowly wise as any sons can or may", the boys thank their father for "our green gowns now sent unto us to our great comfort, beseeching your good lordship to remember our porteux" (breviaries) "and that we might have some fine bonnets sent unto us by the next sure messenger, for necessity so requireth." (Were these requests made at their mother's insistence?)

This letter winds up somewhat unkindly: "Please it your Highness to wit that we have charged your servant William Smyth, bearer of these, for to declare unto your nobley certain things concerning and touching the odious rule and demeaning of Richard Crofte and his brother. Wherefore we beseech your gracious lordship and full noble fatherhood to hear him in exposition of the same, and to his relation to give full faith and credence."

Perhaps some hint of this complaint is given in the second letter, written a few months later, in which they rejoice in the news of their father's triumph over his enemies. It implies that both young-sters had been given bad reports by their tutor, for after noting their father's instruction "to attend specially to our learning in our young age that should cause us to grow to honour and worship in our old age", they assure him they have been diligent in their studies ever since coming to Ludlow, and will continue so to be, which assurance the Duke, if he remembered his own childhood, doubtless took with a grain of salt.

They conclude: "by the which we trust to God, your gracious lordship and good fatherhood shall be pleased. Also we beseech you to send us Harry Lovedeyne, groom of your kitchen, whose service is to us right agreeable; and we will send you John Boyes to wait on your good lordship". Incidentally, in later life Edward made amends to Croft by granting him a reward.

[3]

England was a savage, gloomy land in the years during which the two boys came to adolescence. For several decades of the fifteenth century, war lords, whose dependents, retainers, servants and yeo-men, were compelled by law to fight for them, contended for supremacy under a feeble-minded King—Henry VI. Gradually these conflicts crystallized out into a struggle between two great houses—Lancaster and York—for succession to the throne. The reigning monarch was of the house of Lancaster. Richard of York's father, Edmund, Duke of York, had lost his head for conspiring against Henry V. His son, determined not to follow his example, gave no trouble at first, and during this period Edward, Earl of March, now his heir, for the weakly first son had died, passed out of the schoolroom into active life. He was carefully trained in the arts of war, and was to be seen toddling about in armour specially made to fit him, flourishing a miniature sword. Most of his time was passed at either Ludlow or Wigmore Castles. In 1451 he was made constable of Bristol Castle.

Merely by holding so important a position as first prince of the royal blood, with what many considered an unassailable claim to the throne of England, since he was descended from the *third* son of Edward III, whereas the King claimed descent from only the fourth son, York acquired enemies. On the 9th December, 1447, he was packed off to Ireland as "Lieutenant" of that country for ten years, obviously to get him out of the way. It was not until 1449, however, that he left England, taking with him Cicely and his second son, Edmund. Sailing from Beaumaris in Anglesey, he saw the shores of his country slowly recede.

York resented his dismissal from the Court, and in September, 1450, returned unexpectedly to England, bringing with him the nucleus of an army, and the secret intention to claim either the throne or the succession. It was believed in some quarters that he had come expecting to find the rebellion of Jack Cade successful, and the throne his for the taking.

Henry VI's Queen, Margaret of Anjou, was a remarkable and handsome woman, of enormous will-power, courage and per- tinacity. Born on the 23rd March, 1430, the fourth child of René of Anjou, she was bethrothed to Henry by proxy at Nancy in March, 1444, and officially married at Titchfield Abbey, near Southamp- ton, on the 23rd April, 1445. Intelligent, attractive, a literate woman loving the works of Boccaccio and the French romantics, she was also arrogant, grasping, unscrupulous, arbitrary, and care- less of justice when it ran counter to her own wishes. An extreme nepotist, a meddler in the lives of those around her, she lacked both money and possessions until she became Queen of England. Her ambition, when later her husband's mind suddenly gave way, was to become Regent, but the powerful York was an ever- present obstacle to this aim and a source of irritation to her. She used her position and influence, therefore, to promote and reward her favourites and thwart his aspirations.

She prodded her husband until he sanctioned the raising of an army, which was promptly marched to the Welsh border to inter- cept the Duke and give him battle. Warned of this royal advance, York side-stepped, eluding the Queen's force, and reached the out- skirts of London. He "beat down the spears and walls" of the royal chamber to obtain audience of the King, but not yet powerful enough to carry out his secret design, protested loyalty, and demonstrated it by helping to try the followers of the defeated Cade, in proof that he had had no part in that rebellion. At the same time he denied having come to claim the succession, and presently withdrew to his estates on the Welsh marches.

[4]

For about eighteen months all was quiet, but in 1452 the Queen and the chief minister, Edmund Beaufort, Duke of Somerset, persuaded the King that York was but biding his time while quietly he prepared for an eventual assault. Together, they planned his destruction, but York forestalled them. Still declaring himself a faithful subject, and having raised an army, he once more advanced, asserting that Somerset was responsible for the loss of previous territory in France and an evil influence about the King. He reached the Thames and crossed it at Kingston, was in Dartford on the 1st March, and was well-provided with guns and ships. The royal army advancing to meet him camped on Blackheath, and Margaret, remembering the trick so effective in 1450 with the rebel, Jack Cade, sent the Bishops of Ely and Winchester to confer with the Duke and his friends, the Earls of Salisbury and Warwick, in the hope, perhaps, of buying him off with false promises. Warwick, created Earl in 1449, was the cousin of young Edward, but fourteen years older.

It was eventually agreed, probably on Salisbury's advice, that the King should retain his crown for life, but York was to be acknowledged successor to the throne, and this succession should pass to his heirs. He was granted 5,000 marks, young Edward, Earl of March, receiving a similar sum. Somerset was to be imprisoned on a charge of endangering Calais, of which he was then "Captain", and held in the Tower pending trial.

This compromise accepted, the Duke rashly disbanded his army, and went to Henry's tent at Blackheath, unarmed, to pay his respects to his sovereign. He had walked straight into a trap, for Somerset was still there, and by the Queen's orders he was seized and compelled to ride before the King like a captive when the royal army returned to London, being released only after swearing an oath of allegiance.

There were good reasons for his release. Firstly, the King's mind had given way, and he had had to go into retreat, a virtual imbecile. Fresh disasters were reported from France, where more territory had been lost. But the best reason of all was the temporary incapacity of the Queen, who gave birth to a son on the 13th October, 1453. This infant's paternity, too, was the subject of much slanderous comment. It is also suggested that his release took place when a rumour spread that Edward was marching on London with 10,000 men.

York's hopes of the succession were destroyed when the Queen's child was accepted as Prince Edward, heir to the throne. The basis of the Duke's own claim to the throne was acknowledged by some, but not by all. He determined, therefore, to have himself declared Regent. With Henry helpless and Margaret prostrated by maternity, he came back to London, bringing his own Edward with him, and without needing to fight, was offered and accepted the office of Protector on the 2nd or 3rd April, 1454.

Somerset was promptly sent to the Tower and held without trial. The Lancastrian ministers were dismissed and replaced by men of the Duke's own party. Nevertheless, the new Protector filled his office honourably and well, though his position was far from secure. The Queen, now a tigress devoted to her new-born son, remained his implacable and tireless enemy, her tongue never still, her brain ever scheming. As 1454 drew to a close, the King recovered his wits, and at once Margaret set to work to eliminate the Protector. Given charge of Calais again on the 7th February, 1455, Somerset was freed and restored to office. The Earl of Salisbury, Richard Neville, father of the great Earl of Warwick, was deprived of the Great Seal, which was transferred to Thomas Bourchier, Archbishop of Canterbury. Whoever held this seal was the highest executive authority under the King. York ceased to be Protector on the 9th of the month.

Margaret lost no time. Secretly, she mustered and equipped an army with which to shatter the Yorkist party, whom she suspected of preparing to depose her. The Duke, gathering his own forces together, tried vainly to settle the dispute around the conference table, but was forced to give battle. Meeting the royal army under Somerset at St. Albans on the 22nd May, he won a brilliant victory. The struggle raged in the streets of the town, the Yorkists meeting heavy opposition as they sought to reach the Lancastrian centre, based on the main street. By way of gardens and houses, however, they burst through the defensive ring, reached the street, and charging to the sound of trumpets, their men, uttering savage war cries, broke the Lancastrian centre, and after bitter street fighting from house to house, routed and massacred them. John de Vere, 12th Earl of Oxford, should have brought up men to support Somerset, his commander, but failed to arrive in time. John Dudley was captured and sent to the Tower, but was later set free. The Earl of Wiltshire threw his weapons and armour into the nearest ditch and escaped.

Henry VI was struck by an arrow in the neck, but the wound was not grave, and he was made prisoner. Many nobles died, among them Henry, the second Earl Percy, and Somerset himself. The tradition persists that Somerset had been told by a soothsayer that he would die at Easter, and as in his dreams Windsor Castle kept recurring, he would not enter its gates. In the end he was killed, the story goes, outside "The Castle Inn" at St. Albans, whose sign depicted Windsor Castle.

Some writers have declared that Edward was with his father in this battle, but he probably came no nearer than Leicester.

Returning to London in triumph, York brought Henry with him. It is said that the King had walked into a tanner's cottage after the battle, was captured there, and taken to the shrine at St. Albans, then to York's own room. The terror occasioned by the defeat was believed to be responsible for his second illness, which struck him in the October of 1455, when he went once more under a cloud. York at once took over government of the country as Constable of England, and Edward was certainly with his father in London on a day in January, 1456, for his signature accompanied the Duke's on a warrant issued after a meeting of the Privy Council, which both attended.

In the following month, however, the King recovered sanity, and Margaret, now active again, took him into the Midlands. York accordingly laid down his office on the 25th February, though whether voluntarily or because the Queen dismissed him is uncertain. She continued to plot and intrigue against him, and calling Parliament together in Coventry on the 7th October, obtained changes in the administration. However, York was too powerful to be imprisoned, and at length an uneasy truce was declared. At St. Paul's in March, 1458, a "reconciliation" officially took place, being made public by a procession and a ceremony, but it was soon obvious that neither peace nor friendship between the two factions could be for long preserved. At one Grand Council meeting at Westminster, for example, Warwick's servants came to blows with the royal lackeys, the Earl himself, who had earlier been made Captain of Calais, Somerset's former post, being assailed by cooks and scullions, so that he had to be rescued and escape to the city in his barge. Most unjustly the Queen accused him of causing this disturbance himself, and fearing imprisonment, he went off on the 9th November, to Calais, of which he was still Captain.

Margaret continued to plan the overthrow of the Yorkists. It had been suggested that York should go back to Ireland, but he refused. Scenting danger, however, he took the precaution of entrusting the young Earl of Rutland to Salisbury and Thomas Neville, who rode for three or four days with him till they reached Wakefield, then carried him on to Middleham Castle in Yorkshire, a Neville stronghold. York himself retired to his castle of Wigmore in Staffordshire.

In August, the French raided, burned and pillaged the port of Sandwich in Kent, for which disaster the Queen was held responsible.

[5]

The administrative condition of England at this period was bad. Money was owed in all directions by the King. The great barons were intent only on furthering their own interests and piling up vast fortunes. The wars in France had resulted in a long succession of defeats, and the French attacked English ports with ever-increasing impunity. In some quarters it was asserted that since the birth of her son, the Queen had but one thought in her head—to get rid of her husband and put the young Prince in his place. To do this she would, if necessary, eliminate the Yorkists without mercy.

When he saw that she meant real mischief, Salisbury came from Yorkshire with about 4,000 men, meaning to join York at his castle at Ludlow. Warwick was on his way from Calais early in 1459 with 600 men of the garrison there, under Andrew Trollope and wearing red jackets with white ragged staves, Warwick's badge. York went to Ludlow to prepare for the conflict now seen to be inevitable.

Learning of Salisbury's move, Margaret, in Cheshire raising men from that county and Shropshire, turned back to Eccleshall in Staffordshire, ten miles south-east of Market Drayton, and despatched a superior force of between 6,000 and 7,000 men to intercept and "arrest" him. On the 22nd September, 1459, they lay about four miles north-east of the town of Market Drayton, while Salisbury's army lay encamped a mile south of Black Heath, between Drayton and Newcastle under Lyme.

Next day, as the sun was rising Salisbury led his men through an extensive forest, which concealed their advance, especially as mist was still thick in the foliage. Coming out at last into the open, they saw ahead of them a hedge, tall enough to hide them but not tall enough to hide the fluttering pennants of the Lancastrians on the opposite side of a brook. Their approach unobserved, they dismounted the better to conceal themselves, and took up order of battle, resting one flank on the forest. To protect the other, Salisbury drew up his supply carts in a defensive ring, tying the horses to the carts, while his men dug a deep trench for themselves behind this rampart. Sharp stakes were placed in front of the trench to hinder the enemy. This done, the men confessed their sins to an accompanying priest, and filed into the trench, kissing the earth as they did so.

Meantime they had been detected, and Lord Audley, the Lancastrian commander, ordered his men to attack. The archers advanced first and discharged a volley of arrows. When their quivers were empty, the cavalry followed. From their well-defended position the Yorkists shot back, doing such heavy execution, particularly among the exposed horses, that the attackers were driven back and out of range.

Reforming his ranks, Audley once more launched his men, but mounted troopers had little chance against well-entrenched bowmen. Heavy losses resulted, and for a time he was baffled. Presently, however, he ordered his men to dismount and charge on foot. Some refused, abandoning the field, and 300 are said to have gone over to the Yorkists. Such desertions were not uncommon in medieval warfare. Since the wars were primarily between rival factions, national honour did not enter into them, and to change sides, even in mid-battle, was not regarded with odium, since many of the combatants had no love for their own commanders.

The battle was fought at Blore Heath, or, rather, Mucklestone, a mile north of the Heath. After a struggle lasting between two and four hours, the Lancastrians were decisively defeated. Lord Stanley should have brought up 2,000 men to reinforce Audley, but did not appear, for which he was later impeached, being, however, pardoned by the Queen. Audley himself was slain, and a commemorative monument marks the presumed site of his fall. John Dudley was wounded and went over to the Yorkists. There were many other dead, including Thomas Harrington. Some of Salisbury's men, going too far in a two-hour pursuit of the fleeing Lancastrians, were turned upon and the pursued captured Sir Thomas Neville and John Neville, the latter an important person in the life of Edward IV, who will reappear in these pages as Lord Montagu, and later still as Earl of Northumberland. The battlefield is still called Deadman's Den from the number of dead. Margaret of Anjou, tradition relates, watched the defeat of her forces from the tower of a neighbouring church.

After the fight, Salisbury joined York. Instead of linking up with them, Warwick, who had landed, set off on a march right across England to Warwickshire, whereas it had been expected he would sail to Wales and proceed thence to Ludlow. Reaching London unopposed three days after Blore Heath, the Earl pressed on, and although the Queen planned to intercept him at Coleshill, near Warwick, she arrived there too late.

As the Yorkists were still protesting loyalty the royal advisers recommended that the King should offer them a general pardon on condition that they submitted within six days. This offer being refused, the King's army at once moved on Ludlow.

We now hear again of Edward, then an adolescent of 17, for he and his brother, Rutland, took the field with their father and the

Earls of Warwick and Salisbury. A fierce and heroic struggle should have taken place, but influenced, no doubt, by the victory of Salisbury at Blore Heath, the Duke resolved to adopt similar defensive tactics. Taking up a position shielded by a river then in flood, and having caused a great trench to be cut, he packed into this embryonic Maginot line all his guns and waggons, protecting the weaker points with sharp stakes driven into the ground. Unfortunately, the haste with which he had been compelled to take up arms again had given him too little time to muster men; Salisbury had not yet replaced his heavy losses; Warwick's force was small, being limited by the numbers he could bring over by sea; and York's men were not battle-hardened.

The King's army, on the other hand, which advanced at great speed, numbered some tens of thousands. A chronicler says 30,000 —an exaggeration. The Paston Letters go to the other extreme, suggesting 1,000. Many of these men were, however, not well-armed, if armed at all. "Naked men" the chronicler terms them. When they were less than half a mile from Ludlow, the royal heralds went forward, proclaiming a free pardon for all who begged for mercy, except a few named persons. There was no response.

It has been earlier said that the men of Calais accompanied Warwick. Their commander was Andrew Trollope, a man of lowly origin, who had fought in France. If tradition is to be believed, these men had refused to sail until assured they would not have to fight against their King. Trollope had, however, already determined to betray York and Warwick, having secretly corresponded with the young Duke of Somerset—heir of the defeated Duke, his father—who had reproached him for taking up arms on their behalf. Somerset offered him a pardon and great honour if he would return to his true allegiance.

Accordingly Trollope put seamstresses to work all night, making coats showing the badge of Warwick, with which he provided all his men, carefully coaching them in their actions on the morrow. Then he and Sir James Blount, having marched to Ludlow with about 4,000 men independently of Warwick's small force, came into York's lines. York, overjoyed, put Trollope in charge of his vanguard.

It was the evening of the 12th October, 1459, and the sun was setting. As the King's heralds withdrew after making their proclamation, a few arrows were exchanged. Somerset advanced, and Trollope promptly marched his men out of Ludlow town ostensibly to engage the enemy. York expected them to attack, but instead, Trollope passed over to the King, bringing into the royal tent the plans and battle dispositions of the Yorkists.

This defection opened the way to Ludlow, and Somerset drove fiercely forward. Dismayed and greatly weakened, York put up no great fight, but fled with his associates. The royal army at once marched in, took the town, and hanged all stragglers found in its streets and environs. Others were, however, fined and afterwards pardoned, but Ludlow was put to sack, many women being raped, and the royal army disgracing itself by its behaviour, the men going "wet-shod in wine". The Castle and its womenfolk were, however, left unharmed.

Cicely Neville, with her youngest sons, George and Richard, was sent under escort to the Duchess of Buckingham, her sister, who became her guardian, "with many a great rebuke". Craving an audience of the King, she threw herself at his feet, begging that her husband might come to Court to plead his own innocence of treason. The King agreed, offering a pardon to all who would come in within eight days and surrender, which included York and his followers.

[6]

York, however, now in flight, moved from point to point in Wales, destroying every bridge over which he passed, as a means of delaying pursuit. Reaching Beaumaris, he sailed to Ireland, where he was welcomed and made Lord Lieutenant of the country for the second time. He presently introduced new coins with a crown on one side and a cross on the other, and made new laws.

As York had not surrendered, Margaret arraigned him before Parliament at Coventry in 1459, and with him coupled the Earl of March, the Earl of Rutland, the Earls of Warwick and Salisbury, and other influential members of the Yorkist faction. The Yorkist ministers were all dismissed from their posts, and all Acts passed at Westminster after the battle of St. Albans were annulled.

Edward, Earl of March, whose father had seemingly scant desire for his company, had been entrusted to Warwick and Salisbury. On the Eve of St. Edward, they rode with Sir John Wenlock, who had been Captain of Calais in 1455 and will be heard of again, into Barnstaple in Devonshire. There, aided by an Esquire, John Dynham, they hired a small vessel with a crew of four, paying 120 nobles—gold coins worth about 6s. 8d. each—on pretence of going to Bristol. Once at sea, however, they revealed that their true destination was Calais. The skipper pretended not to know the Channel well enough to steer them there, so without more ado Warwick had the sails hoisted, took the helm himself, and guided the ship on her way.

A furious gale drove them to take shelter in the harbour at Guernsey, where they were compelled to await a favourable wind and the assurance that Calais would grant them refuge. Then, on the 3rd November, their little fishing smack sailed into Calais just in time to thwart an attempt by the royal forces under Somerset to take over the port.

Here they remained for about nine months, Warwick's men of the garrison being loyal to their commander rather than their King. This great baron, the Earl of Warwick, Edward's cousin, towered over his early years like a beetling cliff. Bold, aggressive, powerful, he possessed estates so vast that he could summon up under feudal law great numbers of armed men to fight for him. He never attended a Parliament without taking several hundreds of retainers with him, all clad in his livery. Not content to remain an exile, he determined to return to England at the proper time and restore York and himself to their original offices, corresponded with the Duke in Ireland, and mustered an army of about 2,000 men.

On the 15h January, 1460, between 4 and 5 a.m., he attacked the already ravaged town of Sandwich with a fleet under Dynham, Richard Clapham, William Elyot and a number of worthy Calais traders and men. They waited an hour at the dunes before sailing in, and being taken for foreign ships bringing in timber, achieved a complete surprise, capturing Lord Rivers (Sir Richard Woodville) and his wife, the widowed Duchess of Bedford, in bed, as well as Anthony Woodville, their son. All were whisked back to Calais,

Rivers's ships being seized and taken across the Channel, except for one found unseaworthy. Salisbury and Warwick would not bring their prisoners into Calais by day for fear they would be recognized and attacked, so their arrival took place at night, illumined by the flaming of sixty torches. Edward joined his seniors in reviling Rivers and his son for calling him and his father traitors.

This success strengthened Warwick's determination, and encouraged him as greatly as it distressed the Queen. He now left the French port to confer with York in Ireland, sailed unchallenged down the Channel, and kept a marine rendezvous with the Duke. Together they sailed into Waterford, Edward being left with Salisbury and Lord Falconberg, later Earl of Kent, to defend Calais.

The Queen sent Lord Audley with money and reinforcements for her unpaid and discontented forces in France, where Trollope now was, and if she had been luckier, might have retaken Calais during the Earl's absence, but Audley's ships were so badly battered by a storm that they had to seek refuge in the harbour of Calais itself, and were at once captured, Audley and his officers being imprisoned. In desperation the royal forces outside the town attacked, hoping to liberate them, but were heavily defeated near Boulogne.

Having concerted his plans with York, Warwick left Ireland on the 1st June. The Duke of Exeter, in command of the royal fleet, waited for him with two carricks and some smaller vessels in the Channel to prevent him from getting back to port. Warwick sighted the Lancastrian squadron off Cornwall and prepared to engage them, but Exeter's men, unpaid for months, mutinied and refused to fight. The Queen's ships had to stand idly by without firing a single gun while Warwick sailed contemptuously past them to reach Calais unharmed, to Margaret's dismay and disgust. The royal seamen later sailed their ships into Dartmouth, saying they would rather rescue their former Admiral than fight him.

Once more a fleet of supply ships was got together in Sandwich port under Osbert Mountford, Treasurer of Normandy, with pay and reinforcements for the army of England in France. It was ready to sail when, for a second time, the port was raided by the Calais men under Dynham, Sir John Wenlock and Lord Falconberg. This time, however, the surprise was not complete. Dynham received an arrow in the leg and was doomed to limp for the rest of his life. A severe struggle began, but the raiders captured Mountford, killed many of his men, and seized the town, which they had instructions to hold. Falconberg was appointed Commander, and remained there. Mountford was shipped to Calais, where three seamen cut off his head and the heads of two of his men.

Everything was now ready for the invasion of England. On the 26th June, 1460, Edward, Earl of March, Warwick, Salisbury, Sir John Wenlock, and Falconberg, who had returned from Sandwich, together with Lord Audley, who had turned his coat, boarded Warwick's ship with joy, and landed about 1,500 men at Sandwich. They were welcomed by Lord Cobham, the Archbishop of Canterbury, his cross carried before him, and other representatives of the county, and with them came also Francis Coppini, Bishop of Terni, an emissary of Pope Pius II. Coppini had been in England the previous year, but having achieved nothing, had now been deputed to preach peace to the royal court.

Edward and Warwick were soon at the head of rather more than 6,000 men, whose banner was that of the Church. By sunset they were outside the walls of Canterbury, where they expected opposition, but after a brief parley, the town gates were thrown open, and the Yorkists, marching in, knelt before Becket's tomb in the Cathedral. Many men joined up with them in the town, and the lords of Kent swarmed in to meet the two leaders, declaring themselves ready to live and die with them. Asking Warwick what they should do, he replied that he would "test their courage".

The Earls marched from Canterbury to Rochester, which they surprised and captured, then crossed the River Medway and spent the night in Dartford. A conference was called attended by Thomas Bourchier, Archbishop of Canterbury, the Bishop of Rochester and high officials of Warwick's entourage. It was agreed to ask for passage through London on the pretext that their advance was for the good of the King and his country.

The Bishop of Ely took their request, and was challenged at Southwark by Lord Scales, who had held the Tower against Jack Cade, and was now holding the bridge. After Ely had stated his mission, he was allowed to go into the city to consult the Mayor.

Scales had come into the city with an armed force, seeking to be made captain, but the populace would not have him, saying they could do what was necessary "without any aid of lords". It was agreed, however, that the Yorkists should be opposed. The city gates were guarded, strangers espied, the drawbridge gates closed, and soldiers posted on the gatehouse top to let down the portcullis. Edward and Warwick were warned that their entry would be resisted. On the 29th June, however, a reply from Warwick to this warning turned the townsfolk from their purpose, if they had truly entertained it. They now offered a welcome to the invaders, sending aldermen and commoners to receive them.

Scales, with Robert, Lord Hungerford, Francis Lovell, Earl of Kendal, and some of the leading men of Kent, now took over the Tower of London. Other nobles appealed for support to the Mayor and leaders of the guilds, but their appeal was rejected. Warwick consequently moved in force into Southwark, being joined there by his younger brother, George Neville, Bishop of Exeter; halted overnight; then poured his men in hundreds over London Bridge. As they went they removed the heads exposed on spikes, burying them at the church of St. Magnus. It was the 3rd July.

In the rebellion of Jack Cade, 1450, a great battle had been fought on this bridge, some part of which had been destroyed by fire. Repairs had been effected with more haste than permanence, and there were still holes to threaten unwary steps. The crowd streaming over the bridge to welcome the Yorkists was so great that some soldiers in the retinue of the two bishops fell, could not rise again for the weight of their armour, and died where they lay, crushed underfoot by the eager, onrushing mob.

The newcomers penetrated into the city unopposed, and riding to St. Paul's, performed the usual ceremony of thanksgiving, being received by the Archbishop of Canterbury, the Mayor, Aldermen, and representatives of every branch of the city legislature. The Yorkist leaders now declared their aims, and on Thursday conferred at Greyfriars, their men bivouacking in Smithfield.

The following day they visited the Guildhall, where they indicted and imprisoned those considered dangerous, a few being executed at Cheapside. It was known that Henry had left Coventry, leaving behind his wife and son, to raise an army much stronger than their own, under the Duke of Buckingham, who was gathering men at Northampton by enticing but ludicrous promises of unrestricted plunder. Warwick and York had already discussed whether York should take the field at the head of his army, but this was thought to be too risky as he might be killed in battle. The truth may well be, however, that Warwick preferred to direct the campaign himself rather than rely on the Duke's not too brilliant generalship.

A messenger, escorted by one of the bishops, was sent to the King, saying they had no wish to take up arms against him, but merely desired to defend themselves and be heard. The Privy Council hid this letter from Henry and rejected it out of hand on the grounds that the King was not in a fit state to discuss matters of such importance. The royal army would give battle next day. York remained in Ireland, therefore, while Warwick and young Edward collected together men and guns, of which they soon had an ample supply. With Lord Falconberg, Edward, the 1st Baron Abergavenny, Lord Audley and others, they rode out. Many of their men came from Kent, Sussex and Essex. The Archbishop of Canterbury went back to his Cathedral, taking with him Coppini and young George Neville, then about twenty-seven, and later to figure frequently in these pages.

To guard the city of London, Salisbury, Edward Brooke, Lord Cobham and Sir John Wenlock were deputed. Obviously the loyalist, Lord Scales, could not be left in command of the Tower. Cobham and the sheriffs aimed their guns, therefore, to batter the fortress on the city side, while Wenlock and a mercer named Harrow bombarded it from St. Katherine's Wharf. Considerable damage was done by both batteries; the guns of the Tower, replying, also proved effective. Meantime a strict watch was kept in the city for fear of treachery.

[7]

At 2 p.m. on the 10th July, after attempts at mediation by the clergy had failed and a couple of bishops had gone over to the King, Warwick with 4,000 men met the royal army at a point beyond Northampton known as the New Field. The Earl of March (Edward) and Falconberg each had a command. Lords Scrope and

Stafford led the vanguard till all had assembled, after which it was entrusted to Falconberg. The Lancastrian van was led by Sir Edmund Grey, and this time Lord Stanley and his men were present. The King spent the night at Friars.

It is said that Edward commanded his men to kill all lords, knights and esquires, yet to spare the King and the common soldiers, but an alternative suggestion is that this order came from Warwick as commander-in-chief. Warwick sent his herald to the royal general, the Duke of Buckingham, declaring his intention to fight. Buckingham replied that he would never abandon the field without a struggle.

The Lancastrian army occupied a valley, "beside the Nunnery" with the River Nene behind them, commanded by the hill on which the Yorkists stood. They cut deep trenches full of stakes in a "new field between Harrington and Sandiford" at a point flanked on both sides by the river. At a signal, Falconberg and his men rushed down the hill, Edward and Warwick following at the head of the centre and rearguard. The hand-to-hand struggle that followed was fierce. Buckingham, the Earl of Shrewsbury, Lords Egremont and Beaumont and many other men of rank among the Lancastrians, were slain, together with at least 300 commoners. When Sir Edmund Grey of Ruthven turned his coat during the battle and went over to Warwick, the Yorkists triumphed, despite the armour and guns of their adversaries, rendered useless by incessant rain. Many of the Lancastrians were drowned in fleeing from the field (Grey was later rewarded in 1465 by being made Earl of Kent). Another heavy blow to the defeated royal force was the capture of the King himself, for the second time, by an archer named Henry Montfort. It was the King's misfortune to be taken like a pawn at almost every fight. The three leaders of the Yorkists did him homage, however, promising he should come to no harm and retain his throne. He was led captive first into the Abbey of St. Mary, then into Northampton town, where he was preceded by Warwick, carrying the sword of state erect before him.

The Queen and Prince Edward had awaited the result of the battle in Coventry, and according to one improbable account went to London with the King and lodged in the Bishop of London's palace near St. Paul's. Another version says that she went to Eccleshall, and endeavoured to raise a new army, but was pursued and nearly caught by one of Lord Stanley's men, John Cleger. Her own servants now turned against her and stole her treasure and jewels, but rescued by John Combe of Amesbury, a boy of 14, she began with him a perilous and difficult ride into the Welsh mountains until she reached the Castle of Harlech, when she proceeded to the little town of Denbigh, where she remained for a time. This appears to be the more probable account. Cicely Neville, after this battle, went to live in Southwark in what had once been Sir John Fastolf's house, to await her husband.

After three days Edward and Warwick returned to London. Scales and Hungerford in the Tower, having offered prolonged and courageous resistance, were near to surrender. Food ships from Gascony meant for them had been intercepted, and they were now suffering severely from hunger. The Lancastrian defeat outside Northampton depressed them, and they began negotiations on the very day the victorious Yorkists entered the capital. On the 18th or 19th July they surrendered, on condition that Scales and Hungerford should go free. Not trusting his conquerors, Scales tried to slip away to sanctuary in Westminster, but a woman, seeing him, warned some river boatmen, who followed and killed him as he fled by water. They threw his body, after stripping it of every stitch, on to the open ground near the porch of St. Mary Overy, where it lay for some hours. Edward and Warwick buried him with full honours. Anthony Woodville, Rivers's son, was later to acquire his title.

There is proof that Edward was in London, without his brother Edmund, Earl of Rutland, on the 10th August, for he wrote a letter from there to the Duke of Milan on that date, signed in a shapely, clear, legible, upright hand. That Edward was more than usually literate is shown by the way in which the Earl's name, spelled by him "Eduarde", and the M of March are linked together. The individual letters are smoothly formed and characteristic, while the signature ends with a noteworthy flourish. This letter was written three weeks before the battle of Wakefield, which will be described later. It is in the British Museum manuscript collection.

[8]

It was now possible for York to return to England, but by reason of delay in getting ships together, two months elapsed before, on the 8th September, he crossed the Irish sea, landing at Redcliff, near Chester. He brought but a small band of supporters including Edward's brother, the Earl of Rutland, and seems to have had "divers strange commissions from the King to sit in divers towns", for he made but slow progress towards the capital, which he did not reach till about the 10th October. His entry into the city was impressive. Fanfares sounded, the full arms of England were displayed, and his sword was carried upright before him. With about 500 armed men and a much larger number of hangers-on, he came to Westminster, forced his way into the King's chamber, and compelled him to transfer himself to that previously occupied by his wife.

After six days spent in taking soundings, during which he received no great encouragement, York formally claimed the throne before Parliament, but the session was not well-attended, many lords keeping to their houses, while others, fearing for their lives, fled to their country castles. However, eventually the Duke's sons, Edward and Edmund, swore loyalty to Henry while ever he lived, and the Duke, accepting once more the office of Protector, was acknowledged heir apparent. Warwick had recommended acceptance of this compromise because of the lack of solid support for the bolder claim.

York now left for the north with Salisbury to put down a rising under Somerset, but after an engagement at Worksop, where he suffered heavy casualties, he took refuge in Sandal Castle, near Wakefield, on the 21st December, whereupon Somerset occupied Pontefract.

The Queen, with the Duke of Exeter, had previously taken ship from Wales for Scotland, and throughout the summer was sheltered by Mary of Gueldres, the Scottish Queen, a niece of the Duke of Burgundy. Receiving Margaret with full honours, Mary sumptuously entertained her, and later a marriage between Prince Edward and Marie, her daughter, was proposed, Margaret undertaking to surrender Berwick to the Scots. This town was, in fact, handed over on the 28th April.

Margaret raised an army in England against the Duke, but the Christmas festivities were approaching, and a truce was therefore arranged to last till the 8th January. Relying on the Queen's word, York allowed his men to disperse in quest of food and enjoyment. He paid dearly for this second such error, for the Lancastrians, assembling in great strength, treacherously surrounded Sandal and sat down before it, meaning to starve the Duke into surrender. Holinshed suggests that on discovering this, York summoned Edward, then at Shrewsbury, to come to him with every man he could raise, but if Edward received any such message, either it did not come in time or he was unable to act upon it.

Whatever his qualities as a statesman, York was a poor general. Warned not to leave the castle, he declared with remarkable inconsistency that it was dishonourable to stay cooped up in a fortress "caged like a bird", asserting that he had never done so when commanding in France. With his men, reversing his tactics at Ludlow, he charged down the slope to give battle to the besiegers.

The moment they reached level ground they were encircled by superior numbers and heavily defeated. The Duke was killed in combat, his head cut off and set up on the walls of York. Salisbury, captured by a servant of Andrew Trollope, was carried to Pontefract and his head sent to join York's on the walls. The young Earl of Rutland, escaping over Wakefield Bridge with his tutor after the battle, was caught and murdered in cold blood by Lord Clifford, known as 'The Butcher'. According to Hall, Clifford said to Edmund: "By God's blood, thy father slew mine; and so will I do to thee and all thy kin."

Edmund's head was set up beside his father's on the battlements of York, a space being left on the other side for that of the Earl of March, who seemingly owed his life to his frequent absences from his father's side. The author of the Lancastrian victory is said to have been that same Andrew Trollope as had betrayed York at Ludlow.

TWO

1460 – 1461

[1]

EDWARD HAD NOT followed his father into Yorkshire. Possibly he revisited the pleasant landscape of his childhood at Ludlow, for later he came to Hereford, where one account says he waited daily upon the King and Queen when they were there. What is established is that he spent Christmas with the Friars of Shrewsbury, but was at Gloucester when he received the dreadful news of Wakefield. The young man was distraught, and returning to Shrewsbury, appealed to the surrounding countryside for support, but the towns were cautious and dilatory. Far more enthusiastic and loyal to him were the men of the villages and farms, who joined him in great numbers. When he learned that, heartened by York's death, Jasper Tudor, Earl of Pembroke, with James Butler, Earl of Ormond and Wiltshire, had raised a strong force of Welshmen, French and Bretons to seize him, he redoubled his efforts.

Before long, thousands more came riding in to join the tall, handsome young Earl. When ready, Edward marched, and on Sunday, the 2nd February, Candlemas Day, 1461, confronted Jasper's army, having cut across their line of march, at what until fairly recent times was an open common, Mortimer's Cross, five and a half miles north-west of Leominster in Herefordshire.

It was early morning, and the grey dawn was stealing into the bedroom of night when in the sky a strange brilliance appeared, aweing and astounding all who saw it. No fewer than three golden suns "shining full clear" rose into the firmament. What strange atmospheric refraction caused this well-attested phenomenon cannot be said, but with characteristic superstition Edward's men, perceiving this triple effulgence in advance of their opponents, since they were on the eastward side, took it to represent the Father, the Son and the Holy Ghost—a direct token of victory. Edward, kneeling, offered up prayers and thanks to God for this propitious sign. Crossing themselves and with unshakable confidence, his soldiers rushed to the attack, whereupon, it is said, the three suns united.

No precise details of the battle have come down to us, except that the Earl's men, having left the walls of Hereford behind them, hid themselves in the swampy land known as Wig Marsh. They won a significant victory. Edward's crest had been a panache of many azure feathers issuing from a crest coronet, his badge being a white lion. Now he also adopted a sun in full glory as his emblem. Jasper Tudor and the Earl of Wiltshire, who had commanded a wing of the beaten army, fled, and disguising themselves, made off towards Hereford with what men they had left, designing to rejoin the Queen.

Altogether some 3,000 men, knights and esquires, were killed or captured at Mortimer's Cross, it is believed. It was indeed an unhappy day for the Welsh Tudors, because Owen Tudor, Jasper's father, who had fought with him, was taken, carried into Hereford market place, and there beheaded, his head being afterwards impaled on the topmost step of the market cross. Owen was convinced he would not be executed, and only when he saw axe and block carried to the scene and heard the excited cries and jeers of the onlookers did this conviction wane. Nevertheless, not till the red velvet collar of his doublet was torn away did he perceive that neither mercy nor respite awaited him. The story goes that he lamented: "That head shall lie on the stock that was wont to lie on Queen Katharine's lap", the allusion being to his marriage to Henry VI's mother, daughter of Charles VI of France. He was her second husband, if indeed they were truly married.

After he had been beheaded, a "madwoman" came to him, combed his hair, sponged away the blood from his severed head, and producing an enormous number of candles, lit them and left them flaming around the corpse. (Was she mad, or was she rather a woman who had dearly loved him?) His body was buried in the

Chapel of Grey Friars in Hereford. Executed on that same day were
also Sir John Throckmorton and six other knights. Sir William
Herbert, later to become Earl of Pembroke in place of Jasper
Tudor, fought on Edward's side that day.

It was shortly after Wakefield (Sandal) that Margaret, who had
been with her son in Edinburgh, left Scotland at the head of an un-
disciplined, ruthless mob of Scotsmen, Welshmen and men from
the north. They came roaring into England, pillaging and laying
waste. Had she learned first of Mortimer's Cross, she might have
hesitated.

[2]

Edward's cousin, Warwick, one of the most famous men in
English history, was at this period a mature, experienced statesman
of 32, eldest son of the Earl of Salisbury. He took his title from
Anne, his wife, heiress to the Warwick estates. York had left him
in charge of London when he went north, but Warwick knew that
he would soon be called upon to fight, for everywhere Margaret
was active and her army growing and formidable. He advanced
with what forces he could muster, mainly of men from London and
Kent, and on the 12th February, left London, taking Henry with
him, and coming presently to St. Albans, where he remained for
four days. In London the Duchess of York fearing the outcome of
the coming battles sent her younger sons, George and Richard, to
Utrecht in Holland, where they remained for some time.

Siting his main force between St. Albans and Sandridge on a
section of high ground, open in character and known as No Man's
Land, the Earl carefully prepared a purely defensive position. He
possessed guns of good calibre and some smaller hand guns served
by Burgundians, expert gunners. These fired "pellets of lead and
arrows of an ell of length with six feathers, three in the midst and
three at the other end, with a great mighty head of iron at the other
end, and wildfire withal".

The Earl had also introduced some novel means of protecting his
camp, such as cord nets bristling with nails; boards studded with
more nails and placed in the likeliest positions; "caltrops", iron balls
with four evil spikes, to be tossed on the ground about the encamp-
ment to injure attacking horses; and loopholes for firing, shuttered

when not in use. Unfortunately, not all his conservatively-minded soldiers took kindly to these innovations, preferring the orthodox infantry weapons. Indeed, many of the new devices are said to have done more harm to their users than to the enemy.

Warwick was also badly served by his scouts, for on the 19th the Queen's army, having come through Grantham, Stamford, Peterborough, Huntingdon and Royston, turned sharply west, and appeared suddenly at St. Albans by way of the Dunstable road. The 200 men holding the town were taken completely by surprise. The alarm given, however, a few of Warwick's admirable archers, defending the town, took up their stance by the market cross, and killed so many that the advancing Lancastrians were forced to withdraw, but after a council of war, the attackers turned north, crossed St. Peter's Street, and moving across the meadows, met the Yorkists face to face. Despite fierce opposition they forced their way back into the town, which they took, whereupon Andrew Trollope ordered his men to make a rapid night march towards Warwick's camp. (There is a legend that this attack was conceived by Margaret of Anjou, but this is doubtful. The idea was probably suggested to her by her commander, and received her formal approval. It was not uncommon for Kings and Queens to be given the credit for the bright ideas of their generals.)

Warwick is said to have believed the Queen to be still nine miles off. Prevented from learning the truth by the death of the entire St. Albans garrison, he was surprised by a sudden flank attack—unusual in medieval warfare—and was beaten back to Sandridge, about three miles distant. Nevertheless, his rearguard of a few thousand men fought so well that the result remained in doubt. However, his new hand-guns proved largely innocuous, doing more damage to those who used them than to the enemy, while in the confusion of battle no proper commands could be given, so that men were not thrown in at the right points at the right time, while some commanders either failed to receive or chose to ignore their orders. Indeed, one body under Lovelace deserted to the Queen.

Eventually Warwick's men gave way, and thoroughly beaten, galloped wildly from the field, praying for darkness to hide them. John Neville (later Lord Montagu), wearing his crest—a griffin issuing from a ducal crown—was captured. The poor, simple King, left under an oak tree a mile from the battlefield, guarded by Lord Bonville and Sir Thomas Tyrell, had passed the time chuckling and singing to himself as men fought to decide his fate. After the battle, he was collected up by Margaret and the Prince, taken to Lord Clifford's tent, then lodged for the night in St. Albans' Abbey.

Andrew Trollope, said to have planned this victory, was knighted on the field, but had not done much fighting himself, having a "calletroppe" in his foot—one of Warwick's four-spiked iron balls. He modestly remarked that he had not earned his honour, having killed but fifteen men!

Next day Bonville and other captives were ruthlessly beheaded. Warwick, too resolute and hardy to be easily discouraged, gathered up the remnants of his force and retired westwards to link up with Edward, coming up fast from Wales. The two commanders met five days later at Chipping Norton in Oxfordshire, Edward having been unable to reach St. Albans in time to redress the balance of the battle with the Queen.

[3]

The Edward Warwick now met was an altogether different person from the callow youth who had been his ward in Calais and his companion through Kent. Here was a young Earl at the head of his own army, having just won a considerable victory over an experienced commander. From his towering height of over 6 ft. 3 in., the Yorkist general looked down with new self-confidence, pride and the dignity born of sorrow upon the sturdy Warwick, almost as tall as himself. He had the bearing now of a true leader—even a King, perhaps. Both Nature and his own intelligence and valour seemed to fit him for high position. By contrast, the babbling, amiable, half-witted Henry was featureless, a mumbling zany. There and then, it may be, Warwick, the "idol of London", the "Kingmaker", as he came to be known, decided to throw all his wealth, power and influence behind this youth, seeing in him a genuine claimant to the throne if ever there was one.

His spies were keeping Warwick well-advised of affairs in the capital, and he therefore suggested an immediate march there to forestall the Queen.

Edward was still deeply depressed by the death of his father and brother, and the loss of many gentlemen he knew well and esteemed. Warwick's defeat at St. Albans did nothing to cheer him, and when the Earl declared that the commons were eager to welcome him and that he had a right to claim the throne, he lamented that he had next to no money with which to wage war, his followers having mostly paid their expenses out of their own pockets. Warwick comforted him, however, telling him he could count on popular support, and that once he reached London, his supporters there would keep him in funds. A visit to the capital was just what was needed to raise the young Earl's spirits, and he agreed to Warwick's suggestion.

[4]

The part played by the ordinary citizens and countrymen of England during the Wars of the Roses was less active than has sometimes been supposed. As indicated, much of the fighting was done by the relations, friends, retainers, yeomen and servants of the great barons, many of whom had to provide for themselves during the campaigns, and because of this were accustomed to live off the land through which they passed. They did not hesitate to rob and strip the dead or wounded on the battlefields, and to sack whatever towns or villages they took. Many of the horrors of the Wars of the Roses were the direct result of the great demoralization of the English soldiery after their consistent defeats in France and the barbarity with which the concluding stages of the Hundred Years War were fought, as indicated in the Prologue. The burning at the stake of Jeanne d'Arc in Rouen was but one example of this. The successive failures of the English armies embittered both them and their commanders, and made them more savage and desperate than they might otherwise have been when opposing the rival factions.

Behind and beside these marauding baronial armies agriculture and trade went quietly on. Those responsible for the more humdrum activities went daily about their business, shrewdly watching their betters rob and kill one another, ready at a moment's notice to gain an advantage, take a quick profit, or run away and hide till it was safe to return, as fortune directed. The rivalries and conflicts of the aristocrats had in the main no shattering effect on the country's economy. In fact, it is now generally accepted that the disturbance of the national machinery was not nearly so great as that caused by the comparable struggles in France and other lands during the same historical period.

Undeniably there was great misery among the combatants and their families and dependents, a marked decline in the moral standards of men and women, and much social discontent. Nevertheless, the towns emerged with no essential change. Throughout the long years of civil war, the laws were obeyed over the greater part of the land. Judges sat, sheriffs and their officers did their duty, trials were held and civil wrongdoers apprehended. Comparatively little destruction took place, the English mostly refusing to indulge in the frenzies of their contemporaries in Europe.

In particular the administrators of the towns avoided the excesses of the nobles. Surviving all vicissitudes they adapted themselves to both King Log and King Stork, rarely supporting a cause with little more than romantic hope behind it. Their main wish was to keep out of trouble, preserve their comfort and watch over their own interests. Like sober citizens caught up in a brawl, they did their best to keep out of the way and get home to their own firesides as quickly as possible.

In effect, they did not openly take sides, but dropped little "sweeteners" into the pockets of whoever came for a time to the top. Any movement backed by a well-established and flourishing town was likely to be the one that offered a more convincing promise of sound and stable government. Of course, where a town had grown up around a great baron's castle or fortress so that its defence, safety and order might thereby be guaranteed, the inhabitants naturally supported the "great house", but all the same they did not always interpret their obligations too precisely.

When the weak, imbecilic Henry and his dominant, restless, intriguing, unpopular Queen failed to give the land security and peace, opinion hardened against them. Throughout the reign there had been great discontent. A popular Duke (Humphrey of Gloucester) had been murdered, a Marquis poisoned. Many great prelates had ground down the people with their avarice. Cherished English territory in France had been shamefully surrendered, and English ports cruelly sacked and burned by the French. The popular rebellion of Jack Cade had been put down by trickery and with great severity. A new king, men felt, could not be worse and might be much better.

During his brief Protectorate York had been a reasonably sound and considerate governor. In so far, therefore, as they committed themselves at all, the towns, where not tied by feudal law to the House of Lancaster, favoured the Yorkists. Their backing, and especially that of the City of London, was essential, because they were the main source of money.

London had seen something of young Edward, and what she had seen she liked. When he appeared at Warwick's side in the streets he was greeted with enthusiasm. For a few days he lodged at the Bishop of London's Palace, then moved to Baynard's Castle, close to Blackfriars Bridge and directly below St. Paul's. (It was destroyed in the Great Fire of London.)

On the morning of the 1st March, George Neville, Bishop of Exeter, assembled commoners, citizens and soldiers in St. John's Fields, Clerkenwell, enumerated the errors of Henry and his unfitness for the throne, indicated the basis of Edward's just claim to the crown, and asked if they would declare him their true and worthy king. All roared enthusiastically: "Yea! Yea!", which was all the leaders needed.

At Baynard's Castle next day a deputation consisting of "Captains", including Warwick, Norfolk, Lords Fitzwalter and Ferrers (Thomas Grey), with many leading knights and citizens of London, notified Edward that both his party and the commons had chosen him as their king. They promised full support if he would accept the crown. Edward pretended reluctance, pointing out his youth, and suggesting that he was barely able to bear so great a burden. Nevertheless, when the Archbishop of Canterbury and the Bishops of Exeter and Salisbury, speaking for the Church, joined with the political leaders to press the crown upon him, he agreed, thanking first the Deity for having honoured him in this way, and then the leaders for their confidence and trust.

Two days later the council proclaimed his accession to the

throne. Edward solemnly vowed that he would not be crowned until Henry and Margaret had been expelled from the country or put to death.

[5]

The reign of Edward IV began officially on the 4th March, 1461. When the city knew he had accepted the throne, they thanked the Lord and rejoiced. A saying current in the city was, "Let us walk in a new vineyard, and let us make a gay garden with this fair white rose and herb, the Earl of March". A rhyme of the period ran, "He that had Londyn for sake, wolde no more to him take."

This same day Edward rode in solemn procession with his company to the river, where they took barges and by water came to St. Paul's, which they reached at 9 a.m. A great crowd followed them after they had landed, and were asked once more by George Neville if they would have Edward for their king. Again the cries of "Yea! Yea!" rebounded from the walls. The new King now proceeded towards the city, followed by thirty-two knights wearing blue gowns and hooded like priests. He dismounted before the great hall of Westminster, and entering the chancery, vowed in the presence of the Archbishop of Canterbury to do all a monarch should. He was then dressed in the robes of his new dignity and the cap of state, and inducted into the royal seat beneath the canopy. From this he addressed the assembly, expounding his right to the crown. A third appeal to the people brought once more the "Yea! Yea!" of assent.

From Westminster Palace the new King moved to the Abbey, where the Abbot and his monks presented to him the sceptre of St. Edward the Confessor. Proceeding to the altar and to the Saint's tomb, he made his oblations. Then, occupying the throne, he again proclaimed his legal right to the crown, being greeted with renewed acclamation. After the lords had paid him homage, a Te Deum was sung, and presently, having resumed his customary dress, the King returned by way of the river to the city, where he dined.

Soon afterwards he received in the palace the Mayor, Aldermen and principal citizens, who asked him to be "good and gracious" to their city, and to grant and confirm their former rights and franchises, as in the days of his noble forbears. This he willingly undertook to do, and in his turn bade the Mayor do his best for London while he was absent, and keep it in good state for his return.

[6]

Edward was popularly known as "the White Rose of Rouen". The original white rose of his house was said to have been carried and worn by his father in right of his ownership of Clifford's Castle, York. After his formal acceptance, his royal work began. It was clear that however just his claim to the throne, he would not keep it unless he made himself supreme throughout England. This was impossible while ever Henry and Margaret preserved their army and could threaten him from their immediate positions. Therefore it was essential, as Warwick and the rest of his council agreed, to raise, assemble and supply an army of his own, powerful enough to defeat any force the Lancastrians might bring against him. Trumpets accordingly summoned all men to join him in the field.

His efforts in this direction were facilitated because England had been for so long in a state of continual warfare that men were habitually ready to arm at a moment's notice to meet whatever danger might threaten. Nevertheless, raising an army took time, and few commanders were ready to move before weeks had elapsed after the original muster. It speaks well for both Edward's popularity and his genius as a commander that he was able to take the field in about eleven days, an admirable military and logistical achievement.

Many messengers were sent into the country to proclaim that the new King meant to "reform the hurts and mischiefs and griefs that reign in this land". This increased the enthusiasm for his cause, especially with the commons of London and Kent. In reply, Kent offered to receive and unite with him, expressing regret that he had been proclaimed traitor by the Coventry Parliament. Most of his men came, as before, from Kent, Surrey and East Anglia.

On the 7th March, Warwick, leaving London with a sizeable force, advanced northwards displaying the royal standard, and gathered up supporters from the midlands and west. Stanley, who had at last joined Warwick, undertook to besiege Hornby Castle.

Two Lancastrians, Sir Baldwin Fulford and an esquire named John Heysand, who had come to Britain by sea to stir up the people against Edward, were caught on their way over, taken to Bristol, hanged, drawn and quartered.

Falconberg and his foot soldiers left on Wednesday, the 11th, and Wenlock, with men and guns, set off to attack Thorpe Waterfield, a Northamptonshire stronghold of the Lancastrians. On the 12th the King sanctioned the execution of a grocer, Walter Waller or Walker, at Smithfield, for disrespect towards him. Normally an executed man's goods became the King's property, but this time Edward allowed the widow, an attractive woman, to keep them. Lovelace, the turncoat of St. Albans, reputed to be the country's supreme exponent of the arts of war, was also beheaded, his head being set on the tip of a lance on London Bridge.

After a meal in his private room on the 13th, Edward rode northwards with Norfolk, Stanley and a glittering array of lords, knights and esquires, followed by archers and footsoldiers, with many chariots and carts laden with food and artillery. Riding on a horse covered with a great cloth showing the arms of England, he took the road through Bishopsgate to St. Albans. Hundreds lined the narrow streets to watch him go, crying: "God save King Edward! Dear Sire, venge us on King Henry and his wife!" He told them he had left his mother in their care.

At Bernay he waited for Stanley with 400 archers of his company to catch up with him, as well as Lord Audley, and with them spent the night in St. Albans, where they feasted well. The following day they moved on to Dunstable, where they again halted for two days to allow the foot-soldiers to overtake them. It had turned wet, and heavy rain was falling, but as soon as there was a lull the King remounted his horse. Three days later he paused at Barkway in Hertfordshire, and at Cambridge on the 18th. He did not stop again till he reached Northampton, where he was met by Suffolk, Marshal of England, with his own contingent and that of Norfolk. By the 27th or 28th he had reunited with Warwick and Falconberg, and together they entered the little Yorkshire town of Pontefract.

His force probably consisted of no more than 15,000 men, but all of these, as well as their horses, were well-fed. The Lancastrians were more numerous, totalling, it has been estimated, about

20,000. (Lt.-Col. Burne argues for 36,000 Yorkists and 40,000 Lancastrians, but gives no indication of how such great forces could have been kept fed and supplied along the wretched roads of the period. It is true the old chronicles suggest these large numbers, but their compilers were not present, and probably had little first-hand experience of warfare in the times of which they wrote. I have suggested a smaller number, but it is impossible to be dogmatic, and the reader must carefully weigh the arguments and decide for himself.)

THREE

1460 – 1461

[1]

AFTER DEFEATING WARWICK at St. Albans, the Queen's army halted at Barnet, St. Albans and Dunstable itself for eight days, being short of food and in no shape to march against the intruders advancing towards the capital. Many of her men were still unpaid and consequently mutinous. The various detachments scattered over the countryside had been looking forward eagerly to the sack of London as a recompense for their lack of pay. When Margaret's advisers told her it would be unwise to urge them southwards, proposing instead a retirement northwards to pick up reinforcements, her troops, fearing their anticipated booty would be denied them, were enraged, and went about cursing and muttering, until before many days had passed hundreds upon hundreds deserted.

The wise course was obviously to withdraw until she could bring the Yorkists to battle again at a place and time favourable to herself, but even before the two Earls reached London, Margaret learned of their reunion, and had at once sanctioned the retirement northwards. Edward's rapid and unexpected seizure of London had, indeed, come as a shock to her. She had been attempting to obtain cash and food from the city for her troops, but by the time her messengers reached them, the wily civic dignitaries knew that the Yorkists, despite their defeat at St. Albans, were still in the field, and that young Edward, Earl of March, had won a victory in the west. They knew also that both he and Warwick were moving on the capital. Torn between hatred of Margaret and fear for their lives if she gained the upper hand, they 'stalled', chaffering and dragging out the negotiations as long as they could. When carts had at last been loaded for the royal forces, John Bishop, head cook to Sir John Wenlock, incited the common people at Cripplegate to steal and share out the contents among themselves, which they gladly did. Both the Queen and Henry were refused access to the city, and in revenge some Lancastrian officers pillaged and ransacked the Aldgate region, but being set upon by furious citizens, were beaten, and retired leaving dead and wounded behind.

The medley of men that trudged northwards after the Queen were from many different counties. They were no longer a unified, high-spirited body, but an array of squabbling, ill-behaved boors. As they saw the fleshpots of Smithfield and the city recede and the wild Yorkshire moors approach, they made up for their disappointment by plundering the country through which they marched, increasing their unpopularity. Margaret's emissaries tried to whip up support and reinforcements for her, but with little result except in the strongly Lancastrian areas. The uneasy provincial townsfolk knew themselves the iron between hammer and anvil, and without actively engaging themselves on either side, if they could help it, wriggled out of danger by means of pretty speeches and lavish promises.

[2]

The Lancastrian army came presently to a small village south of Tadcaster, named Towton. Here they halted, taking up a position beside the high road at Sherburn, a couple of miles to the south of the village, roughly midway between Doncaster and York. Their front was protected by the River Aire, which recent heavy rains had caused to rise high up its banks. Farther south, a road, first built by the Romans, traversed the river at Ferrybridge, near Knottingley. John, Lord Clifford, the 9th baron, a young man of 26, was assigned to command a detachment of horse and prevent the Yorkists from crossing the river at this point. The brutal executions carried out by the Queen after her victory at Wakefield and again after St. Albans had appalled many, and when she allowed her savage soldiery to pillage and sack the districts through which they passed, the whole character of the struggle changed. The country ceased to be a unity.

Nevertheless, the Queen had many supporters. New recruits and reinforcements of trained men came swarming in, as well as supplies, and these more than made up for the losses and desertions, so that her army now outnumbered the Yorkists, who were following up her retirement. She and her commanders were confident of throwing them back, but had no suspicion they were so close at hand.

The Yorkists, in fact, advancing by forced marches, had already posted a few men on the river bank at Ferrybridge to spy out the dispositions of the Lancastrian force and their preparations for defence or attack. At this juncture the main body was reinforced by the Duke of Suffolk's men. The plan was to take the Lancastrians by surprise and capture a bridgehead on the opposite bank, but on Saturday, the 28th March, the spies were detected, and guards sounded the alarm. Clifford and his men promptly charged, hurling the Yorkist task-force back to the foot of the bridge, which was damaged.

Edward countered by sending Falconberg and the vanguard, with full supplies, to ford the river at Castleford, near Wakefield, four miles to the west. Falconberg crossed successfully, and went forward by the road to Brotherton, meaning to cut the highway between Ferrybridge and York, which the Lancastrians had deployed strong forces to protect. After a council of war in Edward's camp it was decided to await the rearguard under Sir John Wenlock, which was still coming slowly up, before attacking the enemy. With his vanguard safely on the northern bank, Edward's threat to the Lancastrian right flank and centre would then become dangerous. Presently Wenlock came lumbering in from Pontefract giving the Yorkists ample reserves.

Clifford, believing he had thrown back merely a few outriders, well ahead of the Yorkist main force, was quite unprepared for the sudden appearance of the mass of manœuvre under the King. With the brilliant generalship that marked his battles, Edward flung his men in great numbers towards the bridge. Advancing with élan, they cut Clifford's detachment to pieces, retook the bridge, and put men at once to fortifying and repairing it against the expected counter attack. Clifford, gathering up the remnants of his force, prepared to fall back on the main body, but in the heavy armour of the day few could fight for long without rest and re-freshment. Removing his gorget or throat armour, either to cool himself or because it was chafing him, he received at that very moment a Yorkist arrow, which pierced his now unprotected throat, and he fell dying to the ground. The arrow is said to have been headless.

His seven-year-old son fled, and lived disguised as a shepherd boy for several years, to fight one day at Flodden Field. Warwick also stopped an arrow with his leg, and Lord Fitzwalter, a Yorkist leader, was killed.

The skirmish at Ferrybridge is said to have lasted for six hours, but Clifford's rout and death gave free passage across the river. Throughout that night Edward passed men over it until, by dawn, he had enlarged the bridgehead on the north bank into an admir-able jumping-off point. Meantime, winter had returned like a savage, counter-attacking old general. As they tramped over the repaired bridge, the Yorkist footsoldiers had to struggle unpro-tected against biting winds, and shelter as best they could when they arrived.

[3]

Palm Sunday saw a great spilling of blood. When daylight came, Edward placed his men in order of battle, to save time and prevent confusion if the enemy attacked before they were expected. He now rode on horseback along the entire battle line so that all might see their leader, and exhorted his troops, declaring that any man afraid to fight could leave the field, either at once or before the battle began, but the moment it was joined, whoever turned his back could be legitimately killed, and his slayer would be re-warded by doubled wages. All who stayed to fight would receive great reward.

He now dismounted, took sword in hand, and with it slew his horse, to show that he would not leave the field, but would live and die with them.

The Yorkists were stationed on gently sloping ground close to Saxton village. From the top of this slope they could see the Lancastrians encamped upon the opposite ridge, overlooking the dale of Dinting, through which the highway ran from Ferrybridge to Tadcaster. The dale stretched between Saxton and Scarthington, being about half a mile long. In the centre of the Queen's army was her Commander-in-chief, the Earl of Northumberland. Their position had been well chosen, for to reach it Edward would have to descend and climb the slope above which they lay, under a hail of arrows. A rural lane marked the Lancastrian boundary. Their right wing under Somerset and Exeter was well-protected by a small stream or "beck" known as the Cock, a tributary of the Ouse. This, swollen by rain, could hardly be crossed by an attacker without heavy loss. The royal troops here were posted behind a deep trench, whose front was protected by sharp-pointed stakes and brushwood. The water of the beck had been diverted into this, but unfortunately the heavy downpours at that time had raised the water level in and around the trench so high that the guns sited immediately behind it were swamped and could not be fired.

Moreover, there were weaknesses in the position, which the Yorkist high command detected. The enemy left wing under Thomas Courtenay, Earl of Devon, and Lord Dacre, stood on the highroad, unprotected by natural obstacles, and wide open to any attack across the road and the flat fields beyond, which would cut their line of retreat along the road between Saxton and Towton. Moreover, the Aire, but a few miles off, ran behind the Queen's force, and should retreat become necessary, could be safely crossed at two points only.

King Henry had learned of the defeat of Clifford's detachment at Ferrybridge, but when on Palm Sunday morning Edward's rear-guard was still coming up in dribs and drabs, and his main body was not yet wholly across the bridge, Henry would not give permission for attack, though at this moment the Yorkists were at their most vulnerable. To the pious, weak-minded King, Palm Sunday was a day of great solemnity, which should, he said, be spent in prayer rather than in bloody combat. The Lord would be more likely to grant them victory on a secular day. So he stayed in his tent telling his beads while his army fretted in idleness, seeing their opportunity go by.

Finally, neither Margaret Northumberland, nor Somerset—

young son and successor of the Duke killed at St. Albans—saw
sense in further waiting. They ordered the line to be held at a point
beyond Barkston Ash, and made ready for battle.

For his part, Edward had already entrusted his left wing to
Falconberg, he and Warwick taking over the centre and the Duke
of Norfolk the right. Wenlock had charge of the rearguard. The
two armies closely watched each other's movements. For easier
recognition, Edward's knights had tokens of white silk on their
shoulders. Then, as they shivered in the bitter cold wind, snow fell,
thick, blinding, heavy, that terrible moorland snow all Yorkshiremen
recognize as frequent and typical of a dying March in their county.

Sliding down, it was snatched up by the howling, buffeting
wind and flung full in the faces of the Lancastrian archers, half-
blinding them, wetting their bowstrings and putting them at a
great disadvantage. Falconberg cunningly ordered his own archers
to fire but one arrow each, then drop back out of range, so that
the enemy should believe they were nearer than they were. The
trick worked. The Lancastrians peering desperately through the
curtain of moving white flakes, fired blindly in return at where
they thought the Yorkists were. Their volleys consequently fell
badly short, and as soon as their fire ceased, the English rushed
forward again, gathered up the fallen arrows, but left behind a few
which had stuck in the ground as extra impediments to charging
enemy foot soldiers.

[4]

The tactics of battle at that period had changed but little for many
years. There were few dashing cavalry charges carried out on swift
horses, no preliminary sustained bombardments with heavy cannon
of great range and precision. It was, indeed, some time before guns
played more than a terrifying or demolitionary part in warfare,
being used chiefly against fortress walls to effect breaches through
which footsoldiers might pass, rather than to slaughter the enemy.
Normally the archers, discharging sheaves of arrows at one another
and at advancing horsemen and footsoldiers, ended their exchanges
only when their quivers were temporarily empty, whereupon the
men-at-arms came to close quarters and fought hand to hand.

Archery was the speciality and pride of the English soldiery, as marksmanship with the rifle was of the British Army of 1914. The bow was the weapon of commoners rather than of nobles and esquires, who regarded archery as primarily a sport for occasional tournaments and competitions for silver arrows. Edward later laid down that every man must possess a bow as tall as himself. Those who failed to keep the shaft in good order were fined a halfpenny and lost much face. Clergy and judges were the only ones exempted from this law. Butts had to be set up in every township, and on every Sunday and feast day target practice had to take place, those not turning up for this being also fined a halfpenny.

Great numbers were killed outright in sustained battles of the age, especially knights. In medieval warfare it was normally a matter of chivalry to spare a vanquished foe, apart from the material consideration of probable ransom. The War of the Roses, however, bred such a high degree of family hatred that no quarter was given or asked. A wounded knight, encumbered by his armour, was often easy prey and could be stabbed through exposed parts of his armour, or mercilessly battered to death by mace, flail or spiked ball-chain. Even a common soldier could rip plates from his armour with the hook on the back of his halberd and despatch him with the point.

The knights and nobles usually fought on foot, side by side with the pikemen, not on horseback, as might be supposed. The commanders and their lieutenants and messengers alone remained on their steeds, either to intervene with the reserve at critical moments or to save themselves at speed if the battle went against them. Usually they dismounted only to lead their men to the charge, then remounted. On horseback their elevation enabled them to oversee the conflict and be recognized as a rallying point by their men. Edward, however, led his men invariably on foot, it is said. Probably this was because his great height enabled him to survey the fluctuations of battle better than his fellows.

This same pattern of combat was followed at Towton. The Yorkist archers having the snow and wind at their backs were less hampered than Henry's, and could therefore shoot at their adversaries as if at target practice. When their quivers were empty, Edward sounded trumpets and launched his men not against the obvious weak point, the Lancastrian left, which he was convinced Northumberland, the commander-in-chief, would have shielded with every power at his command, but in a massive frontal assault upon the centre, hoping to take them by surprise. In this, however, he seems to have failed.

The savage struggle lasted, it is said, for about ten hours. The Lancastrians, yelling "King Henry!" made a terrific din and clamour, hoping to intimidate their foes, and led by Lord Rivers and his son, Anthony Woodville, now Lord Scales, fought with the cruel weapons of the time—battle-axes, swords, daggers, flails and terrible bone-shattering leaden mallets designed to smash the helmets of the enemy and their skulls with them.

The outcome was for many hours in doubt, but the execution done by Edward's archers, particularly among the leaders of the opposing army, had given him an advantage greatly heightening the confidence of his men, already stimulated and encouraged by the sight of their giant young leader in the forefront of the fight, towering above the stumpy Lancastrians.

Henry, it is recorded, was browbeaten and badgered into coming out of his tent at last to urge his men to greater efforts, but after a few feeble admonitions, retired from the field altogether, accompanied by a few horsemen, and stood at a point from which he could watch the conflict in safety. This retirement, contrasting with the ferocious valour of the handsome, dominant Edward, must have taken the heart out of the Lancastrians, who slowly gave way.

When the Yorkists reached the first line of defence, the water-filled trench and the flooded land on its verges, they plunged in without hesitation, expecting to be met by fierce opposition at all points. To their delight, however, at one place the Lancastrians under Lord Grey lent them a hand as they tried to climb the perpendicular wall of the trench and the parapet above it. Grey had changed sides in mid-battle. In half an hour, therefore, they had overcome the most difficult obstacle to their assault.

An illegitimate brother of Warwick's, known as the Bastard of Salisbury, was killed during the fight. He, too, was exceptionally tall. Warwick, still on horseback, as was his custom, heard the news, and hastened "like a man desperate, puffing and blowing", to the King, to whom he is reported to have said: "Sir, I pray God to

have mercy of their souls, which in the beginning of your enterprise have lost their lives. And because I see no succours of the
world but in God, I remit the vengeance to Him our creator and
redeemer.'

Dismounting, he then, like Edward before him, killed his horse
with his own sword, saying: "Let him flee that will, for surely I
will tarry with him that will tarry with me," and kissed his sword
as token that these words constituted a solemn vow.

After vicious combat, marked by many heroic individual contests, Edward and Warwick poured in more men, driving a wedge
between the two wings of the royal army and separating them one
from the other. With the enemy centre penetrated and held,
Edward now turned his attention to the less well-protected enemy
left. At last Norfolk and Wenlock, who had been waiting on the
right for their numbers to reach full strength as men and supplies
came steadily over the bridge, sent Sir John Howard storming
over the level fields to cut off all retreat. This was the decisive
movement. The enemy here were pushed helter-skelter across the
road linking Saxton and Towton, then destroyed as a fighting
force on the slopes leading to the ford over the Cock stream.

Meantime, Northumberland had thrown his own reserves under
Lord Rivers, his son, and Andrew Trollope against Edward's left,
forcing it down the slope up which they had charged. A number of
faint-hearted Yorkists panicked, taking to flight and making for
Ferrybridge. The Lancastrians on this wing made the crass error of
rushing pell-mell after them, chasing them for eleven miles under
the impression the day was theirs and their right wing keeping
pace with them on the other flank. In their onrush they came upon
Edward's baggage train, which they stopped to plunder.

Northumberland was consequently faced by the defection of
Grey in the centre, the rout of his left wing, the sudden disappear-
ance of his right, and a dangerous penetration of his line as a result
of Grey's treachery. Into the gaps thus torn the Yorkists poured,
so that what had been a struggle of equals became a fight against
odds. The remnants of the Lancastrian army were overcome by
furious warriors. All cohesion vanished, the Lancastrian foot-
soldiers fought on the retreat, then, seeing the battle lost, turned
and ran.

Between them and safety ran the Cock, into which they plunged at the ford, crowding together in mad haste, so that some were swept off their feet into the swollen waters, and unable to swim, were drowned. Those surging behind trod these bodies down further into the water, others being killed by arrows as they crossed the swirling stream. Bodies are said to have piled up at one point to such an extent that they formed a bridge over which their comrades hurried towards the farther bank, lapped as they ran by the foaming Cock.

The lucky ones, more familiar with the district, picked out a crossing point where the water was shallower, and passed safely over, among them Somerset, their commander. He and these few survivors, dispirited, cold, their armour buckled and bent, their sodden clothing clinging to them, straggled across the snowy fields in ones and twos, making their slow way to York.

The fleeing men left behind were hampered by their own numbers, and the slaughter was so great that, it is said, the snow was stained crimson and the Aire ran blood-red. The bodies littering the field covered an area of six miles by a depth of half a mile, having to remain unburied for two or three days. Later, however, they were decently interred near Saxton church. The burial pits, runing from what was then Castle Farm to a small gully known as Towton Dale, were still partly visible in 1896, but are so no longer.

[5]

Edward's victory at Towton not only gave him security, and reassured those in London who had backed his claim to the crown, but also eliminated many nobles and leaders of the Lancastrian party. According to a reasonably trustworthy source, forty-two knights and 3,500 commoners were slain in the skirmish of the 28th and the battle of the 29th. Among Henry's supporters who lost their lives were, besides Lord Clifford; the Earl of Northumberland; Lord Neville; Lord Dacre—said to have been transfixed by an arrow from the bow of a boy hiding in an elder, just as he lifted his vizor to take a drink of water; Sir Henry Stafford, a son of the deceased Duke of Buckingham; Sir Andrew Trollope, the treacherous knight who had betrayed York at Ludlow; and many others.

Edward had had his aristocratic losses, too, but these were slight in comparison. Dead were Lord Fitzwalter, Sir John Stafford, and Robert Horne, Captain of Kent, while John, Lord Scrope, the 5th baron, who had fought for Warwick at Northampton, was "sore hurt".

Many prisoners and wounded were taken. When his men returned from pursuing the enemy, Edward asked the fate of their friends and the names of those who had held fast under pressure. He then gave thanks to God for this great victory, and allowed his troops, who had fought so bravely and for so long, to take their ease. A troop of light horse was detached and sent in pursuit of Henry and Margaret, who, as soon as they knew they were beaten, had fled for their lives; but the pursuers were too late.

Determined to cut off as many heads of the Lancastrian Cerberus as he could find, Edward ordered the execution of all captive leaders. As soon as his men were refreshed and ready to march, he had the head of Sir Thomas Tyrell, Henry's guard, cut off and impaled.

Edward was not one to dawdle when his enemies were in flight. On Monday, the day after the battle, taking the advice of his council that York should be seized, he advanced on that city, entering it unopposed, with full dignity. With his men, some riding, some marching, he passed in procession through the gates and along the narrow, miry, unpaved streets. The priests presented themselves before him in great humility, begging for grace if they had offended. This he freely granted.

His first action was to remove the grisly, shrunken heads of his father, brother and uncle from the city gates. They were sent in rich caskets to Pontefract for burial with the bodies. The Earl of Devon, lying sick in Clifford's Tower, was seized with other Lancastrians and immediately beheaded. Devon's head was placed where the Duke of York's had been, while that of the Bastard of Essex replaced that of Edmund, Earl of Rutland. Other heads of captured men were impaled in the same way. The bodies and heads of Edward's own kinsmen and friends were buried with full ceremony, marked by loud lamentations and copious tears.

The King's vengeance was not yet complete. He had never forgiven the insult to his father by death, mutilation and public display. If on this occasion he was vindictive and harsh, he was akin to others of his period. These men had acted cruelly and disgustingly towards his own flesh and blood. They had known what to expect if fortune went against them. They themselves, if sincere, would not have reproached him for doing what he felt he had to do.

[6]

The new King remained in the northern capital for almost three weeks, legislating to ensure a firm hold on the wide expanses of Yorkshire and the neighbouring counties. The Lancastrian rout had left him militarily unchallenged.

Henry, Margaret and the young Prince Edward, having gathered up all they could conveniently carry, did not linger in York, knowing the townsfolk would not defend them. With what remained of their following they paused briefly in Newcastle, then departed for the border town of Berwick, where they waited, sick at heart, for a safe-conduct which would allow them to take refuge in Scotland. There was great mourning throughout Lancastrian territory, for many a grande dame had lost husband, son or both in the battle.

When the news of Towton reached London, however, a Te Deum was sung on Easter eve in St. Paul's and every parish church. Thereafter, on each succeeding Palm Sunday the victory of Towton was celebrated. In Warwickshire a "Red Horse", as it was called, was cut out of a hillside to commemorate the horse killed by Warwick before the battle.

On the 16th April, Edward left York, and on the 22nd advanced to the Percy fortress of Durham, which surrendered without resistance. He aimed to capture the royal fugitives, or drive them out of England, and halted at Newcastle on the 1st May. The Earl of Wiltshire, captured in Cockermouth on his way to Scotland, was now beheaded. Wiltshire's head was too significant a token of victory to be left shrivelling on a provincial city gate, and was therefore packed off to London, joining its predecessors on the vertical fangs of London Bridge. The news of his death distressed Queen Margaret, who is said to have loved him greatly.

Edward now rooted out as many northern traitors to his father as possible. The lords, gentry, mayors and aldermen of the entire area were compelled to swear allegiance and to obey his edicts. It would have been unwise to remain here longer. North of Newcastle the country was hostile, and there was always the danger that the Scots, mistrusting his intentions, might attack in strength. Moreover, the French King, taking advantage of his absence, might once more sack the Cinque Ports. His enemies, too, would have time and opportunity to stir up the people against him.

Learning that Henry and the Queen had crossed into Scotland, he took Warwick's advice and turned west. After a brief stay at Middleham, Warwick's castle in Wensleydale, he moved into Lancashire to display his military might, reaching Preston, Manchester, Chester and Stafford, and proceeding thence to Eccleshall, Lichfield, Coventry, Warwick, Daventry and Stony Stratford. Re-entering London on the 14th June by way of Cheapside, to St. Pauls, he came on horseback amid many fanfares of trumpets and clarions to the river, where in full dignity he boarded the gaily-decked royal barge, followed in other barges by princes, barons, knights and esquires. All landed at Westminster Palace, whose ramparts rose from the riverside, and whose interiors were richly furnished and covered with gorgeous tapestry. Here he addressed Warwick and Falconberg, saying: "Sirs, you have been my father and my friends, from whom all goods I have and hope to have spring. God give me grace to deserve them."

Wenlock was made a baron. Edward was immensely popular now, so that "no man was spoken of, no person was remembered but only he". His mother so swelled with pride, that she won herself the title of "Proud Cis".

[7]

Notwithstanding calamities galore, Margaret refused to abandon her husband's cause. Riding towards Scotland, in which wild country she had decided to take refuge, she was hopeful that both the Scots and France, her native land, would become their firm allies. She had already offered Berwick town for Scottish aid, but Towton had dismayed the Scots, who would not now risk Edward's anger, and even when in addition the titbit of Carlisle was thrown in, they still refused. When the Queen learned that Edward was moving north to capture them, she and Henry crossed the border in desperation, and were granted refuge in Scotland. Margaret stayed first at the Palace of Linlithgow, then in Durisdeer and Lanark, and finally in July, 1461 in Lincluden, the Dominican Abbey of Edinburgh.

The royal exiles now allied themselves with George, the "Red Douglas", fourth Earl of Angus, who was promised lands between Trent and Humber for his military aid. The pact was signed by Henry, whose signature was "as long as the whole sheet of parchment, the worst shaped letters and worst put together that I ever saw."

Edward, furious, reacted sharply, demanding that the Duke of Burgundy should abandon his existing alliance with the Scots. Burgundy agreed, sending two nobles to arrange this. Edward's young brothers, George and Richard, now came back from Utrecht and Bruges by way of Calais. They were cordially received by their monarch and brother.

FOUR

1461 - 1462

[1]

NOW THAT EDWARD was master of England, it was felt that he should be formally crowned, with all the spiritual impressiveness of a royal coronation ceremony. The date fixed was Wednesday, the 14th June, 1461, but was altered because Margaret and the Scots, having finally plucked up their courage re-crossed the border, and were threatening Carlisle. Carlisle was quickly relieved, however, and the King remained in London instead of taking the road north to meet the invaders. Another date was fixed, the 28th, but this was abandoned because Sunday, the feast of Holy Innocents, was declared to be "a bad day". The new date was the 29th, the day of St. John the Baptist.

The coronation preparations were exhaustive and exhausting. Extra staff were engaged for the kitchens. Workmen were kept busy knocking up extra tables and making repairs. Delicacies such as swans, peacocks, pheasants and other foods were made ready. The King bought a new sword for £4, and his royal barge was repaired for £6 13s. 4d. The total cost of the affair came to at least £1,000, a colossal sum for the time.

The young King spent a week or two in the royal manor house of Sheen, now Richmond, Surrey, on the right bank of the Thames, of which house only a gateway remains. He then transferred himself to the Bishop's Palace at Lambeth, to which, two days before the ceremony, the Mayor, aldermen and 400 commoners, all well-horsed, came as his escorts to the Tower. They made a colourful spectacle, the city dignitaries in scarlet robes, the commoners in green. A knight in armour, lance in rest, rode forward, and passing before the King's table, challenged any person to deny the right of Edward of York to the crown. The Mayor then formally presented the sword of justice to the King, who, taking it, held it for a moment then handed it to another knight directly behind him. After the meal, the King took the sword again, returned it to the Mayor, and charged him to do justice and guard the rights of the merchants and commons of the city.

From the Tower he was led to Westminster Abbey, followed by thirty-two Knights of the Bath he had created as a reward for their loyalty and valiant service. They were hooded in silk like priests, and wore pieces of white silk over their left shoulders. A Te Deum was sung, and in his royal robes, but not wearing the crown, Edward was anointed by the Archbishop of Canterbury and the Archbishop of York before the high altar, then inducted in a separate room into the chair of St. Edward the Confessor. Holding the sceptre and wearing the cap of estate, he received St. Edward's crown, kept at the Treasury under lock and key in a small iron-bound leather casket, to which it was not returned until the 12th August.

Now, under a canopy of cloth of gold, carried by the Wardens of the Cinque Ports, he walked to Westminster Hall, where a banquet had been prepared. By ancient tradition the Mayor and the leading citizens of London had the right to the first table on the left of the Hall "next the cupboard". It was also the Mayor's privilege to offer the new King a draught of watered wine in a golden cup, which, with the ewer used, became the Mayor's perquisite, as the canopy was of the Wardens of the Cinque Ports.

On St. Peter's Day, Monday, Edward, wearing his crown, returned to the Abbey, and from there went to Lambeth Palace, where he conferred dukedoms on his brothers. George became the Duke of Clarence, from the Suffolk town of that name, and Richard became Duke of Gloucester.

Edward wore the crown in public again in St. Paul's "in the worship of God and St. Paul". A chronicler says: "Then an Angel came down and censed him at which time there was a great multitude of people in Paul's."

[2]

It was but natural that the young King, after his martial exploits, should enjoy himself, and the coronation over, he spent much time in hunting and hawking in the green spaces around the capital, being lavishly entertained by nobles and rich citizens. On the 27th July he redeemed his father's jewels, pledged to raise money, so maintaining the honour of his house.

His reign began with a sombre episode. John Davy, one of his household, had assaulted a man in the presence of the justices at Westminster, a breach of the law punishable with death. The King assenting, he was beheaded at the Standard in Cheap, as a deterrent to others.

Another of his acts was to erect a catafalque at St. Paul's in memory of his father. So many candles were burned on this that 80 lb. and more of wax was needed to make them. The catafalque itself, sprinkled with golden suns and silver roses, was covered by a cloth showing Christ seated on a rainbow, fifty-one gilded images of kings and 420 smaller images of angels.

In the mellow harvest days Edward made another royal progress, showing himself to his southern peoples and his armed supporters in the west. Sending his navy by sea and accompanied by the Earl of Essex he left Westminster and rode first to Sittingbourne, Canterbury, Sandwich, Ashford, Battle Abbey, Lewes, Arundel and then on the 27th August to Bishop Waltham, where William of Waynflete, Bishop of Winchester, had been seized by his tenants to prevent him from leaving the country. (The Bishop had fled when Edward was crowned, and had been in hiding until now.) The tenants were refusing to pay rents for the manor of East Meon, his property. However, Edward released him, insisting that his rights must be respected. If they had a good case, the tenants must submit it to Parliament, not take the law into their own hands.

When the King came to Salisbury, the townsfolk, wearing dark green robes and hats of black felt, gave him a golden cup, £20 in cash and a pageant. After Devizes, he reached Bristol, entering through Temple Gate. Here a man in the guise of William the Conqueror accompanied by three "lords" recited this welcoming verse:

"Welcome, Edward, our son of high degree!
Many years hast thou lacked out of this land.
I am thy forefather, William of Normandy,
To see thy welfare, here through God'y's sond".

The town keys were then handed to the King by a giant, and at Temple Cross, "St. George", mounted, was seen "upon a tent, fighting with a dragon", the King and Queen high in a castle and his daughter standing beneath a lamb. "And at the slaying of the dragon there was a great melody of angels."

After Bristol followed Gloucester, Ross, Hereford, his beloved Ludlow Castle and other towns in the midlands. Edward re-entered London on the 6th October and sailed down the Thames to residence at Greenwich. At that period the river was a busy thoroughfare, stippled with bright boats and gaily ornamented barges, many displaying the banners of their noble owners. It was the London highroad for every walk of life. Gentlefolk and others would hail watermen as today one hails a taxi. The river made for much quicker transit than the streets, many of which were ill-paved, winding labyrinthine cracks between blocks of overhanging wooden or mud and wattle houses, whose upper stories almost met. Every pathway was holed and rutted, littered with stinking garbage, and traversed by rivulets of foul water.

Edward was in a good humour, however, having found acceptance everywhere. The landed knights, the gentry, the yeomen and the commons, had one and all acknowledged him their liege lord, and had been told that he meant to be as kindly and generous a king as any before him. What had pleased him most, perhaps, was that the clergy also submitted to his rule.

His military position was strong, for apart from Harlech, not a fortress in Wales or on the Welsh border held out against him. Jasper Tudor, Earl of Pembroke, and the Earl of Ormond were fugitives in the hills, hiding and helpless. Lord Herbert had occupied Pembroke Castle and in it found Owen Tudor's son, Henry. Edward gave Herbert both the castle and charge of the boy, who was well and kindly treated. None could foresee that in due time this four-year-old would one day be King Henry VII of England.

All the other fortified places of Wales admitted him, their inmates declaring themselves his loyal subjects.

Sir Baldwin Fulford and John Heysand, the rebels, were, as earlier stated, beheaded at Bristol, but not every voice was friendly. John Burney grumbled in July that the King was welcoming "tyrants" and "great enemies of his county of Norfolk". His motive was probably envy, for his concluding remark was that "such as have assisted him have not been rewarded".

[3]

During October, 1461, Paston of the famous "Letters" incurred the King's renewed displeasure, having failed to come to Court to defend himself against a complaint made to the King. Edward told him sternly that disobedience to this final warning would mean death, for he would "make all other men beware by him how they shall disobey our writing . . . we will not suffer him to disobey our writing".

In December, Edward advised Paston that any Norfolk man, whatever his station, with a complaint against another must submit it to the arbitration of the local sheriff, who would give his decision. If this were not accepted, the matter must be put before the King himself, and once the royal ruling had been given, any who disobeyed it would be punished unless there were good reason to the contrary.

Edward now called a Parliament for the 4th November, and was lucky in that most of his countrymen were weary of the weak-minded Lancastrian king, who could not control either his nobles or his wife, and of the anarchy into which the country had been plunged. The Lancastrians had also forfeited much sympathy by their harsh treatment of those opposed to them or whom they sought to victimize. None felt free from persecution or could be sure he would not be tossed into a fire of faggots at the will of some baron, while those who had had their lands and crops ravaged by the troops were deeply resentful.

The sober, earnest folk of town and city, the merchants and craftsmen, artisans and shopkeepers, were only too glad to see a strong leader assume power, and were in no mood to dispute his claim to the kingdom. The turbulent, aggressive, northern barons, more concerned with increasing their own wealth and influence than with the welfare of the nation, were almost alone in supporting Henry.

One of Edward's objects in calling Parliament was to impeach Henry of Windsor and all, living or dead, who had followed him into that hostile country, Scotland. On the date appointed, the House met in the Painted Chamber at Greenwich. (Some historians have claimed that it met at Westminster.) The Speaker was Sir James Strangways, and the proceedings opened with an address by George Neville, Bishop of Exeter, brother of Warwick. This young man, born in 1432, had already risen fast, and was of considerable intelligence, colder and more dispassionate than his illustrious brother. He was above all a wirepuller and intriguer, having been trained in a good school, that of the Italian papal colleges, where he had been brought up. Ambitious, especially for political and ecclesiastical office, he had been appointed Bishop of Exeter when only twenty-five, and was to become Archbishop of York at the age of thirty-two.

A man without deep feelings, he lacked the main essentials of greatness—scruple, breadth of mind, principles, vigour and boldness. On the other hand, he was a boon companion, polished in manner and speech, devoted to hunting and similar pursuits, witty in conversation, talented rather than brilliant, with much knowledge and ability in the management of men. A glutton at table and a pedant in attitude, he paid great attention to his dress, being often seen in a short coat and surcoat of deep gold, and wearing the fashionable "piked" shoes, turned up at the toes in a fantastic manner, reaching sometimes midway to the knee. (These long-pointed shoes were first worn for comfort by a French noble after an accident, but when he was seen in them, everyone believed them the latest fashion, and flocked to buy similar shoes.)

The Bishop fastened his garments with gold buckles studded or inlaid with jewels, and whenever he went riding in the country a greyhound ran by the side of his horse. He had a sense of humour, lacking in his brother, the Earl, but was inclined to irony rather than open jest. At this period he was living in St. Clement Danes.

He opened the House with a text from Jeremiah (vii.3): "Amend

6

your ways and doings, and I will cause you to dwell in this place."

Parliament proceeded to attaint Henry of Windsor, Prince Edward, his son, and their supporters, as usurpers and traitors for handing Berwick to the Scots. Their estates and property were declared forfeit. The Duchy of Lancaster, which Henry had held, was awarded to the King. Henry's supporters when named included seven living peers, seven dead, and at least 100 others of all ranks.

The Commons formally accepted Edward as their lawful King by right of inheritance, and he heard two petitions—that the franchises held by cities and towns should be renewed, and that judicial decisions reached after 1399 should not be annulled.

Knowing the importance of keeping the towns favourably disposed towards him, Edward granted both petitions, but did not immediately confirm and ratify the security for £18,000, lent to Warwick by the Calais traders in wool and cloth for the wages of the garrison there and for the invasion of England. Advised by Warwick himself, the King would not admit personal responsibility for this debt, which he argued had not been incurred by him, but by John Butler, the new Earl of Wiltshire, then Lord Treasurer of England, who had negotiated the loan. Nor would the King admit owing the Customs Officers money advanced for the same purposes. There is a long history attached to this controversy, which it would be tedious to relate. In all other respects Edward's treatment of the Calais traders was scrupulous and just.

Waynflete's trouble with his tenants also came up (p. 78), and the tenants were formally ordered to pay what was due. As for the judicial decisions, the King excepted those only listed in the Bill of Attainder, which, drawn up by the royal advisers, was submitted as it stood, and the Commons had to agree whether they liked it or not.

Among other legislation enacted was that the Justices in Petty Sessions should take over from the sheriffs of the various districts the right to try criminal cases. Corruption had occurred under the sheriffs, many complaints to this effect having been forwarded by the owners of rural estates. It was also made illegal to play at dice or cards except during the twelve days of Christmas. This is the first allusion to playing-cards in the history of England.

No monetary grant was made to the King, who probably did not ask for one, the revenues from his estates now making it unnecessary. He repeated his pledge to be a good and merciful sovereign who "would always be ready for their defence, never sparing nor letting for any jeopardy".

Parliament was then prorogued till the 6th April, 1462.

Many parts of England were at this period in a state of chaos, and traversing the highroads became so dangerous that wherever possible long journeys were avoided.

[4]

Once she had reached Scotland Margaret could breathe freely again. Delay in leaving Newcastle—waiting for a safe-conduct—had nearly proved disastrous, for she and Henry were overtaken at the castle of Wark, near Carham, and besieged by Robert, Lord Ogle—a prominent Northumberland Yorkist—and Sir John Conyers, of Hornby Castle, near Richmond, Yorkshire. The siege was not raised till the new Earl of Northumberland had collected some thousands of men, all supporters of the House of Lancaster, and driven the besiegers back. Five thousand men are said to have died in this battle, but once again this is an exaggeration.

In Scotland Margaret was not idle. She persuaded the Scots that England was too weak and divided to withstand a well-armed, well-led army. In May or June of 1461, as indicated, she and the Duke of Exeter led a Scottish army over the border to besiege Carlisle, and on the 26th Henry crossed the Tyne to Brancepeth, south of Durham, having ridden, standards streaming in the wind, through Ryton. Commander of his troop was Sir John Fortescue, a famous lawyer and judge.

The King had created John Neville "Lord Montagu", and deputed him and Warwick to hold the border against the Lancastrians and Scots. This was why Warwick could not attend the coronation. Montagu threw back the Queen from Carlisle, and when, before Michaelmas, Sir Ralph Percy, holding Dunstanburgh for Henry, changed sides and declared for the White Rose, the immediate danger passed. Dunstanburgh Castle, on the North Sea shore, crowned a magnificent frontage of black cliffs, being the largest in area of all the northern fortresses, with an impressive gatehouse.

As autumn moved towards winter a truce reigned. The Queen's fortunes were at an ebb and her spirits not lightened by the prevailing gloom and drizzle of her Scottish surroundings. All of England remaining to her husband was the castle of Harlech. The Scots were proving a broken reed, being torn by internecine struggles and having neither the will nor the courage to attack the formidable English. Nevertheless, Margaret refused to lose hope, and turned to France, whose King might prove more generous and resolute.

Accordingly the young Duke of Somerset was sent to Guienne to seek his aid. Her plan was that the Scots, crossing the border once more, should ravage the north country in great force; the Lancastrians under Pembroke should rise, using Harlech as their base; and simultaneously a French contingent should land at Sandwich, linking up by prearrangement with her friends in the south and west.

Annoyed by the assistance "my rebels of Scotland" were giving to the Lancastrians, Edward negotiated with the rebellious Scot, James, the ninth "Black" Earl of Douglas, seeking at that time to regain his confiscated estates in Scotland. Douglas and the Earl of Ross discussed this matter in England, and in October Edward undertook to protect any Scots who fought for Douglas.

Early in 1462 John de Vere, 12th Earl of Oxford, a great favourite with the King, incited Lord Aubrey de Vere, his son, together with Sir Thomas Tudenham, Sir William Tyrell and a body of Lancastrians, to rise against the King, but their plot was discovered. Arrested in Essex on the 20th February Aubrey was drawn from Westminster to Tower Hill on a sledge and beheaded on a scaffold 8 ft. high. Tudenham, Tyrell and Montgomery, an Esquire, met the same fate. Worcester gave Aubrey and the others no trial.

Three days later Oxford himself was briefly tried before the Lord Constable, on the charge that in treasonable correspondence with Margaret he had proposed a landing on the east coast. Found guilty, he was taken on foot to the place of execution. A large fire had been kindled close by the tall scaffold. He was tightly bound, his stomach cut open, his entrails roughly pulled out, and after castration he was tossed, still living, into the flames. When life had left him, his skin was stripped from his back and given to two lay friars, who, wrapping it in a cloth, buried it in a chapel. The body was quartered, and the members left hanging at the city gates. The remains of the three earlier victims were decently buried in the Church of the Augustine Friars, their heads joining the gruesome array on London Bridge.

[5]

Edward now visited Sandwich to settle a quarrel between nobles and seamen, then, by way of Cambridge, advanced to Peterborough to overawe the Lancastrians, if they contemplated a disturbance, by show of force. Warwick and Norfolk remained behind to guard London and the south coast. The King paused at Newark, then returned via Lincoln to Leicester. Falconberg, made Earl of Kent in June, 1461, was sent north to hold the border. With the retirement of the Scots the danger passed, Newcastle was relieved, and George Lumley knighted and made Sheriff of Northumberland. His father, Lord Lumley, was installed as Governor of Newcastle. George had the task of holding Tynemouth against invasion or attack.

The alliance with Douglas was strengthened by a treaty signed in London on the 13th February, whereby John of the Isles and his lieutenant, Donald Balloch, were given leave to subdue and share all Scotland north of the Firth of Forth, and Edward pledged himself to aid the "Black Douglas". Ample funds were allotted to the three Scots. Meantime, Louis of France, having but recently come to the throne, was naturally and habitually cautious, and unwilling as yet to embroil himself with England.

Failing in his mission, therefore, the young Somerset consoled himself by harrying Calais almost every other day, causing casualties. The Queen of Scotland, Margaret's friend, having lost her husband, James II, killed by a bursting siege gun when attacking Roxburgh Castle, had become Queen Regent. Margaret decided to go to France to plead with Louis herself, and borrowed £190 from her to pay for the journey. She sailed from Kirkcudbright on the 10th April, 1462, taking Prince Edward with her. Henry was left in Edinburgh. She landed in Brittany on Good Friday, the 16th, but had to wait for an audience until Louis returned from the south. The intervening period she passed in Anjou and Touraine, spending a few weeks with her father, who had to borrow money to meet the expense of keeping her. She had pledged her own plate as security for the loan from Mary of Gueldres.

Louis eventually agreed to give her material aid, demanding as his price no less than the restoration of Calais to France. They met again in Rouen towards sunset on the 13th June. Louis then undertook to provide 2,000 men under Pierre de Brezé, Seigneur of Varennes, and Count Malevrier, both experienced generals. De Brezé had been under lock and key for some months, having incurred his sovereign's displeasure, and possibly Louis gave him this command to get him out of the way. The French King also supplied 20,000 fr. in cash. Later, in 1462, he signed a formal treaty recognizing Henry as rightful King of England, and declaring a truce between their two countries to last for 100 years. This was virtually a declaration of war on Edward, and indeed Louis made no secret of his intentions, giving Margaret leave to enlist troops in Normandy and press any vessel found in Norman ports into her service.

Now nominally master of Calais, Louis prepared to besiege the town, but the Duke of Burgundy, who favoured Edward and feared the French, showed signs of assisting the defenders, so Louis, drawing in his horns, contented himself with allowing the Lancastrian expedition to sail without further delay. At the same time, behind Margaret's back he put out feelers for peace with both Burgundy and England. In fact, Wenlock, Essex and the Archbishop of York came to St. Omer in 1463 for discussions with Burgundy and France.

[6]

In England Warwick, now almost supreme, had every reason to avoid foreign conflict. He proposed, therefore, to the Queen Regent of Scotland that they should discuss the future relations of their two countries. Ever anxious, in view of her difficulties at home, for peace with her powerful neighbour, Mary of Gueldres met him in secret at Dumfries. Warwick is said to have suggested she might marry Edward, but Mary was in no way enchanted by this proposal, while Bishop James Kennedy of St. Andrews, head of the Scottish Lancastrians, was hostile to the notion. The idea was therefore quietly dropped.

Another proposal was that Henry VI should be handed over by the Scots, but this, too, came to nothing. Warwick then captured a fortress on the border, and the Earl of Ross raided Atholl, doing great damage. Mary "saw the red light", and in Carlisle a truce was signed, Warwick agreeing to hold Douglas in check.

The Scots being no longer a menace, Warwick and his generals mopped up the north country. Hastings and Montagu—made Warden of the East Marches towards Scotland—took Naworth Castle. Alnwick Castle also surrendered to Hastings in July after a long siege, and was placed under Sir Ralph Grey.

Somerset had planned that Margaret should go to Rouen, wait there and sail from Boulogne, but de Brezé, in command of her army, preferred to sail from Normandy. He landed in Scotland with Margaret and 800 men, mostly mercenaries. Somerset, who had earlier returned to Scotland, now crossed the Scottish border into Northumberland at Lent, and retook Naworth.

Montagu and Hastings quickly recovered this stronghold, Somerset being compelled to withdraw, but just before the Queen landed, further insurrection broke out in England. Sir Richard Tunstall, Henry's former friend, captured Bamburgh Castle, hitherto guarded by Sir William, his brother. Sited on the edge of the North Sea, it was the key point any invader of Northumbria had to take and hold. Dunstanburgh was also treacherously surrendered by Sir Ralph Percy, brother of that Earl of Northumberland killed at Towton. It fell without a siege. Alnwick, strongest and handsomest of the northern fortresses, was also retaken after a brief investment, being short of food.

The Queen now gathered her supporters about her, and into her enticing pool like spawning salmon swam those loyal warriors Somerset, Pembroke, Roos, Hungerford and the treacherous Percy, who, though not yet of age, was virtually chief of his clan, many of whose stoutest fighters he brought with him. Having paused long enough in Scotland to pick up Henry, and knowing the Scots could no longer shelter her in view of the truce, Margaret came into England again, making Bamburgh her headquarters.

FIVE

1462 - 1464

[1]

BY THE 30TH OCTOBER news of the invasion and of the loss of the northern fortresses had reached Edward in London. Warwick was already in the north preparing to meet the Lancastrians. The King sent commissioners south and west to raise money, and in November marched, taking his Master of Ordnance and ample munitions of war. His big siege guns, however, went to Newcastle by sea in ships hastily provisioned and manned, and were carried on thence by road. All were named. "Edward", the largest, was a bombardel; "Newcastle", next in size, an iron gun; "Dijon" was of bronze. The smallest was "London". After unloading these, the ships sailed up and down the Scottish coast to prevent surprise landings and raid the enemy seaports.

Edward, satisfied that his generals had the situation well in hand, slowed down his advance to gather more men in York, which he reached on the 19th November. Here he was laid up with the pox ("pocks"), which may have been measles, chicken pox, smallpox or some less reputable ailment, for he was no austere monarch. He took no part, therefore, in the ensuing military operations, but sent his own men forward to Warwick, and as soon as cured, returned to London.

Warwick, setting up his headquarters at Warkworth, a small port seven miles south-east of Alnwick, besieged the three strongholds—Alnwick, Bamburgh and Dunstanburgh—simultaneously during December, riding each day from one to the other to control the operations and ensure that his men received their supplies without stint from their base in Newcastle. Dunstanburgh town, now commanded by Sir Henry Bedford, was besieged by John Tiptoft, Earl of Worcester, Warwick's brother-in-law. The castle of the town was defended by Sir Richard Tunstall, Sir Philip Wentworth, Dr. John Morton and some hundreds of men.

Bamburgh, besieged by Montagu and Ogle, was defended by Somerset, Percy, Pembroke and others, with but 300 or 400 men. When Hastings marched in from the south, Greystoke and Powys continued the siege of Alnwick, while Warwick and Hastings, joined by Scrope and Fitzhugh, went on to threaten Bamburgh. The Queen, seeing her danger, fled to a French "carvyle" or caravel, a light, small, fast ship, meaning to seek refuge again in Scotland. De Brezé, eager to muster another army, accompanied her. Their small fleet was passing Lindisfarne—Holy Island—when a storm blew up. The wind howled, great green waves advanced in savage rushes, and the frail craft were tossed this way and that until their cracking, groaning timbers could take no more. The caravel let in water, and was soon sinking fast. Margaret and her entourage succeeded in transferring to a fishing boat which was weathering the gale, and in this cockleshell, exposed to the elements, were soon driving helplessly towards the frowning, spray-smothered rocks of the coast.

The caravel presently went down before their eyes with all the Queen's treasure, but Margaret and her companions landed safely near Berwick, after a narrow escape from drowning. The three larger ships, unable to make headway against the fierce wind, were forced relentlessly aground, till they struck the rocks of the island. Altogether 406 French soldiers with De Brezé's second-in-command, the Sieur de Graville, scrambled ashore, and failing to re-float their vessels, set them alight. Helpless, wet, shaken, they could but huddle forlornly where they were till the tide turned. Then they crossed the sands and sheltered in the church.

Bamburgh was now so closely invested that they saw no chance of rejoining the garrison there. Warwick sent a party to take them, and after a short, sharp fight they surrendered. Taken prison were not only de Graville, but also Sieur Cardot Malorte, an Admiral of France, with his son Louis, who were held captive till ransomed on the 16th June, 1467. The Queen's goods were recovered according to one story, and presented to Edward for his use.

As the besiegers narrowed the noose around the fortresses, the garrisons were reduced to eating their horses. Bamburgh and Dunstanburgh held out till Christmas, then capitulated. Their garrisons were turned loose and left to find their way back, carrying white staves, to Scotland. Alnwick alone remained, stubborn and indomitable.

On the 5th January, 1463, intense cold was followed by heavy snow, and now men could travel over the ice. The Yorkists, worn out by the protracted siege, carrying on under depressing conditions of wind, rain, sleet and bitter frost, had no more stomach for battle after all they had endured, and when Angus and De Brezé returned with a new Scottish force, withdrew half-starved to the river bank. The Scots took the castle without opposition, relieving the defenders, and Lord Hungerford took charge. Had they been bolder, they could have attacked the wretched Yorkists with every prospect of victory over these dispirited men, silently watching their approach.

Fearing a trap, however, the Scots stood irresolute, not even discharging an arrow, and finally Hungerford withdrew, taking the garrison with him, and leaving the castle empty, its gates standing wide. Warwick's men took fresh heart, and next day entered the abandoned fortress, regaining warmth and shelter. Once more Harlech alone held out for Henry.

Edward gave the Abbot and Convent of Alnwick an honorarium of £100 for the losses sustained during the siege.

[2]

Somerset and Sir Ralph Percy now made their peace with the King, and it was agreed that their confiscated possessions should be restored. The two nobles took the oath of allegiance in Durham, and the King, having taken a fancy to Somerset, a handsome young man, gave him and Percy new livery and rich presents. Percy went back to his fortresses in Northumberland, being allowed to retain Bamburgh and Dunstanburgh. Sir Henry Bedford, the original Governor of Dunstanburgh, accompanied the King to London.

Confident that his recapture of the three Northumbrian strong-holds meant no more trouble from that quarter, Warwick followed Edward to Fotheringay Castle. Here Edward had the catafalque used in St. Paul's (p. 78) sent to him. It was draped with a rich cloth and four large banners showing the royal arms. A month later he celebrated the anniversary of his father's death, arranging for permanent burial of York, Salisbury, Warwick's father, and Sir Thomas Neville, in Bisham Abbey. The impressive funeral was attended not only by the three chief mourners, but also by other relations and members of the Court, male and female.

The King then moved on to Hertford Castle, and by way of the nunnery at Sion to London, where he was again warmly received, though a plan to meet him on the road had to be abandoned because he came in by water. Montagu had been left in full command of the Scottish border, but presently he, too, came after the King to London.

Once again the Yorkists had reckoned without the implacable, indefatigable Margaret of Anjou. Not only did she stop the faint-hearted Scots from making peace with the English, but also she and De Brezé raised another strong force of Frenchmen, Scots and refugee Lancastrians to conquer all England.

This strange woman never won affection from those below her, to whom she remained cold and distant. Nevertheless, by her courage and bearing she won great respect. She could be charming when she liked, but relied primarily on intelligence, will and craft rather than on warmth of affection. With promises of ample assistance from France, she crossed the Tweed again during Lent, 1463, with De Brezé, Exeter, Roos, and about 2,000 men. Taking the Yorkists completely by surprise, she quickly recaptured Bamburgh and Dunstanburgh, aided by new treachery, for Percy, turning his coat again, surrendered both fortresses the moment she presented herself before them. Defended with spirit, Bamburgh at least could have held out for a considerable time.

Overjoyed at her success, the Queen drove southwards to Alnwick. Sir Ralph Grey had hoped to be made Governor of this Castle, but Sir John Astley, a brave knight who had fought well at Smithfield, had been preferred. At the first opportunity, therefore, Grey avenged himself by going over to Henry. On the 1st May he threw Astley out, admitting Hungerford and the Lancastrians. Astley was first imprisoned, then handed to the French. Strong forces of English, French and Scots were left in all three captured strongholds, and for a time Margaret commanded an extensive area of the north of England. To consolidate her position, however, she needed to link up with the Lancastrians of the shires.

The commons roundabout gave her no enthusiastic welcome, and none joined her colours, the yeomen of Rock and Beadnell in particular remaining passionately Yorkist. Percy brought his men into Dunstanburgh, of which he was made once more Governor.

[3]

The new invasion alarmed London. Montagu came posting back to prevent Newcastle from falling into Lancastrian hands. Warwick and his lieutenants left London for Westmorland, with power to summon all the county to help him repel the Scots. Edward stationed armed men on every coast to prevent invasion, and ordered his constables in the southern half of the country to refuse the Queen shelter or support on pain of being regarded as enemies of the crown. Guards screened the border everywhere to stop the Lancastrians from coming over it to reinforce the Queen.

After Parliament had been prorogued on the 18th June, the King with the reserve moved towards Northampton in support of Warwick. There he remained till the 28th, awaiting news. Montagu threw back the Lancastrians under Grey from the walls of Newcastle, and to Margaret's dismay, four ships sent to Bamburgh from France with supplies and men were intercepted and brought by seamen of Newcastle into the Tyne. Montagu also relieved Warkworth, besieged by Grey and De Brezé. In the west James, Earl of Douglas, was foraying into Scotland, so keeping the Scots on tenterhooks throughout spring and summer. Towards midsummer, Margaret and Henry, with the young King, James III of Scotland, sat down before Norham, which held out stubbornly for eighteen days until relieved by Montagu and Warwick.

The capture of the French ships was now seriously handicapping Margaret, who was short of supplies, which Louis showed no signs of replacing. The Yorkists advanced, crossed the Alne, and on the

10th July met a strong force, mostly of Scots, at a point near Great Ryal on the right bank of Devilswater. They prepared to attack, but the Scots, just when they should have held fast, succumbed to fright, and without striking a blow, fled back to their own country. Margaret had to snatch up her young son, and with a few followers regain the border with what equipment could be gathered together in haste. Thieves or brigands pursued her, pouncing upon her jewels and baggage.

The chief, sword drawn, grabbed the Queen's garments, seeming about to end her life, but weeping, she knelt, praying him to spare her. By a lucky chance, her captor detected his men sharing out the spoils unfairly, and letting go of her dress, went over to protest. A fierce quarrel broke out, during which the Queen, approaching a young man left to guard her, whose features suggested humanity and gentleness, begged his help, and moved by her distress he agreed. All three stole away on a single horse, the young Prince in front and the Queen behind. In Dipton Wood, a common refuge of villains, outlaws and cutpurses, one of these, savage and cruel in appearance, heard the sound of hooves, and came up to them, ordering them to halt. Margaret addressed him boldly, and according to her own account said: "Man, you were born under a lucky star. After all the evil you have done, you now have it in your power to do a good deed that will never be forgotten. If I, the wretched Queen of England, have fallen into your clutches, it is because you are meant to turn from your old way of life. If you believe in God and his Passion, take pity on my misery. At all events save this boy, the King's only son. For doing such a merciful deed all your past cruelty shall be forgotten. Hide him in your woods and thickets. Let him eat roots and acorns with the swine and pass his nights on the cold ground. His life will be safer on such a royal bed and in such baronial company than if he endured the fitful fortunes of a throne. Save my son! Keep him for me! And if God grant his restoration, you can be sure He will well reward a service such as no man of your sort has ever before had to perform."

The robber, prostrating himself, swore to die rather than forsake the young prince, and to lead him by secret paths to safety in Bamburgh Castle. He pleaded for pardon as if she were still on the throne, and convinced the Prince would be safe with him, she rode off with her companion. Together they reached Berwick, and the outlaw kept his word, restoring the young Prince to his friends.

Her goods lost, Margaret was so reduced that for five days she and her escort had but a herring between them, and one day not even a loaf of bread. At Mass on the 20th July, the feast of St. Margaret, her patron saint, she could not even offer a "black penny", having to borrow a groat from a Scottish archer, who took it from his purse with obvious reluctance.

Now, learning that a treaty was being negotiated between Burgundy, France and England, and that the English army was close at hand, the Queen embarked in one of four fishing vessels, aiming to reach Flanders and herself make a pact with Philip of Burgundy before it was too late. Landing at Sluys with De Brezé, the Prince, Exeter, and her Council, she was in a sorry state, having neither money, furniture, jewels nor royal robes. She had but seven attendants, and as credentials only an old safe-conduct Philip had once given her. De Brezé had to lend her the money for their food. She had promised Henry, left behind in Bamburgh with her equipment and horses, that she would return in the spring with a new army, but in the event she never set eyes on him again.

There is a story that when she sailed, one brave French drummer stayed behind, determined not to give way when Warwick arrived. Standing alone on top of a sandhill, he played his pipe and drum by the postern gate of the town, cheerfully and stoutly refusing to move. Warwick, taking a liking to him, eventually won him over and took him into his own service.

Philip of Burgundy sent Philippe Pot, his chamberlain, to welcome the Queen, but a destitute exile who had so signally failed to establish herself was unlikely to weaken his resolve not to abandon the alliance with Edward. Though compassionate towards her, a royal personage in misfortune, he continually deferred the meeting she desperately sought until he had completed his talks with the English plenipotentiaries.

The audacious Queen, losing patience and determined to have her way, took matters into her own hands, notifying the Duke that she was coming to see him. Without awaiting his reply, and disguised as a peasant woman to conceal her identity from the English soldiers who were seeking her everywhere, she set off in a rustic cart drawn by four horses. A French aristocrat sheltered her near Lille, giving her food for a couple of days more and lending her money. The English nearly captured her at Béthune, but Philip had sent her an escort of archers, and they dared not attack.

The Duke treated her with great courtesy, and on his return sent her 2,000 gold crowns, 500 more for De Brezé and 400 for each of her ladies. The Duchess of Bourbon and her daughter were appointed her companions for the day, and the Duke promised to remember her when bargaining with the English.

Still protected by his archers, she returned to Bruges, where she was entertained by his son, Charles the Bold, Count of Charolais. Having now to rest content with the Duke's assurances, she revisited her father in Bar, near Nancy, who gave her a house in St. Mighel en Barrois, where she first told the Duchess of Bourbon, now attached to her suite, the story of the forest robber.

Sir John Fortescue, who had been at Towton and had already spent two years with the Queen's household in Scotland, was appointed tutor of Prince Edward. He wrote: "We be all in great poverty, but yet the Queen sustaineth us in meat and drink. Her highness may do no more than she doth." The Queen was to remain here for seven years.

[4]

In England things were going badly for her cause. Louis, Burgundy and Warwick had agreed upon a truce, and so her most powerful ally had abandoned Henry. Faced with this fact, the Scots, she believed, would now desert her, and his hands thus freed, Edward would crush her husband once and for all. As 1463 ended, Henry's prospects were indeed at their lowest. Only the remote castle of Harlech still displayed his standard. Nevertheless, Margaret's personality was such that her followers did not readily abandon her or their King.

Edward, who had not forgiven the Scots for their impertinent invasion, determined to punish them as soon as he was ready. A brief stay in the capital was followed by a visit to Dover, where he ordered Worcester to load ships with supplies for Scotland, but these vessels seem to have been lost at sea. Before the news of the

French truce had come through, Douglas was badly beaten in the field, his brother and many more being taken to Edinburgh and beheaded.

Edward's preparations for attack dismayed the Scots, and Henry begged them to put him in a safe place. Early in 1464, therefore, they sent him to St. Andrews, then to the coast, and so to Bamburgh.

Edward came to York via Pontefract in October, and stayed there for a time. The Queen-Regent of Scotland now sought peace. Her envoys came to him and a truce was signed, the absent Bishop Kennedy agreeing; the truce was to last till the 31st October. Before this date both Mary of Gueldres and the Earl of Angus were dead.

Despite many grumbles, Edward had extracted from Parliament a considerable grant for his Scottish campaign, and when this came to nothing, the tax-payers naturally demanded its return, but they did not get it. For a time the King lost popularity, and quick to perceive this, he later wisely restored a good proportion of the money—£6,000—no doubt with great regret.

As indicated, Somerset, whose friends had pleaded for him, had been pardoned, and had pledged his loyalty. Greatly trusted by Edward, he was given money, the Castle of Bamburgh and the Captaincy of the Royal Guard. The King took him on a journey through Yorkshire, the guards being men of Somerset's own command. A chronicler wrote: "It was like putting wolves to guard a lamb. But Almighty God was shepherd."

The King now spent a couple of months at Westminster and Windsor enjoying himself. To everyone's surprise and irritation he continued to make a great fuss of Somerset, sharing a bed with him on several occasions when they hunted together. Parliament restored the Duke's titles and estates, while Edward granted him money to cover his immediate expenses. He was promised an annuity of 1,000 marks, but this he did not receive, the King himself being short of money. It was not uncommon for medieval kings to make generous promises, discovering later they could not keep them. Sometimes, too, their ministers of finance conveniently "forgot" to see that they were kept.

The King now sought to console Somerset for his defeat by

Henry VI, 1421–1471, a fifteenth-century painting in the National Portrait Gallery, by an unknown artist

The Earl of Shrewsbury presenting Margaret of Anjou with an illuminated manuscript, *Poems and Romances* (1445). Fragment of a page from the book

arranging a tournament at Westminster, and requested him to arm himself and ride in the lists, but the Duke refused to do battle with mere knights. The King urged him to "be merry, and sent him a token", whereupon Somerset took part in the tournament, using as his helmet "a sorry hat of straw".

Edward also saved him from serious injury at Northampton, where, when he arrived on the 18th or 19th June, men sought to kill him under the King's roof. Edward cleverly gave the angry Northampton men a cask of wine to drink in the market square, as well as "many fair pieces of silver". They broached the cask gleefully, filling basins, cauldrons, bowls, pans and dishes. Afterwards, Edward packed off the Duke to Wales for his own safety, sending his bodyguards to Newcastle.

Secretly Somerset was chafing at his new servitude. Taking advantage of the remoteness of North Wales, he occupied Holt Castle, assembled his Lancastrian friends there, and galloping through the night rode with them northwards. He knew his men, now in Newcastle, were loyal to him, and believed they would open the city gates when he appeared. Bad luck nearly ruined this scheme, for he was recognized in Durham when he took a lodging for the night, and warned of impending arrest, escaped barefooted and clad only in his nightshirt. Two of his servants were captured, and also his treasure chest. Sending a messenger to his men in Newcastle, he hurried there as fast as he could.

[5]

Edward, wounded to the quick by the Duke's defection, had believed with Montagu that the Scottish truce ended the Lancastrian hopes, and that Somerset was completely won over. He now marched in strength to Newcastle, seized Somerset's men before they could move, and executed some of them, making Lord Scrope governor of the city. Somerset found the gates firmly closed against him, and had to fly to Bamburgh. The King had no compunction in arresting his mother and suspending her annuity. Her tenants promptly ceased to pay her their due rents, but friends lent her money and other necessities.

Why did Somerset risk his head in a seemingly lost cause? Had

7

he been a man of high principle, he would not have accepted friendship, honours and privileges from the King, nor, having accepted them, so quickly have betrayed him. Possibly slights from Yorkist nobles at Court irked him, or he suffered remorse for his desertion of Henry. On the other hand, secret correspondence and his own observation may have taught him that Edward was not so popular as he had been. Like all romantic peoples, the English loved battles, but hated paying for them. Edward had faults to set against his virtues—a love of good living, a passion for women—and of these his enemies made the most.

Many with short memories looked back nostalgically to the days of Henry VI. The rewards anticipated from a change of sovereigns had not materialized. The new King spent time and money on his own, sometimes undignified, pleasures, leaving Warwick to do the fighting and govern the country. In addition, the land was riddled with Lancastrians as an archery target with holes. Reading between the lines, Somerset may have believed little was needed to topple Edward from his throne. Gathering up the threads of discontent, he wove them into a tapestry of plot and betrayal. Having obtained many pledges of support, he became convinced that the resourceful, tireless Margaret would break the unstable pact between Burgundy, France and England, or find another backer among her influential friends abroad.

In short, the Duke believed Henry's restoration practicable, and tried at Bamburgh to inject into him his own enthusiasm. His hopes were strengthened by the unexpected arrival of two staunch and useful Lancastrians, Sir Henry Bellingham and Humphrey Neville of Brancepeth, both enforced collaborators with and prisoners of the Yorkists, whom they had deserted.

SIX

1463–1465

[I]

GROWING DISCONTENT IN ENGLAND was matched by trouble in
North Wales, where Pembroke was operating. To counter him
Norfolk was rushed to Holt Castle in Denbighshire, recently abandoned by Somerset, while Edward moved swiftly towards the
west. In Coventry towards the end of January he rode on to
Worcester, rested briefly, then came via Tewkesbury to Gloucester,
staying six days. The chief justices of the county rode with him,
doing summary justice after trial to disturbers of the peace.

No sooner had the King made his heavy hand felt in this quarter
than he was off again to Norfolk and Cambridgeshire, Kimbolton,
Waltham and St. Albans. Meantime, the Duke of Norfolk rooted
out Somerset's friends in North Wales. Some fled, but most were
taken and eventually pardoned. Small risings in Lancashire and
Cheshire were more severely dealt with.

Parliament, called to meet at York, was adjourned owing to the
King's absence. In London, a day or so later, Edward met an envoy
from Burgundy with a proposal that he should marry Isabella of
Castile—eventually the bride of Ferdinand of Aragon. This offer
he politely declined, backed up by Warwick, a Francophile,
though it would have had many dynastic and practical advantages.
Edward, it will be seen, had other ideas of his own.

The Scots, wishing their truce to become a firm peace, offered
to negotiate. Montagu undertook to meet their delegates at the
border as Warden of the Marches, and bring them to York, George
Neville, the Chancellor, accompanying him. Somerset and Percy
were already burning, pillaging and destroying the country around

Bamburgh, and were besieging Norham Castle, a stronghold on the border, which promptly came over to them. Next, their rapid, daring attack surprised Skipton Castle in the Craven district of Yorkshire, which fell without a fight, having always been a Clifford stronghold.

With eighty spearmen and a body of archers, Sir Ralph Percy determined to ambush Montagu and his troops, who were in no great strength. Occupying a wood near Newcastle, he awaited them as they set out to meet the envoys.

Learning that a hostile force was hiding at this point, Montagu changed course, eluded Percy, and came safely to Newcastle and the Tyne, aiming for Norham Castle, which he perhaps believed back in Yorkist hands. He paused to collect up more men, then moved forward with Greystoke and Willoughby. On the 25th April, 1464, St. Mark's Day, he was furiously attacked by Somerset and Percy when about nine miles short of Alnwick. Their men were largely from Alnwick and Dunstanburgh and were defeated. Percy was killed, crying as he died: "I have saved the bird in my bosom", which is taken to mean that by keeping faith with Henry he had saved his honour. A rough column, Percy's Cross, is reputed to mark the spot where he fell.

Known as the battle of Hedgeley Moor, it was a tribute to Montagu's skilful tactics, for he was inferior in numbers. Later he met the Scots envoys at Norham, and brought them to York, where they were welcomed by the Lords Commissioner. Meantime, the miniature Court of the Lancastrians at Bamburgh was extremely active. Somerset had told Henry that all Wales and the west of England were loyal to him. Behaving as if they were indeed a nation state, the Privy Councillors of the royal exile received and entertained an envoy from Louis. Advised by Somerset of the distubances in England, and ever distrustful of Burgundy, Louis took the chance to meddle in Edward's affairs, but was particularly offended when the Scots signed a peace treaty with the King, negotiated at York on the 1st June by George Neville, Bishop of Exeter. It was proposed it should last for fifteen years.

Louis was not the only one to be upset, for the treaty was received with unease in England, where it was said that if the Scots were true, the treaty might run its full course, "but it is hard to trust the Scots; they be ever full of guile and deceit". Later in the year George Neville was rewarded for his good work by being made Archbishop of York, and enthroned on the 23rd September, 1464.

The Duke of Burgundy sought to insure himself against trouble arising out of the treaty by himself sending an envoy to Bamburgh. Meantime, Margaret was hard at work seeking to win support, especially from the Duke of Brittany and other potential allies. The French envoy at Bamburgh was asked by the Lancastrians to visit her on his return and instruct her to persuade Charles, who would be the new Duke of Burgundy when his father, Philip died, to send them food. She should also ask her father, René of Anjou, to send her cannon and culverins.

[2]

Hedgely Moor had after all been a comparatively small affair. Somerset and his men, though badly mauled, did not turn and run, but spent three weeks gathering up every man they could, biding their time till Montagu was once more escorting the Scots back to the border. Having dumped Henry like a sack of coals at Langley and Bywell Castle on the north bank of the Tyne, they moved cautiously towards Newcastle in the wake of the departing Scots.

On the 14th May they came to Hexham, on the south bank, and camped at Linnels, a field of about twenty acres beside the stream known as Devilswater. Shielded from the cold northern winds, it was as good a position in comfort and concealment as could have been chosen, but was tactically bad, being virtually a blind alley. There was but one good way in and no easy way out. A mass of bushes lined the stream, and elsewhere were only steeply-rising, thickly-wooded hills.

When scouts reported to Montagu in Newcastle that Somerset was on the move, he hastened westwards with Greystoke, Willoughby and Scrope—healed of his Towton wound—and followed the Tyne to overtake them. On reaching Linnels, he first made sure of the open end of the field, then sounded the charge. The Lancastrians resisted, striving to hold their position, but as the battle went against them, they sought to escape across Devilswater. At this critical moment Grey and his men took to their heels, and weakened by their desertion, Somerset and 500 spearmen fought for their lives on one of the hills enclosing the field. Many ran after Grey, others surrendered, and eventually Somerset himself fled, but was pursued and taken by Sir John Middleton's men. With him went Sir Edmund Fitzhugh and 'Black Jack', a border brigand said by some to have been the young Prince's protector when Margaret escaped. All were brought into Hexham.

There the master cook, in his apron, struck off the spurs from Somerset's heels with his knife. The King-at-Arms and the heralds tore his coat of arms from his body. Stripped of title and knighthood, dressed in a coat of "thin arms reversed", he was compelled to walk through the town, lie on the usual sledge, and be drawn to the scaffold. His headless body was buried in the Friary.

Roos and Hungerford were caught hiding in the woods and beheaded at Newcastle on the 28th, together with Sir Thomas Fynderne and six others. Sir Thomas Hill was beheaded at York, Sir Philip Wentworth and Sir William Poynington at Middleham, while at least fifteen were executed at York, including Sir Thomas Hussey and Robert Watts, one of Henry's "porters". The scattering of these executions over so wide an area in the space of eleven days was designed, no doubt, to cow dissidents.

During May Sir William Tallboys was found lurking in a coalpit with much gold and silver on him meant for the soldiers' pay and to buy armour and ordnance. He was beheaded at Newcastle.

These punishments were probably the work of Montagu and Warwick, though Edward could not have been ignorant of them. It was rough justice, but it was a rough age.

Montagu had lost many men as well as wounded and sick. Those who survived shared Tallboys's cash among them. Langley and Bywell Castle surrendered without resistance. The jubilant Yorkists had hoped to find Henry there, but he had escaped: "how and whither God only knows, in whose hands are the hearts of kings", a chronicler wrote. Henry had, in fact, ridden back to Bamburgh under the wing of Sir Henry Bellingham, leaving behind his "bycocket" or cap of estate, a turned-up peaked cap richly garnished with two golden crowns, pearls and jewels. A week later, Montagu presented this to Edward at Pontefract. Also captured were Henry's sword, the trappings of his horse and three of his servants clad in blue samite, a rich silk interwoven with threads of gold.

[3]

Hexham was one of the more important minor conflicts of this reign, but although victorious, Edward was still insecure while ever Henry and Margaret were at large, even though Scotland was no longer their refuge and ally. In York on the 27th he created Montagu Earl of Northumberland in place of the new Earl, son of the Percy who had fallen, and now immured in the Fleet prison in London. Warwick, leaving the north, returned to the capital on the 14th June.

Edward remained in the Palace of York for some weeks, intent on crushing the Lancastrians once and for all. The new Earl of Northumberland (Montagu) now attacked Henry's remaining strongholds, and Alnwick hoisted the white flag on the 23rd June as soon as he approached. Dunstanburgh and Norham surrendered to Hastings and Wenlock respectively, the besiegers observing the Feast of St. John within the gates. Bamburgh, however, held out, Grey, having fled there from Hexham, knowing he had nothing to hope for, having twice betrayed the trust placed in him.

Warwick was now back with the army, and told the defenders through the Chester herald that he was prepared to sit down before their walls for seven years if need be, as the Greeks had sat before Troy, and that for every cannon shot that damaged the walls, a head should fall. If they surrendered, all would be pardoned except Grey, Sir Humphrey Neville and "other that kept his rebellious opinion". No reply being made, the siege guns "Newcastle" and "London" opened fire, and the castle was badly battered, stones from the walls being blown into the sea, while the balls of "Dijon" smashed into the Governor's own rooms. The cascade of rubble and stone stunned and wounded him, so that when Warwick's archers and footsoldiers stormed through the gaps torn in the defences, Grey's men, shaken by the bombardment and the collapse of their commander, capitulated. It was about the 10th July.

When Grey, who had told Warwick he would live or die in the castle, next opened his eyes, he was a prisoner. Taken to Pontefract Castle, then to Doncaster, he was tried by the Earl of Worcester and executed, his body being buried in the cemetery of the White Friars. His head joined the others on London Bridge. Two days later, Edward came to Doncaster and by stages proceeded to Leicester.

Those defeated Lancastrians who could sailed to the Continent, but Jasper Tudor fled back to Wales, wandering from place to place "nowhere finding safety, comfort or support".

[4]

A new and powerful influence upon Edward now approached. Twenty-two years of age, he seemed to be what England badly needed, a strong, brave, handsome, healthy King. But was he more?

Hitherto he had merely executed Warwick's will, for the experience and ability of the elder statesman were unrivalled. For a time Edward was perfectly content to indulge his private whims while leaving the arduous work of government to the great Earl. So much so, indeed, that in March, 1464, Louis of France had remarked: "They tell me that they have two rulers in England— Monsieur de Warwick and another whose name I have forgotten."

When not in the field the young King passed the time in feasting, philandering, the chase and the spectacle. Nevertheless he was well-liked because of his good looks, courtesy and bonhomie, and his freedom from affectation. Even ordinary citizens found him approachable, and their wives even more so. An example may be given.

A midsummer feast was given by the King in 1463 to the Mayor and Officers of the City of London, seated in strict order of precedence. Within the city gates the Mayor was almost as powerful as the King, and in many matters second to him alone. By some mischance, however, the Mayor, Matthew Philip, a goldsmith, coming in late, found Worcester in his place at table. Incensed, he went straight home without bite or sup, taking with him most of his aldermen. At his own house he put on for them, at the city's expense and as quickly as possible, a feast of magnificent proportions, including cygnets and other delicacies, begging them to set to and enjoy themselves, and promising that next time everything should go right at the royal feast.

The "greatly ashamed officers of the feast" told Edward what had happened, and he appreciated the Mayor's loss of face. He at once despatched masses of meat, bread, wine and many other good things to the Mayor's house, but when his servants arrived, they were, it is said, embarrassed because what they brought was no better than the fare already being enjoyed. Nevertheless, the King's accompanying message was so kindly and apologetic that he was held to have made full amends, and not to have intended a slight upon the city.

Free from a hard, military life Edward, as is not surprising, behaved like the young man he was, spending money freely, eating enormously, feasting his friends, and tasting to the full the pleasures of kingship. He loved a good tournament, a pageant, a band of well-trained minstrels. The nation's business—a bore—he was well content to avoid. His circle considered him a bold, brave, dashing young soldier, handsome, fond of field sports, inclined to be thoughtless, a favourite with the ladies, whose favours he greatly enjoyed, a lover of food and liquor, indolent, self-willed and improvident, an opinion not altogether unjust.

Nevertheless, beneath his gay and reckless exterior lurked a powerful will and a keen brain. He was eloquent, with also the ruthlessness of a medieval monarch, but with these he had a degree of compassion, tolerance, good humour, trust and magnanimity. Although inexperienced in statecraft, he was greatly interested in the administration of the law, and Stow records that in 1462 he sat for three successive days in the King's Bench in the great Hall of Westminster to hear cases tried and sentence passed.

His private purse was small, and his generosity and extravagance consumed money like a prairie fire. A good deal of it went on medicaments and drugs, for though his general health was good, his doctors had often to cope with the maladies of an amorous young man.

[5]

During these first years of his reign England was in a bad way. The winter had been hard, prolonged and marked by intense frost, during which many cattle were destroyed for lack of fodder. In mid-March a severe drought lasted till the morning after Mid-summer Day, the skies staring brazenly down, not a drop of rain refreshing the upturned, imploring faces. The crops withered, prices rose and parsons prayed in vain, not for the first time, for the salvation of the crops. Then plague broke out over the entire kingdom. Money was terribly short, wheat costing 4d. a bushel, but wine remained cheap.

The nation in general and the King's advisers in particular now felt that Edward, having sown his wild oats, should marry and beget an heir to the throne. Even during his early years there had been several proposals that he should marry. It was first designed to marry him to Magdalene, the daughter of Charles VII of France, but this fell through. Then, in 1453, the proposal was made that he should become the husband of the daughter of the Duke of Alençon. In the following year this idea, too, seems to have been dropped, and the new bride offered was the daughter of the Count of Charolais, later to become Duke Charles of Burgundy; but even this project was abandoned. Some aspect or other of shifting national policies was probably responsible for the failure of these matrimonial suggestions to materialize. Hitherto, the consorts later proposed to him had been politely but firmly rejected. One of these was, as stated, Mary of Gueldres, Queen Regent of Scotland, a widow. Another was Isabella of Castile, sister of the King of Castile. A proposed betrothal to Lady Elizabeth Lucy came to nothing (p. 109). But now the Earl of Warwick took a hand in the game, having made up his mind to marry him off, preferably to Bona of Savoy.

King Louis of France, under the dual pressure of Burgundy and Brittany, ambitious powers horning in on two sides of his realm, was seriously considering alliance with England for self-protection. He now proposed to Warwick, whose basic foreign policy was for *rapprochement* with the French, that this young woman, daughter of the Duke of Savoy and sister of the Queen of France, might be a suitable match. Warwick agreed, and she was brought to the French Court for him to meet her.

Accordingly in July Warwick left London (p. 110) with a retinue of ninety attendants and 100 horsemen, and sailed from Dover, first stocking up one of his ships with "muttons, veals" and other provisions to ensure that his men had enough good English food. Infuriating King Louis, the St. Malo Bretons put to sea and captured this vessel, but Warwick himself landed safely in Calais, and with Wenlock and Whitehill went to Hesdin.

He did not know it, but his mission was fruitless, for Edward had a secret he did not wish to reveal.

SEVEN

1464

[1]

ON THE 30TH APRIL, Edward—to go back a little in time—had secretly set off for Grafton Castle, seat of the Duchess of Bedford and about five miles from Stony Stratford. On and off for some time he had been visiting this castle in the intervals of hunting in Wichwood forest. The attraction was Dame Elizabeth Grey, born in 1436, daughter of the Duchess and widow of John Grey, Lord Ferrers of Groby, a Lancastrian knighted at the second battle of St. Albans, and later killed in action. The Duchess, her mother, had been remarried to Sir Richard Woodville, now Lord Rivers, 'a country squire but the handsomest man in England'.

John Grey's estates came to Elizabeth by a jointure, but were forfeited when the Yorkists came to power. Edward had first visited Grafton for rest and refreshment, and on that occasion she had asked him to restore her possessions. A woman of striking presence, sober and dignified carriage, engaging smile and un-doubted beauty, she enchanted the King, who granted her request and fell violently in love with her.

Quick to see the value of her conquest, Elizabeth, some years older than he, was both intelligent and calculating. She saw that by cheapening herself and becoming merely another of the King's mistresses she would lose a magnificent and unanticipated oppor-tunity. So, when the amorous Edward in his customary cavalier fashion sought to seduce her, she refused him her favours, but in so doing was clever enough not to chill his ardour or give him offence. Indeed, according to Holinshed, the less she gave, the more she allured.

Presently the King was imploring, offering rich gifts, vowing all the vows of men desperate to achieve their ends, but Elizabeth declared that nothing short of honourable marriage would win her. Unaccustomed to refusal, Edward is said to have held his dagger to her throat on one occasion, vowing to use it unless she yielded. She told him "she knew herself unworthy to be a queen, but valued her honour more than to be a concubine".

That she was both chaste and courageous transmuted Edward's passion into something akin to worship. He swore to marry her, but it must be soon, or his Council might force him into a marriage of state. Wealth, power, the throne, mattered nothing to this man, ensnared by one "moderate of stature, well-made and verie wise".

Not daring to consult his Council, whose opposition and refusal could be expected, Edward declared his purpose to but a few most intimate friends, who, seeing he had the bit between his teeth, made no attempt to stay him. His mother, however, fiercely opposed the union, partly because of his earlier affaire with Lady Lucy, who had borne him a child. It was senseless, she said, to marry a widow with two children of her own. Edward laughingly replied that although a bachelor, he had a few children himself.

Heywood, in his "Edward IV, Part I", makes Cicely say: "Married a woman? Married indeed? Here is a marriage that befits a king! It is no marvaile it was done in hast. Here is a bridall, and with hell to boote, you have made worke". Nevertheless, one chronicler at least favoured the marriage, rating an earlier "lewde fellow" for "disordrid writing for lakke of knowledge".

The marriage was secret. Early in the morning the King and a few friends slipped away to Grafton, and there, on the 1st May, Edward and Elizabeth were married in a secret place, the only witnesses being the Duchess of Bedford, two gentlewomen, a priest and the boy serving him. After the ceremony the couple went to bed, remaining there for two or three hours. From his bride's arms the King returned to Stony Stratford as if just back from a hunt, and retired for the night.

He went back there a day or so later, and received with every honour, spent three days in the Castle, his wife being smuggled each night into his bedchamber by stealth, so that virtually none but those who had attended the wedding knew of it. Certainly no one at Court knew, Warwick least of all. Matters were so arranged that whenever the King hunted, he did so near Grafton, slipping over secretly to see his wife. So things stood when the Privy Council met on All Hallows Eve at Reading to discuss once more the vexed question of the currency, a subject previously raised in Stamford. Edward came to this Council from a short stay at Ludlow.

The lords now urged and recommended him in the name of God to marry and live under "the law of God and Church". If he did not care for Bona, they said, they would willingly scour Europe for some maiden of royal blood who would make him a suitable Queen. Meantime, Warwick, as stated, had gone to France to see Louis and meet Bona. Thus harried, Edward could no longer evade the issue, and told them bluntly they were too late. He had been married for nearly five months to Dame Elizabeth Grey.

The Council, shocked, considered this a bad, wholly undesirable match. She was five years older than he, her family were dyed-in-the-wool Lancastrians, and although her mother was of good blood it was rumoured that she had had two children before her marriage. As for Elizabeth's father, he was a nobody, his only money and lands having come to him from his wife. Warwick had taken him prisoner at Sandwich in 1460, and he had been merely the Duke of Bedford's steward, a rustic knight. In marrying him after the Duke's death, the Duchess had married beneath her. The Council suspected she was an enchantress, who by her wiles had ensnared the King for her daughter. Some whispered that having been to bed with Elizabeth, the King would soon wish he had never married her. There was wild talk of annulling the marriage, but in fact nothing could be done about it.

[2]

When the news reached Warwick, he was enraged. In good faith he had set off to negotiate for the hand of Bona, and his King had let him go, knowing all the time he was married, and without consulting him—indeed, without having given him the slightest hint of his intentions. Louis was bound to believe that the King had deliberately let him go on a fool's errand. Postponing the extension of the truce with France, he rushed back to England, reaching London on the 5th August. It is said he quarrelled fiercely with his sovereign and left the Court without leave, taking his men with him. Louis was told that poor Bona of Savoy would have to go back on the shelf. In justice to Edward, it must be said that he did not know Warwick's mission to France included a proposed betrothal.

A man of striking presence, with thick black hair, worn short, a fringe at his temples rubbed away to some extent by his helmet, and a neatly-trimmed beard, Warwick was tall, lean and powerful, having a long, typically Norman face, an aggressive jaw and an eagle nose. He usually wore a short loose coat over a steel breast-plate inlaid with gold and polished by an underling till it shone. Nearly as tall as the King himself, he had a vizored helmet crested with a sable plume, which made him look taller than he was. Next to the King he was the outstanding personage of the realm.

Returning to Calais five days later with a large staff for confidential talks with the Duke of Brittany, he successfully concluded a secret truce with him to begin on the 1st October, inspired by a report that Jasper Tudor, Earl of Pembroke, was in Brittany trying to arrange a landing in Wales. To complete the treaty, Breton plenipotentiaries came to England disguised as Dominican friars.

[3]

On Michaelmas Day Elizabeth was brought to Reading Abbey by the Duke of Clarence and the still resentful Warwick, presented as their new Queen to the assembled peers, and seated in the chair of state in the chapel. A wedding feast, which lasted eight days, was marked by tournaments, banquets and dancing. Preparations were begun for her coronation.

Born in 1437, Elizabeth was used to Court life, having been one of Margaret of Anjou's ladies of the bedchamber. The nobles continued to fume, some making no secret of their belief that the union was unseemly. The King was sharply criticized. If he could be so blinded by passion for a poverty-stricken widow, long in the tooth and of blemished lineage, they suggested, was he likely to be rational and discreet in affairs of state?

Polydore Vergil suggests without foundation that Warwick had a more personal reason for his anger with the King. Ever a libertine, Edward, as his guest, had once seduced a young virgin of Warwick's family (possibly his daughter), which was not only a dishonourable deed in itself, but also injured the Earl's honour. In this year certainly the seeds of enmity between these two powerful men were sown. Warwick lost faith in the King, while the King, having cast off Warwick's apron strings, felt he had shown his minister he could act without him.

However regarded, the marriage was a humiliation for the Earl, lowering his pride, breaking his hitherto unchallenged hold on the kingdom and ruining his foreign policy. Instead of drawing nearer to France, England would now, he foresaw, inevitably move towards Burgundy.

The rift between the two men slowly widened. Warwick, an old-fashioned elder statesman, grave, humourless, orating in polished, but stilted phrases, lavish in hospitality to the point of gross extravagance, had hitherto had his own way because the young King was inexperienced, lazy and good-natured. As long as he, the King, was left free to enjoy himself, the Earl, who could run the country better than he could himself, might go on doing so. Now, however, having quarrelled with his mentor, Edward would henceforward have to take an active, personal part in the government of his realm. He was still popular, having companions and friends outside the Neville circle, and had been uniformly victorious in the field, while when not himself militarily engaged, he had picked good generals to fight for him.

Infatuation with the Queen and the discomfiture of Warwick went to Edward's head, and he determined not only to show his feeling for Elizabeth, but also to replace the too-powerful Nevilles by his own friends. The Queen, one of seven sisters and five brothers, had a whole quiverful of relations. Her eldest brother, Anthony Woodville, had married Lord Scales's daughter, an heiress. Her eldest sister, Margaret, had married Thomas, Lord Maltravers, son and heir of the Earl of Arundel. Virtually all her family now had distinctions conferred upon them, which was not a bad thing, for the Woodvilles brought intelligence, ability and culture to the Court.

Edward IV, 1442–1483, a contemporary portrait by an unknown
artist (National Portrait Gallery)

Elizabeth Woodville, 1437–1492, a fifteenth-century portrait of
Edward IV's wife, in the possession of Queen's College, Cambridge
(artist unknown)

The King began by relieving the Marquis of Exeter—he had forfeited his dukedom in 1461—of his post as Constable of England, which went to Lord Rivers, his father-in-law, Exeter being packed off to Ireland, always treated as an integral part of England.

On the 30th November, some weeks after arrival at Reading monastery, the royal pair departed for Windsor, and a week later came to Eltham, where Elizabeth was prepared for her formal entry into London. With reckless generosity Edward deluged her with rich Christmas gifts, allowing her over £450 for the upkeep of her chambers, wardrobe and stable. Estates worth 4,000 marks a year were bestowed upon her in addition to the manors of Greenwich and Sheen, while on her behalf over two hundred pounds' worth of rings were shared out. The sojourn at Eltham lasted till early in 1465, after which Edward returned to London for a new Parliament, lodging with his retinue at Sheen. In March he granted his sister, Margaret, an annuity of 400 marks.

Elizabeth was received at Shooter's Hill by Ralph Verney, the Mayor, a mercer, his aldermen, and leading men of the city. In state she was conducted to her temporary lodging in the Tower, her beautiful blonde hair, sleek and shining, reaching almost to her knees. It was this that had most attracted the King, it was said. Such hair was then regarded as the "crowning glory" of woman, and when surmounted, as hers was, by a tall headdress embroidered with fleurs-de-lys and encircled by a diadem of pearls, it aroused general admiration.

Her dress consisted of a tunic with the royal gold and blue stripes, over it a blue satin robe, edged with ermine and having long sleeves stiff with tiny pearls. Though she had a good carriage and strong features, her almost statuesque beauty was marred by a petulant, drooping mouth, and an expression rather shrewd and calculating than queenly. Patronizing and proud, her manner suggested contempt for her inferiors.

The next day she was similarly conducted to Westminster Palace in a horse litter, the newly-created knights riding beside her. The streets were gaily decorated, 200 marks having been spent on them. The new Queen graciously accepted the city's gift of 1,000 marks. Her coronation took place at last on the 26th May in Westminster Abbey, and was attended by her uncle, James

8

(Jacques) of Luxembourg and his many, splendidly-arrayed followers. The Londoners called him "Lord Jakes" or in modern terms "Lord Privy". The ceremony was performed by Thomas Bourchier, Archbishop of Canterbury, in recognition of whose services on this occasion the King later gave a window, showing Becket's martyrdom, to Canterbury Cathedral.

None knew better than Edward the importance of outward show, so to set off Elizabeth's beauty he had bought for her from foreign merchants many gems and much jewellery, which now bedecked her, while a bay and a white horse carried her litter through the streets, the litter having cost nearly £30 for the materials and her pillow.

The King also gave her a golden goblet and basin costing £108, two cloths of gold costing £80 and a plate worth £20 for her food.

On such state occasions Garter-King-at-Arms usually received a reward for his services, as did the heralds, and £20 was distributed among them, while Walter Holyday, conductor of over 100 royal mistrels, received the same sum for himself and his company, most of whom were gipsies, famous then as now for their skill in entertainment. Warwick was unable to attend the Coronation and the jousting that followed.

The Queen was given as her own house Ormonds Inn in Knightriders Street, Smithfield. That same day, the 27th, the Knights of Burgundy, part of James of Luxembourg's retinue, showed their prowess at a tournament in Westminster, Lord Stanley winning a ruby ring.

With all she had received, the Queen was able to set up her own establishment in style, and later the King enlarged Greenwich Park and gave it to her as a dwelling place, introducing a herd of deer into the grounds.

[4]

The clergy, seeing the advantage of the King's favour, contributed generously towards his expenses, and in return he recognized all their claimed privileges, freeing them from earlier restrictions. The King had meantime turned his attention to the country's trade. Competition from abroad had to be fended off if manufacturers were to earn a living. England had built up a wonderful reputation for first-rate wool and high quality cloth. The admission of foreign wool and silk would either force down prices and necessitate the lowering of quality, or pare down wages, which were then honourably paid in cash, not in second-rate goods.

Edward therefore rigorously excluded the foreign materials from his kingdom, and to ensure that home-produced cloth should lose no prestige, as happened when cheaper, foreign-made cloth was made from English wool woven abroad, foreigners were prohibited from buying, and English merchants and manufacturers from selling, home-produced wool on the Continent.

The shipping industry also complained that foreign ships were undercutting English freight rates, being allowed to load at English ports while English ships lay idle at their moorings for lack of cargo. It was therefore enacted that goods should not be shipped in foreign holds if English ships could take them.

Farmers raised their perennial outcry against cheap grain coming in from overseas, and the old decree that such importations should be prohibited was confirmed, with but one small modification designed to protect the home consumer. If home-grown wheat rose above 6s. 8d a quarter, foreign corn could be admitted until the price came down to that level.

Craftsmen who produced materials and objects ready for use were also threatened by competition from Burgundy and the Netherlands. These, too, were now protected, such articles as saddlery, lace, thread, woollen caps, fringe, cutlery, hardware, painted earthenware, hats, girdles, pins, playing cards and tennis balls, feather beds and bed covers, were all excluded from the country. It was argued that such exclusions would not harm the nation as the foreign goods were "disceyvable and nought worth".

Parliament, meeting at Reading on the 14th September, 1464, had to consider the currency of the country. The whole year had been marked by a serious shortage of money, not enough gold and silver metal having been brought to the royal mint to be made into coin of the realm. Better prices could be obtained by the suppliers abroad. Moreover in troublous times such as these men hung on to their stocks of previous metals until they saw more clearly which way the wind was blowing.

Early in August the Privy Council had decided to offer a much higher price for silver bullion. The Reading Parliament in April, 1465, ordered the minting of three new coins, a "noble angel" worth 6s. 8d. in new silver, but sold at 8s. 4d.—a value that had remained unchanged for over fifty years; a half-angel or "angelet" worth 3s. 4d.; and a gold farthing worth 20d. The "noble angel" was so-called because it had an angel stamped on it, but soon became known as an "angel". There were sixty-seven and a half of these to a pound of metal.

This put right an earlier decision to produce a coin called a "royal", weighing 120 grains and worth 10s., as well as a half-royal worth 5s., and a quarter-royal, worth 2s. 6d. New silver pieces—a groat, 4d., a half-groat, a penny and a silver farthing, were also coined by Lord Hastings as Master of the Mint.

The lower silver content of these new coins reduced their intrinsic worth, more coins being produced from the same weight of silver. Each coin was therefore of less value, more of them being needed to buy the same quantity of goods as before. In other words, the silver currency had been debased. Fifteen grains in the penny, for example, had been reduced to twelve.

The King did well out of the new currency, since his commission on the coins actually minted was higher, and he gained £15,428 in just over two years. Moreover, the new pieces bore his portrait instead of Henry's, implanting his features in the minds of his people. The bullion merchants also did well, getting a higher price for their metal. Only the common people suffered. The silver coinage was not at all popular, ordinary folk finding it difficult to reckon and to change. It is said that a man might walk the length of a long street or over a whole parish without finding someone who would oblige him.

Nevertheless, gold and silver still entered the country without reaching the Mint, while consignments were smuggled out, not always successfully.

One other serious matter disturbed the traders. A treaty to prolong the exchange of goods between Burgundy and England was about to be signed when, under pressure from his own mercantile vested interests, Philip of Burgundy suddenly stopped the importation of English cloth and yarn. The English cloth merchants had to act quickly, and to prevent disaster, took their wares to Utrecht in Flanders instead, where they were warmly welcomed and virtually sold themselves.

Trouble was now occurring with the friars, who were accused of stirring up the people, and the King had to ask the Pope to call them to order.

The Parliament that met on the 21st January at Westminster maintained the tonnage and poundage on wine and general merchandise at the existing rates. Duties on home-produced wool were imposed and, more important, the excessive duties on wool from abroad were withdrawn, a total subsidy being introduced instead. Nevertheless the wool import duties were still preventing overseas merchants from selling their wool profitably in England, the only foreign wool being brought in by the Lombards, who had driven a hard bargain with the King for its admission.

This same Parliament, while removing the restrictions on selling raw wool abroad, still prohibited imports of foreign cloth, confirmed Dover's sole right to take passengers to and from Calais, and attainted Sir Ralph Percy, Henry Neville and Sir Henry Bellingham as traitors, together with the defenders of Harlech and Somerset's two brothers.

Of minor importance was their barring makers and repairers of boots and shoes from working in London or within three miles of the city, and from making boots, shoes or galoshes with points longer than 2 in. Such boots could not be fitted or sold on Sundays or certain church festivals. The Pope was primarily responsible for this Act, which produced a sharp reaction. The English obeyed the Pope in matters spiritual, but not when he interfered with personal taste and fashion. They ignored the ban, declaring bluntly that they would do as they pleased, and the Pope could mind his own affairs.

Parliament over, Edward went off to Sheen.

EIGHT

1464-1465

[1]

THE GOVERNMENT BELIEVED Henry VI to be sheltering in Scotland. Edward therefore sent secret agents to discover his whereabouts. Why Henry should now have chosen to cross the border into England is uncertain. Holinshed suggests that he learned of Edward's search for him, and was "past all fear", or was disordered in mind, or knew he could no longer remain in Scotland, where his presence was embarrassing in view of the truce with England. Whatever the explanation, he disguised himself as a "black monk", and in cowl and gown wandered the north country, lodging by stealth with this friend and that.

One pictures the simple, forlorn, incompetent fugitive riding through rain, storm and fierce winds over mountain paths and down narrow valleys, never knowing where he was to lay his head at night. He was sheltered several times by John Maychill of Crackenthorpe, near Appleby. Later he entered Furness Abbey, passing himself off as one of their monks. Thence he moved into the south of Lancashire with his Chamberlain, Sir Richard Tunstall, Dr. Thomas Manning, former Dean of Windsor and Secretary to Margaret of Anjou, and Dr. John Breden, all waited upon by the groom Ellerton.

At dinner one day with Sir Richard Tempest in Waddington Hall in the parish of Mitton, near Bashall in Yorkshire, he saw the door thrown suddenly open. In rushed Sir John Tempest of Colbury, Sir James Harington of Brierley, Sir Thomas and John Talbot of Bashall and Salesbury, and other armed men. Sir Richard sat quietly at table while these men made straight for his guest, and did not oppose the intruders, so that he was probably a party to the plot to seize the ex-king.

Things did not go as planned, however, for Tunstall, sword in hand, despatched or disabled one attacker, seized Henry's hand, pulled him swiftly out of the room by another door, smuggled him out by the back way, and bursting through the ring of armed men outside, escaped with him into a wood. The fugitive went trudging miserably from place to place in Lancashire until, fording the Ribble near Clitheroe at Bungerly Hippingstones, he was over-taken and captured on the 13th July. His captor, Sir William Can-telow, a mercer of London, put him on a horse, tying his legs under the horse's belly so that he could not escape.

The unhappy royal simpleton was led, a pathetic prisoner, to London, where Warwick just returned from Calais met him and made the necessary arrangements. Sir Thomas Talbot was awarded £100, and later some estates. Harington and Sir John Tempest received 100 marks each. John Livesey, Henry's groom, got £20 and two of his valets shared nearly £7 between them, all three having been concerned in his betrayal.

There is a well at Bolton which tradition claims was enlarged to form Henry's bath. Here, relics—his spoon, boot and glove (ex-tremely small) are kept. The glove shows clearly the ex-King's lack of strength.

Henry was given no gay welcome in London, no flags, bunting or cheering crowds greeting his arrival. Two esquires and two yeo-men of the guard had charge of him in the Tower, but he was not subjected to indignities and could receive visitors. A small sum was provided for his expenses, and his chaplain was paid 7½d. a day by the King. He was not handsomely clad, perhaps, but velvet and cloth of "violet ingrain" were bought for his doublets and gowns. "Ingrain" meant "brilliantly dyed", it being believed at one time that the cochineal dye came from a kind of grain. Edward some-times sent Henry wine from his own cellars, but he was not kept so clean as he should have been, standards of cleanliness in medieval prisons being low.

Henry endured his imprisonment patiently and without fully understanding all Fate had done to him. One of a long line, he had reigned for many years and been paid great homage. One day, he believed, God would restore him to his throne, but his intellect was too enfeebled for him to feel more than the discomfort of limited freedom. His companion, Dr. Manning, a "white leper", suffered also from ague, and was soon released. Dr. Breden was held much longer, but his friends by pleading and bribery obtained his liberation. He talked too much on his release, and was once more imprisoned for several months, being discharged only after swearing to behave himself.

Edward and Elizabeth were on pilgrimage to Canterbury when told of Henry's arrest, the good news being brought to them by a monk of Lancashire, perhaps he who had betrayed Henry's presence at Waddington Hall to his enemies. It has been suggested he was a Dominican friar from Abington, a religious house near Bungerly Hippingstones.

Overjoyed, Edward hastened to the cathedral with the Queen and the Archbishop, gave out the news, and after ceremonies of thanksgiving, paused at Beckett's tomb. On returning to London, he lodged at Westminster Palace.

[2]

Margaret of Anjou, still living near St. Mighel en Barrois in a castle belonging to her father, could afford only a limited establishment, having only 6,000 crowns a year to live on, given by her father, yet enforced isolation did not quench her ambitious spirit. Day after day, with unshaken will and the conviction of ultimate success, she worked and plotted against Edward, the "usurper", as she called him, On learning of his secret marriage and its unpopularity, she bombarded the French king with new requests for men and money, writing always without humility, subservience or loss of dignity. So much so, indeed, that Louis himself remarked on the "pride" that filled her letters.

Henry's recapture appeared to shatter her hopes. The hangers-on who had remained merely for what they could get out of her; the soldiers who saw no chance now of displaying their prowess and winning rich rewards in England; the comfort-loving, who foresaw a serious reduction in her income and an impoverished existence for themselves; slipped away. Some entered the service of

French nobles and fought in their battles. Others, desperately hard-up, made their way to Burgundy in the hope of aid or employment. A French observer saw Henry Holland, Marquis of Exeter, Edward's brother-in-law, walking feet bare at the tail of the Duke of Burgundy's retinue, incognito for pride's sake, and even going from door to door to beg his bread. Eventually he was recognized, and his plight reported to the Duke, who thenceforward fed and clothed him, since he was, after all, the next of the Lancastrian line to Henry of Windsor.

[3]

In England, Henry being in the Tower, life became more tranquil. The King offered pardon to all who handed in their weapons and swore the oath of allegiance. Otherwise severe punishment was threatened. The fifth year of his reign was marked by a royal pregnancy, but alas! Elizabeth brought forth merely a daughter—Elizabeth—on the 11th February, 1466. An amusing anecdote of the occasion relates that a know-all of the royal household, Master Dominic, prophesied that the King would have a son and heir. To forestall others in bearing the welcome tidings, he posted himself in a room next to that of the birth, listening hard. When the new-born infant wailed, he called out impatiently, eager to know its sex: "What has the Queen?" A woman in attendance replied bluntly: "Whatsoever the Queen has in here, a fool stands out there."

Dominic went away abashed, without attempting to see the King.

The child was baptized by the Archbishop of York. Outwardly reconciled to his sovereign, Warwick acted as her godfather, while her grandmothers also took part in the ceremony. The next formal occasion was the churching of the Queen, a great opportunity for display. The church dignitaries came first, carrying flaming candles, their voices blending in song. Behind followed the flower of the nation's wives and virgins. Then came trumpeters, pipers, flute-players, fiddlers, and no fewer than forty-two royal minstrels. Next in line were twenty-four heralds and pursuivants, with sixty lords and knights. Finally the Queen herself appeared under a canopy of cloth of gold, accompanied by the two Dukes, her mother and sixty ladies following behind. This impressive procession moved into the Abbey for the service, then proceeded to Westminster Palace for dinner, to which a party of guests from Bohemia had been invited.

On their arrival in London, these men had been given a welcoming banquet of fifty courses, and the best available apartments in the Palace, to which a herald and member of the King's Council escorted them.

The guests at the great churching dinner filled four of the largest halls of the Palace. The Lord of Rozunthal, leader of the Bohemians, brother of their Queen, was honoured by a seat at Warwick's own table, equivalent to the King's, for on this occasion the Earl "stood in" for Edward, whom custom did not allow to be present. The Earl behaved, therefore, exactly as if he were king, distributing the royal largesse to singers, musicians and heralds. The amount must have been generous, for "all who had been rewarded ran around the table shouting out what the King had given them".

The Queen, splendidly arrayed, stately, solemn, and detached by rank and pride from all about her, took her meal seated on a chair of gold in a separate chamber on whose walls rich tapestries hung. Her mother and Princess Margaret, the King's sister, waited upon her, keeping a respectful distance. Whenever she addressed them, they were bound to kneel, not daring even to sit until she had partaken of the first course. The other ladies of the Court were not granted even this relief, having to stay on their knees throughout the entire meal, which lasted three hours.

When Warwick brought the Bohemians into the Queen's chamber, she spoke no word to them or any other, sitting silent, in ridiculous pomp, on her golden chair. The tables having been cleared and stacked away to free the floor for dancing, Elizabeth remained a spectator only. Her own mother, keeping her company, had to fall to her knees, and only when she could bear it no longer was she permitted to rise for a few minutes. Princess Margaret, dancing with sundry dukes, was bound by Court etiquette to curtsey ever and again to her sister-in-law. Her new and high position had evidently caused the former Elizabeth Grey's head to swell.

[4]

Almost certainly at her instigation, Edward set to work to break Warwick's grip on the nation, giving further advancement to her numerous family. Her father, created Earl Rivers, was appointed Treasurer of England in place of Lord Mountjoy, a loyal servant, and Warwick's uncle by marriage. In January, John Woodville, fourth of the Queen's brothers, caused a stir at Court by marrying the Dowager Duchess of Norfolk, old enough to be his grand-mother, and believed to be 75. Edward also married off the Queen's sisters to noble husbands. Thus, Anne Woodville went to the altar with William, Lord Bourchier, son and heir of the Earl of Sussex. Eleanor Woodville married Anthony Grey, heir of the Earl of Kent. Catherine, the youngest, found a husband in the young Duke of Buckingham, grandson of the Duke killed at Northampton. This marriage particularly annoyed Warwick, in whose bosom dark emotions were stirring.

Then came the wedding of Jacquette Woodville, the fourth sister, to Lord Strange of Knockyn, and of Mary to William Herbert, son and heir of Edward's trusted comrade, Lord Herbert. Sir Thomas Grey, the Queen's son by her first husband, married Anne Holland, daughter of the exiled Exeter. Anne had earlier been betrothed to Warwick's nephew, the Earl of Northumberland's son, and this, too, angered the Earl and all the Neville family. Both nobles and commons resented these marriages, regarding the Woodvilles as upstarts. Warwick hid his fury, but those who make it their business to observe the great were quick to detect it.

[5]

Despite her contending factions England was regaining pros-perity. True, occasional rivalries among the landed gentry caused disturbances. True, the forests sheltered outlaws and the roads were infested with footpads. From time to time kidnappers snatched up the unwary and held them to ransom. Nevertheless, as the wheels of trade and employment set going by the new King revolved faster, so these vicious activities diminished. In the capital the clamour of buyers and sellers rose steadily higher than the

mutter of baronial discontents. Merchants were active in every
main thoroughfare. Craftsmen in gold and silver, weavers and
sellers of fine cloth, did good business. And the Bohemians, visiting
the country for the first time, noted that Englishwomen were
beautiful and "not easily bought".

The military conflicts of the period were merely ripples on the
surface of a deep abiding pool. Though the nobles contended for
wealth, land and power, the people went steadily about their
business. What they most detested was the inevitable interruption
of their activities when the fighting came too close, and the damage
done to their crops, homes and communal buildings by undiscip-
lined armed bands fighting, pillaging and burning. In a sense they
resembled an old woman picking up her skirts as she crosses a
muddy road, concerned mainly to keep them clean and get over,
but watching the traffic with a shrewd, experienced eye.

Agitated by no great cleavage of religious opinion, inspired by
no shining dream, they swept up the wreckage after each struggle
and started all over again, in the hope that some day these dismal
feuds would end and a settled, orderly existence for themselves and
their neighbours be re-established.

During the first four years of Edward's reign, this seemed possible. Warwick's firm hand in support of the young King had
given the country the first strong rule it had had for decades, the
weak, unfortunate Henry having brought little but disorder,
rapacity, disaster and distress to his people. Now, the bickering of
the nobles, each seeking only to enlarge his estates at the expense
of his neighbours, declined. Slowly there came into being a number
of great trading families and institutions. Keeping clear of the surly,
cantankerous disputants, these confined themselves largely to safe-
guarding commerce and finance.

In London especially these men were acquiring, and what is
more, exercising, power of a new kind, based not on armed retainers and great estates, but on *money* skilfully used, manipulated
and increased. The barons, the kings themselves, could not raise
armies and march them about the country or abroad without the
means of feeding, clothing, sheltering and equipping them, even
though many provided their own horses, armour and weapons.
Consequently, they had either to tax their supporters heavily or

borrow at interest from merchants and financiers, who would lend only if they had faith in the borrower. Though a king might tax his subjects heavily, and often did, there was a limit to what he could do in this respect without becoming unpopular and therefore vulnerable. Money then became difficult to raise, and without it he might find himself with half-hearted, because ill-provided and unpaid, troops, which usually spelled defeat.

It was imperative, therefore, to win the favour of these large trading bodies, which in return exacted concessions embodied in legislation. Indeed, the City of London was becoming virtually a kingdom within a kingdom, and could on occasion decisively affect events.

Had the rift between Edward and Warwick not deepened and widened much eventual disorder and confusion, greatly hindering full recovery, might have been prevented. Hitherto Warwick had been an able lieutenant, influencing and guiding his commander. Sooner or later, however, such men, their masters feel, must be broken or brought to heel lest they destroy him whom it is their duty to protect.

Now 37, Warwick, Edward's cousin, son and heir of Richard Neville, Earl of Salisbury, and Alice Montacute, an heiress of great wealth, daughter of a former Earl of Salisbury of a different line, was married to Anne, daughter of the previous Earl of Warwick. On her father's death she brought him the title and great possessions, which, united to his own, made him the most powerful and wealthiest of all the barons of England. Comines estimated his yearly revenues at 80,000 crowns, quite apart from his inheritance.

He had been loyal to the young King, teaching him statecraft and treating him almost as a younger brother. During the years of royal intemperance, dissipation and sensuality, he had ruled the land, quelling the turbulent north, managing hot-headed and obstinate men, and holding his own with cunning continental potentates. He had set his heart upon a permanent peace with France, and was generally popular, but it is a moot point whether a French alliance would at that date have been in the best interests of his country. At all events, the King did not think so.

This rift between Edward the "business man" and Warwick the statesman greatly harmed the expanding economy of England.

In medieval times a king had to *be* a king. He could not afford to be—like Henry VI—either the appendage of a self-willed Queen, or that of a too-powerful baron, even one so loyal and able as Warwick. Until Edward's marriage Warwick had decided who should fill what places. What he did not appreciate was that marriage had both given the King a consort and made him a man. Edward meant to be henceforward master of his own country. By blood and victory a king, now as a king by right he would reign. It had not escaped his notice—or if it had, the Queen pointed it out to him—that Warwick had quietly made himself responsible for the administration of the country, and that the time must come when his wings would have to be clipped or he himself would be merely his chief minister's lackey, so to speak.

[6]

During these four years Warwick and his family were slowly earning dislike. Lesser folk deplored their gross extravagance. Whenever the Earl took up residence in London, six oxen were killed to furnish meat for the household breakfast, while his servants' friends were all allowed to slice off and carry away as much flesh as the tips of their daggers would hold.

The banquets of the Nevilles were gluttonous. For example, George Neville, Warwick's brother, celebrated his enthronement as Archbishop of York with a feast for which were provided:

> 300 tuns of ale,
> 100 tuns of wine,
>   1 pipe of hippocras,
> 104 oxen,
> 1,000 sheep,
> 304 veals (calves),
> 304 young hogs,
> 2,000 pigs,
> More than 500 stags, bucks and roes;
>   12 porpoises and seals;
> 400 swans,
> 104 peacocks,

2,000 geese,
2,000 chickens,
1,200 quails,
4,000 pigeons,
13,000 jellies, tarts and custards.

Hippocras was made by straining port and canary wines, bruised spices and sugar, through a flannel cloth or bag. Sixty-two cooks were needed to prepare this immense mass of food. The King and Queen did not attend the banquet, being represented by the Duke of Gloucester. The Archbishop may have performed a second miracle of the loaves and fishes to engender this repast, but the chronicles do not say so. Everywhere around this "man of God" were the starving, the hungry, the sick and the poor, and even if a few were granted the scraps and leavings, one cannot repress disgust at such Trimalchian excess, sanctioned by the second highest of God's officers in the land.

Not that in his early years of kingship Edward was much better. He loved luxury, and was so extravagant that he had to recoup himself by taxing his people, which they disliked. Early in 1466 he visited Scotland, and about the same time, Charles of Burgundy, acting for his ailing father, the Duke, was sorely needing a strong ally against his old enemy, France. He began to consider marrying Princess Margaret, Edward's sister, who, he had been told, combined both intellectual attainments and good looks. Only the desire for English support would have led him to this, for secretly he was, it is said, more attracted by Margaret of Anjou. However, his personal envoy sounded the King on this subject.

Warwick was unwilling to negotiate the match, perceiving in a Burgundian alliance a threat to his own plan for closer relations with France. On his advice Edward made private overtures to Louis. Had he an alternative spouse for his favourite sister? he asked. Nevertheless a French marriage did not greatly appeal to him, and determining to keep the more attractive iron in the fire, he sent Warwick to discuss both the alliance with Burgundy and the marriage of Margaret, at Boulogne. Meeting in April, Warwick and Charles either quarrelled or found each other antipathetic, for no progress was made.

NINE

1466 - 1467

[1]

To WARWICK'S DELIGHT the overtures to Louis succeeded. On the 24th May, 1466, a truce was signed at Calais to last till the 1st March, 1468. Plenipotentiaries were sent to France to work out the details. Louis undertook not to assist Margaret of Anjou, to pay Edward 40,000 gold crowns annually, and to find a husband for his sister, suggesting Philibert of Savoy.

Warwick was mindful that he himself had two marriageable daughters—Anne, the younger, petite, with gentle features, tender eyes and submissive, somewhat despondent temperament, More striking and colourful was Isobel, the elder, tall for her fifteen years, and dark, like her father. The astute Earl turned his eyes upon either George, Duke of Clarence, or Richard, Duke of Gloucester.

Gloucester, a mere stripling of 14, had been born at Fotheringay. George, on the other hand, was 18 and eligible. Born in Dublin Castle, he had neither the stature nor the friendly, open countenance of the King, but was not unhandsome. His features, however, were unimpressive, suggesting indecision, lack of character, and obstinacy. With pale blue eyes and projecting teeth, over which his lips did not meet, he had a false smiling air and a mincing gait. Inordinately vain, and womanish in fancy, he wore many rings on his fingers, loving to show them off so that they glittered and flashed. He shared Edward's love of fine clothes, wearing usually a short outer cloak reaching halfway down his thigh and trimmed at hem and neck with ermine. His sleeves were slashed to reveal white lawn beneath, and his doublet was fastened with gold tags and knots. Sometimes he carried, flung carelessly over his left arm, a costly jacket of velvet and fur. A tall hat or cap crowned by a white plume adorned his head, and garters of ribbon encircled his knees. Around his neck was a crucifix carrying a large jewel.

Warwick's choice of Clarence may have been inspired by the reflection that if ever he broke with the King, Clarence was next in line of succession and might legitimately aspire to the throne. The Duke had few brains, even if Caxton had dedicated to him a book on chess he had printed, but this lack made him all the more manageable by an elder statesman. If Clarence ever became King, Warwick's daughter as his wife would become Queen, and through her and her husband he would rule England as he now ruled her through Edward.

In the autumn he made his first move. The greedy, impressionable Clarence quickly swallowed the bait, seeing himself master through his wife of half the great Neville estates. He had kinship with Isobel, his second cousin, and therefore the Pope would have to sanction their marriage, but both he and Warwick believed this could be arranged.

The first hurdle overcome, the second, more dangerous step had now to follow—the obtaining of Edward's consent.

[2]

On a morning in April an incident took place which was to have a spectacular sequel (p. 131). Lord Scales, on his knees before the Queen, and in conversation with her, had laid his cap beside him on the floor. Around them fluttered the ladies of the Court wearing gold-fringed stays and deep blue kirtles under long, loose gowns of silk and fine linen, with slashed hanging sleeves. One of the ladies now fastened about his thigh, evidently by pre-arrangement, a golden garter ornamented with pearls, and with a "noble flower of souvenance" hanging from it. This, enamelled, carried gems formed into the letters "S.S.", and was a reminder that he was to "take a step fitting the times" and fulfil some chivalrous obligation.

The same lady dropped into his cap a vellum roll tied with gold

9

thread, which Scales, according to custom, took to the King, who, breaking the thread, recited the message. It instructed Scales to enter the lists in London on two successive days to do battle with some noble of high lineage and irreproachable character. On the first day he was to be mounted and use spears and swords. On the second, he was to fight on foot with spear, axe and dagger.

Scales accepted this command—he could do no other—and as Anthony, half brother of Charles of Burgundy, known as "the Bastard of Burgundy", had once challenged him to a contest, he was invited to enter the lists against him in the capital. The Bastard was at that moment fighting for his country, but replied that he would come as soon as possible. Meantime, in token of acceptance, he touched the flower of souvenance.

In the meantime the city of London demonstrated loyalty by inviting the King to a great civic banquet. The King, the Queen, her mother and many peers came in state and were nobly entertained. The meal over, the officers of the feast received the cloth of state, suspended above the dining table, as their perquisite, the others being given the table linen and cloths.

The squalid struggles among the princes and powers of Europe, now at their height, brought much benefit to the English, who, sitting as neutrals "on the sidelines", were courted and flattered by Denmark, Spain, Poland, Burgundy and France. Envoys from all these lands flocked to the Court, while negotiations on various matters were carried on with Frederick of Prussia, the Patriarch of Antioch, the King of Naples, the Venetians, Milanese and Angevins. The critical issue, however, was whether Edward should join Burgundy and Brittany on the one hand or France on the other. All three were near neighbours, whose every action affected his country and himself.

Charles, the Burgundian, was in no hurry to marry Princess Margaret of York. Wishing, nevertheless, to remain friendly with Edward, he determined that the matrimonial contract should be negotiated by the Bastard in England, and at the same time the Bastard should fulfill his engagement with Lord Scales. He therefore requested a safe-conduct for him, but the Chancellor, Warwick's brother, raised objections of detail and caused delay.

Overriding Warwick, Edward signed the binding pact of friend-

ship and defence with Charles on the 23rd October, fearing that the
Earl would ally England with France if he did not. The great
stumbling block to the treaty had hitherto been Philip of Burgundy's prohibition of all imports of English cloth. The new
treaty declared that this matter would be formally discussed, and
Edward assumed that soon all would be satisfactorily settled.
While the Duke was still alive, Charles did not, or pretended he
did not, feel free to make so important an economic concession.
So, to cover himself, Edward sent envoys to the French, proposing
an alliance against Burgundy.

Louis told the Duke of Milan that Edward was virtually in his
pocket, being prepared to give up all pretensions to the crown of
France, and to conclude a military treaty with him. Once this was
achieved Warwick would marry Isobel Neville to Clarence, while
Edward's sister Margaret would be given to Philip de Brezé.
Gloucester would marry Louis's own second daughter, who would
bring him as dowry part of the estates that would be hers after
Burgundy and her confederates had been carved up.

In case this new treaty should not come to fruition, Louis, to
insure himself, summoned Margaret of Anjou to his Court. If the
English King, disregarding Warwick, allied himself permanently
with Burgundy, she might be useful to him. Warwick was obviously having difficulty in controlling his headstrong young
sovereign, and Louis conceived that the Earl would not stand idly
by while his foreign policy was repudiated. Indeed, he might
already be contemplating revenge for the slights put upon him.
The French King was astute enough to foresee that at some future
date Warwick, abandoning Edward, might be willing to combine
with Margaret of Anjou in replacing Henry on the throne.

[3]

Edward, loving a spectacle, threw himself gleefully into preparations for the contest between Scales and the Bastard of Burgundy.
The jousting place was to be West Smithfield, an area of comfortable inns and buildings around an open space of three acres or so.
Here herds of cattle were sold, tournaments held and executions
carried out. The King had specified that the lists must be "120

tailors' yards and ten feet" long, 80 yards and 20 ft. wide, "double
barred with five feet between the bars". Consequently, the lists and
bars having to be completed within nine days, many barges went
sailing up the Thames with sand, gravel and timber. Thirty-nine
days were actually taken in finishing the work. The timber alone
cost 200 marks, much of it being used to build handsome galleries
for the ladies of the Court.

Garter-King-at-Arms had been whiling away the time at
Gravesend, waiting until the lists were completed. At last he set out
in a state barge down the broad, gleaming Thames estuary to meet
the Bastard and bring him and his followers safely into London.
The Burgundian and his four small, timber-built ships sailed from
Sluys, and on the way were attacked by Spanish vessels, which may
have been secretly employed as privateers by Louis. However, the
Burgundians beat off the attack and kept their rendezvous with
Garter, their prows cleaving the air and water of England as they
came up river to Blackwall. Here, as protocol required, a large
body had gathered to welcome them, at their head the Earl of
Worcester, that combination of medieval culture and cruelty
(pp. 187, 205). In magnificently decorated and gilded barges, drip-
ping with rich tapestries, roofed by awnings of cloth of gold and
alive with gay, fluttering streamers, they slowly followed in convoy
the abetting tide.

Presently the great battlemented walls of the Tower rose above
them, and the four caravels were moored at the near-by St. Katharine's Wharf, fringed with beerhouses and a large hospital. The
Bastard was now transferred to a special barge and escorted to
Billingsgate, a "harbour for small ships and boats coming thereto",
thence via Fleet Street to his lodging in the Bishop of Salisbury's
house, lent to him for the occasion. In one room here the lovely
tapestry known as "Arras cloth" elaborately draped the walls, and
in another he slept on a bed smothered in cloth of gold. Such was
clerical luxury in the fifteenth century. The Bishop had also
allowed the Burgundian knight a second house at Chelsea where he
could try out his armour in private.

Early in April, the King had jousted at Eltham with Lord Scales
and was now staying in Kingston, but he returned to London to
receive the Bastard and to attend a new session of Parliament. At

that period much of the road to the city was but a bare track through open country. At one slightly elevated point rose a stone cross marking an inn for penitents at St. Clement Danes, and also a well reputed to heal the sick. Bushes fringed the track, and beyond these were the great houses of the nobles. Shops were little more than enclosed stalls guarded by apprentices, who, caps in hands, bawled at passers-by to attract attention, jeering or cursing if their cries were unheeded.

The King was enthusiastically received by the peers, the Mayor, Thomas Oldgrove, a skinner, the aldermen, and the royal heralds, while the gusty blowings of trumpeters and clarioneers enlivened the ceremony. In procession he moved into the city, Scales at the head holding the great sword of state. Present also were Worcester, Constable of England, and Norfolk, the Earl Marshal. The usual visit was paid to St. Paul's.

As he rode along Fleet Street, the story goes, Scales felt eyes upon him, and turning sharply, saw the Bastard watching him from the Bishop's House.

On the 2nd June, 1467, the Bastard formally visited the King, who in the afternoon went with him to Greenwich, where in the noble Painted Chamber Parliament was opened. Scales also came to Greenwich, but returned to London by water after three days. Glittering in a gown of cloth of gold, he rode in state to Holborn from St. Katherine's Wharf, lodging in the Bishop of Ely's house, as luxurious and resplendent as that of Salisbury. All London eagerly awaited the forthcoming excitements, but none expected the significant event that now occurred. Edward, having long concealed mailed fist in velvet glove, struck suddenly at the Warwick family, showing plainly that he meant to break it.

[4]

George Neville, Chancellor of England and Archbishop of York, holder of the Great Seal, had not attended the opening of the new Parliament, John Chadwick, Bishop of Lincoln, acting in his stead. His excuse was illness. On the 8th, some days before the tournament, the King, who appeared to have resented his absence, mounted his horse and at the Chancellor's hostelry in the village of

Charing Cross "without the bars of Westminster", demanded the
Great Seal at once. This was virtually to dismiss the Archbishop
from his Chancellorship, and was so interpreted.

Handed over a couple of days later, the Seal was left in the safe
keeping of Robert Stillington, Bishop of Bath, hitherto Keeper of
the Privy Seal. The Court seethed with rumour and speculation,
but the King, putting affairs of state aside, suspended Parliament so
that all the members might witness the duel between the Bastard
and Scales, fixed for the 11th.

Already the showmen of the capital had erected their booths in
Smithfield. Innkeepers threw open their doors to country visitors.
The area was dotted with tents, platforms, awnings that covered
stalls where refreshments were sold and knavery was practised by
charlatans. Harpers wearing the royal livery threaded through the
gathering crowds. Mountebanks beguiled the inevitable waiting,
and acrobats performed their feats, among them men who gyrated
intricately on stilts to music. In strict time a horse beat a drum with
its forefeet, a monkey played amusing tricks, a conjuror pretended
to saw off the head of a boy, and gipsies, the girls in particular,
danced wildly in a whirling circle, singing as they danced, their bare
arms brandishing tambourines above their heads. At suitable
moments they went round in their gaudy, tinselled dresses to solicit
cash and catch it when flung in their inverted tambourines. Elsewhere musicians played on pipes and treble flutes or fiddled on
stringed instruments known as "rebecks". Lutes played and pilgrims sang interminable ballads on themes for the occasion.

At other points men were hurling iron quoits, bowling, playing
club ball and trap ball—played with bat, ball and trap, the ball being thrown up by a wooden mechanism and struck as far as possible. Quarterstaff contests were held with stout staves, as tall as a
man, gripped at the centre, the hand gliding along them as required. Professional wrestlers, displaying their prowess, threw out
challenges to all and sundry, and those watching them wore sleeveless leather jackets or coats of woollen or cotton cloth, according to
their station. The girls had ribbons in their hair and brightly
coloured gowns. To refresh the onlookers were hot peas in their
pods, sheep's feet, ribs of beef and mackerel, while for their more
refined entertainment fifes and harps were played and catches

ground out on a kind of medieval guitar. Ale and beef were free to pilgrims and strangers.

The lists at Smithfield were rectangular and enclosed by wooden fences; through openings at each end of the rectangle the two combatants would ride, their tents being pitched adjoining the openings. In the centre of the upper gallery on one long side of the rectangle sat the King and his party, with the ladies of the Court. A separate entrance had been provided for these. Edward wore robes of purple, with the Garter about his knee and a staff or baton in his hand. All knelt when he appeared.

Before him, but not impeding his view, an Earl stood with the Sword of State. About the King his eldest councillors, white-haired and dignified, were grouped. The lower tiers were filled with knights, esquires and bowmen. On the opposite side was another gallery, lower than the King's, for the Mayor, the city fathers and the justices, who were preceded by a sword bearer carrying a sword inverted, in token of submission. The commons occupied the lowest tiers.

At each corner of the combat area was posted a King-at-Arms or chief herald, wearing his crown of office. Close to the steps by which the King and his party reached their seats sat Worcester as Constable, with the Earl Marshal and other officials. The royal party having taken their places, Scales appeared at the "bars" or barriers in gleaming armour, riding a grey horse with rich trappings, and attended by nine knights and peers, gaily clad, spurred and carrying swords. Before them rode the Duke of Clarence on the right, the Earl of Arundel on the left, each bearing a helmet. After these came the Duke of Buckingham, the Earl of Kent and two other peers, carrying among them the spears and swords to be used in the fight. (Swords were rarely carried except in war, daggers being more portable and equally deadly.)

All were arrested at the bars by Worcester and Norfolk, who as the rules required asked if Scales had come to fulfil his challenge to the Bastard of Burgundy. After Scales had assented, the King summoned him to the lists, and he entered them, bowing low to his sovereign. His pages, with his banner, were disguised as those heraldic beasts, griffins—supporters of his coat of arms. For this reason their coats were covered with thin imitation scales of steel, coloured green, on which forked scarlet tongues were painted. Their hands holding the banners were made to look like claws.

Scales, fair-haired and bareheaded, now retired into his tent or pavilion of blue satin, displaying his monogram. The Bastard trotted up next, his helmet carried by John de la Pole, Duke of Suffolk, the King's brother-in-law. Having performed the same duties as Scales, he, too, retired into his tent, and without hiding himself from public view, put on helmet and armour. Scales, however, kept himself carefully hidden as he prepared for the fight.

It had been clearly laid down that neither combatant must harm his opponent's horse nor "charge with an horse terrible to smite or bite". In other words, the prowess of the man was to decide the contest, not the offensive equipment or ferocity of the steed. The weapons to be used were submitted to the advisers of the combatants, who after inspection passed them. The rules of chivalry gave the Bastard first choice, as the man challenged, and they were therefore offered to him. The heralds, standing at their respective posts proclaimed the names and purpose of the combatants, forbade all unauthorized approach to the lists, and all unnecessary noise or demonstration which might disturb or encourage them.

The armour used was not the same as that employed in war, being heavier. The helmet, amply stuffed with padding, was tightly fixed by leather thongs to the cuirass of breast and back, and surmounted by a tall plume of feathers. It weighed about $14\frac{1}{2}$ lb. The armour, also heavily padded, was correspondingly weighty. A knight had to be strong and powerful enough not only to carry it, but also to deliver many blows before needing a pause. His horse had to be equally powerful and protected. The warhorses wore their own armour, and were, indeed, more like carthorses than coursers. In consequence there was rarely a thundering gallop, merely a quick jog-trot across the lists.

The "swords", too, were not the finely-tempered, flexible, piercing or slashing weapons of later years, but specially made with rounded points and blunted edges. The knights belaboured rather than slashed each other, using the flat sides, the object being to knock the opponent off his mount by sheer strength rather than run him through or hack off his head. The padding inside helmet and armour moderated the shock and prevented serious injury if the wearer toppled from his horse.

[6]

The combatants being now ready, the heralds uttered the cry: "Go!" ("Laissez aller!"), which began the affair. The two horsemen trotted, or at the most cantered, towards each other, lances, their tips dulled, held in the correct position. The murmur of busy voices in the galleries stilled. The strong stink of beery breath and unwashed bodies in the lower tiers of seats and the sweating of caparisoned horses passed unheeded by insensitive medieval nostrils. The June sunlight beat down, glinting on steel and golden cloth and feminine finery. The odours of rotting vegetables and sour wine, animal and human exudations, were added to the stench of open drains. The only sounds were the muted beating of hooves on the thick sand of the enclosure, the creak of leather, the metallic clanking of armour in motion, the faint susurration of silken and woollen garments from the crowded galleries, the whinnying of tethered horses, somewhere out of sight.

The two riders met with a sombre clash, not squarely, but at an angle, so that Scales's heavy Flanders bay horse drove its head into the Bastard's saddle armour. What happened is not clear, but as far as can be gathered from the records, some sharp projection hurt the Bastard's mount so badly that it reared up, collapsed and fell, taking its rider with it, and died soon afterwards. The general impression was that an element of craft or cunning could not be ruled out. Stow, writing much later, suggests that Scales's horse was illegally wearing a "chamfrain" or steel headpiece, a sharp "pike" at the head of this doing the damage, piercing the nostrils of the opposing horse so that it screamed in agony, reared up high and fell over. At all events there was a suspicion that Scales had indulged in foul play, for when he curvetted his horse around the fallen man, sword drawn ready for the death stroke, the King stopped the contest by casting down his baton, so saving the Bastard's life, and ordered the Constable to help the Burgundian—unable to rise because of his heavy armour—to regain his feet. "I cannot hold me by the clouds," the Bastard is said to have cried.

He was willing to resume the fight, but Edward, convinced that Scales had broken the rules, would not allow it. Scales, however, is—diplomatically—recorded as having demonstrated to the King that his horse's trappings carried no concealed device or unfair projection. The Bastard, shaken, and aware now that he was in no state to continue the struggle, was given leave to find another horse and do so if he wished, but he declined, preferring to await the following day. "Scales," he remarked, "has fought a beast, but tomorrow he shall fight a man!"

He was as good as his word. Next day no horses were used. The two fought hand to hand on foot with poleaxes and daggers. Scales had wished to fight with throwing spears also, but the King would have none of this. The tournament was a spectacle, he insisted, not a fight to the death. All knew, however, that these men were not in the lists for fun. Consequently the excitement was even greater than on the previous day. The Bastard had his disgrace to wipe out, while unless Scales proved himself the better man, he would lose face for ever.

The "moment of truth" came. Scales strode into the lists crying three times: "St. George!" At once the Bastard sprang forward. They circled one another, hacking, parrying, smiting, with a fury and courage few of the spectators had witnessed until that day. The howls and roars from galleries and benches alike could not be repressed and made a savage din, drowning at times the clang of axe on metal, the panting of steel-clad men, and the spurting of sand scuffed by their feet. The London apprentices, long-haired, flat-capped, carrying stout staffs, were particularly ferocious in their shouts.

The issue remained in doubt for some time, but at last the point of Scales's poleaxe pierced the vizor of the Bastard's helmet and stuck there, threatening to force him to the ground. At this moment, the King, not wishing to have an international incident on his hands, flung down his staff again, crying: "Whoa!" Immediately the Constable, entering the lists, separated the two nobles. The Bastard, indignant, wanted to fight on with daggers, but Edward, surveying the dents and jagged tears made in Scales's armour by the Bastard's weapons, decided enough had been done to satisfy the demands of honour. He commanded them to shake hands and show goodwill. This they did, with what sincerity it is impossible to declare, and after an exchange of courtesies, returned to their separate abodes. Scales had regained much of his reputation by keeping his vizor up throughout the contest, though many considered this was merely to give him an advantage, since he could then see better, not because he was the braver.

Entertainments and festivities had been planned for the Bastard during the remainder of his stay, but learning that his father, Philip, the Duke of Burgundy, had died on the 15th June, he was in duty bound to return to his own country, and left England on the 24th for the funeral and his duties.

TEN

1467 - 1469

[1]

THE TOURNAMENT OVER, Parliament reassembled. Edward now showed the rapidity with which he was learning to run his kingdom. Aware that the heavy taxation enforced to cover his extravagance was greatly resented, he took steps to overcome his financial difficulties, realizing that by hook or crook he had to take himself off the backs of his subjects if he wished to keep his crown.

He told the members assembled that he had decided to live without burdening them with taxes designed solely for his own support. To prove he was in earnest, he set about this in competent, astute and sensible fashion. First, he won by his affability and solicitude for their interests the friendship of both the London and the foreign-merchants, whose well-being, he saw, would promote the financial stability and prosperity of the kingdom. He strengthened his hold on the throne by fostering their trade. (He himself was already making a considerable income by selling wool and cloth from his own estates.) In particular he promoted commerce with the Low Countries rather than with those traditional enemies, the French, judging correctly that his subjects had no love for that nation whose raids on the Kentish and Cinque ports had left scars by no means invisible. A good man of affairs, he determined henceforward to seek allies among those countries and classes of society offering the greatest facilities for this profitable commerce.

In other words, he turned for support not to the feudal barons, with their wasteful and vicious rivalries, irritable and greedy cliques, dreams of glory and wealth, and refusal to subordinate themselves to the common good, but to the thriving mercantile and middle classes, steadily increasing in numbers and influence. There was a growing tendency at this period for all the landed gentry who could to be traders as well as dignitaries. Many wool traders—Merchants of the Staple—were gentlefolk, seeing nothing derogatory to their rank in belonging to a mercantile fraternity. The King, having observed with interest the success achieved by Louis of France in bringing his nobles to heel, realized that the future lay with the bourgeoisie, with whom he was becoming ever more popular.

Himself more of a bourgeois than a prince, he loved to visit the city and attend the banquets arranged in his honour, even going into the homes of the leading citizens and winning the favours of their wives, for he retained all his fondness for the fair sex. Handsome, good humoured, with taking ways and the audacious gaiety of a monarch sure of himself, he made many conquests, at times risking a loss of majesty by indulging too freely his amorous inclinations. The portrait of him in the National Gallery shows a clean-shaven young man with a strong chin, a full, protruding lower lip, level eyebrows cresting a longish nose, and a gentle mouth, while his slender neck adds grace to his appearance.

The London financiers and traders saw in their turn that their best chance of settled prosperity lay in a king who would keep the nation's finances sound, study their interests and promote their commerce, while remaining powerful enough to hold down the feudal barons. In time of need, therefore, the wool staplers or dealers lent him money. The Venetian and Genoese merchants lent him money. His friends in the city lent him money. All these factors combined to favour him, and over most of his reign Edward enjoyed, in his efforts to subdue his rivals, the open or secret support of the city of London.

He had, furthermore, the great virtues of understanding the value and importance of money and being able to concentrate on the details of national finance. He was, in effect, a clever royal economist. Although his marriage had offended the nobles, it endeared him to many in the city, who saw in it a victory over the baronial hierarchy. It was almost as if he had chosen a bride from their own ranks. Moreover, they liked him as a person. He was just, protecting the little man from victimization by the great and powerful, perceptibly knitting the country together, and creating a central authority capable of winning respect and providing a dominant power.

With all this he was, even though he may not have foreseen it, both laying the foundations of that great mollifying middle class that helped to build up the nation, and bringing nearer the day when who should fill the throne would be decided by the people rather than by the barons.

His subjects thought him kindly and human. Those unaccustomed to the Court were scared and embarrassed on first appearing there, but if the King saw this, he would go up to them, clap a friendly hand on their shoulders, and put them at their ease.

One great trouble experienced at that time was piracy. Raiders were constantly preying on British ships carrying cargoes overseas. The matter was raised in Parliament, and the King declared that he meant to suppress it. On the 1st July, however, an outbreak of plague in the capital caused the House to take fright and adjourn. Edward went to Windsor, where on the 17th he restored the quarrelsome Paston's property to him.

He had still some uncertainties and worries. Despite all efforts to seize it, Harlech Castle held out. Its defenders, under Sir Richard Tunstall, having captured Holt Castle, raided the country roundabout so that great alarm spread even to the towns. There had been an abortive rebellion in the Isle of Wight, and the Earl of Northumberland had had to use archers to suppress an insurrection by Humphrey Neville of Brancepeth—still the King's bitter opponent —and Archibald Ridley.

The country as a whole presented superficially a spectacle of sporadic assassinations, outbreaks of mob violence, robbery on the high roads, thefts and rapes. The approaches to the towns swarmed with brutal and violent men, many of them disbanded swashbucklers from the armies, scum from the civil commotions, who robbed and ransacked whenever they saw opportunity. In this they were aided by the absence of lights to guide the lonely traveller after dark. In the cities the watch patrolled, crying: "Hang out your lights!", but those ways bordering on the London Thames concealed many who kept themselves alive by robbery. These were often the fatherless descendants of men killed in the earlier civil struggles. They could be seen in the daytime sitting or lying in small groups before the wretched mud and wattle hovels in which they lurked.

[2]

Another problem came now to a head. As yet, no direct approach to Edward had been made by either Warwick or Clarence regarding the Duke's proposed marriage to Isobel Neville, but Edward had heard whispers, and although not his brother's keeper, was certainly his King. An alliance between the great baron and a man in the line of succession to the throne cut across his private policy. He had no wish to unite Warwick more closely with his own family. Sending for Clarence, he asked if the rumours were true. Clarence, shifty and stupid, would neither confirm nor deny that he had contracted to marry Isobel, but answered that it would not be a bad thing if he had. Furious, his brother rated him soundly for not consulting him first, and wrote privately to the Pope urging him not to sanction the marriage if asked to do so. Against Clarence's name he set another black mark, and an even blacker one against Warwick's, while also warning the young Duke of Gloucester to sign no marriage contract without first asking his leave.

[3]

Warwick still held that a treaty with France would benefit England more than one with Burgundy, and for a time the King reluctantly accepted his advice. Nevertheless his business acumen told him that trade with the French, now largely suspended, would bring greater prosperity, and he was therefore inclined to run with the hare and hunt with the hounds. While willing to do business with Louis, however, he would not give up his ties with Burgundy. Charles remained strongly antipathetic to the Francophile Earl of Warwick and had formed a "League of the Common Weal" consisting of Brittany, Bourbon, Burgundy and Berry, aimed at France. This alliance had led to the truce between England and

France, and Louis was anxious to transform it, if possible, into a firm treaty of peace before it expired in 1468.

Edward promised his ambassadors that Warwick should cross the Channel and talk over the proposal. On their arrival, the Earl and his advisers were royally welcomed, Louis paying all their expenses and making them magnificent gifts. These junketings were cut short, however, by the death of Charles's father, the Duke of Burgundy. Warwick, fearing that the new Duke might cut the ground from under his feet by coming to terms with Edward, dashed back to England with another detachment of French ambassadors hoping to put a spoke in the Burgundian wheel before harm was done. After some delays he reached London on the 1st July, saw the King, reported his gratifying reception by Louis, and was puzzled when his King showed little enthusiasm. It was some time before he divined that the King was no longer so pliable as he had been.

The French ambassadors, however, warmly received by Warwick and Clarence, went up the Thames in a pair of handsomely equipped barges, and took up residence in the Bishop of Salisbury's mansion, which had been long since vacated by the Bastard of Burgundy. Next day, Clarence, Hastings, Scales and others took them to the King in Westminster, and after a short interview, at which Earl Rivers brought them wine and spices, they went back to the capital. Waurin (Wavrin) declares that on this occasion Warwick remarked to the principal Ambassador: "Did you see the traitors round the King?" The Ambassador replied: "Sir, you will be avenged." Warwick added: "These are the fellows who got my brother dismissed from his office of Chancellor. The King has taken his seal from him." Apparently unaffected by fear of the plague, the envoys then set off for Windsor.

They brought with them handsome presents and promises from Louis, who undertook, once he and Edward had destroyed the Burgundians, to throw the Netherlands open to English wool and cloth, and at the same time to encourage trade with his own country. Edward, however, had little faith in the French King's promises, believing that Louis meant only to use him as a catspaw in the feud between himself and Charles. With the traditional English reluctance to see any one great power predominant in

Europe, and increasingly angry with Warwick for his obstinate
support of the French, he marked time, quietly carrying on simul-
taneous discussions with Louis de Bruges, Seigneur de la Gruthuyse,
the distinguished Burgundian whom Charles had sent over as his
representative earlier in the year, and whom Edward found extremely sympathetic.

Uneasily Warwick discerned that he was no longer "the power
behind the throne". His brother had been dismissed from office.
The marriage contract between Isobel and Clarence was in danger.
It irked him also that the King should have turned so many cloth-
merchants and grocers into knights. The King showed no fear of
his displeasure, and Warwick's quick eyes discerned a consequent
cooling of men's affection for him at Court. His fears were confirmed when at the end of June Edward formally signed a new
treaty of friendship and joint defence with Burgundy, and another
treaty with Castile which surrendered all English claims to the
throne of that country, originally based on dynastic intricacies. In
return, the King of Castile undertook to support England against
France if necessary.

De Gruthuyse left the Court rejoicing in his success, and returned to his master. On the 15th July the new Duke of Burgundy
signed the treaty.

[4]

The Queen was pregnant again, and there were renewed hopes of a
male heir to the throne, but when her time came at Windsor
during the first two weeks of August, she bore a second daughter,
Mary, baptized on the 12th. The French ambassadors left on the
14th, taking with them merely a promise from Edward that an
envoy should bring his final answer to their proposals. Warwick
had hardly ridden out of the capital with them when Edward
revealed to his Privy Council the treaty he had concluded with
the Burgundians. (He had never forgiven Louis for calling him "the
son of the archer" and sneering at his mother.) The Earl saw the
Frenchmen off from their port of embarkation, Sandwich, whence
they sailed on the 15th, taking with them parting gifts of such inferior quality (powder horns and leather pouches) that both they
and Warwick rightly interpreted them as a deliberate slight.

10

According to Waurin, about this date, at Cambridge, the Earl put into Clarence's mind for the first time the possibility of a pact between them against the King, complaining that in contrast to Louis, the King had given him a chilly reception. Clarence replied that this was no fault of his. Warwick replied that he knew this quite well, protesting that the Court lacked regal dignity. The Government had become inept, everything being run for and by Earl Rivers and his offspring. Clarence asked what could be done, to which Warwick replied that he wished Clarence himself were on the throne.

He is said, again by Waurin, to have told the French envoys that he and Clarence were of the same mind, which delighted them, but Warwick doubted if the King would grant the French request for a treaty because of his correspondence with the Duke of Burgundy. (We must remember, however, that Waurin, though accurate enough in his account of happenings in France, is not necessarily so when he describes conversations and events in England.)

The fact is clear, nevertheless, that Warwick was so deeply wounded in both pride and dignity by the obvious repudiation of his foreign policy that he would not bring himself to return to Court. Instead, he went straight from the Kentish coast to Middleham Castle, and sat there brooding, a dangerous man. In the meantime Edward pushed on with another plan dear to his heart, the marriage of his sister Margaret to the new Duke of Burgundy. This was not achieved without a good deal of mercantile haggling. Edward, had, for example, to readmit into the country those Burgundian commodities previously excluded by statute. On the 30th November, the Great Council received Princess Margaret at Kingston-on-Thames, where she signified her readiness to become the wife of Charles. Everything appeared to be plain sailing, but the Burgundian ruler was not so enthusiastic as Edward supposed, and much more of an opportunist where trade was concerned.

Taking time by the forelock, the Burgundians rushed across the Channel shiploads of their hats, brushes, baskets and other wares, accepting in their turn from England such items only as did not compete with their own products. They were not quick to lift their embargo on the importation of English cloth. Indeed, they did not lift it at all. Behind Edward's back Charles himself had been corresponding with Louis, and was browbeaten by him into signing a truce with France for a period of six months. Louis, learning of the Burgundian negotiations with Edward, had seen danger and was once more protecting himself.

Edward was enraged. This double dealing—essentially a duplication of his own tactics—put him in a difficult position, for he had acted without consulting Parliament. If he had been able to announce his sister's marriage, a defensive alliance against France, and the lifting of the foreign ban on cloth and wool, he would have been applauded and congratulated. But now Burgundian goods were flooding in to the detriment of English traders, and he had no commercial concessions to set against them. He himself was making a good profit out of the imports from Burgundy, but this would not mollify his subjects when suddenly, and with little warning, they were exposed to heavy overseas competition.

Refusing to ratify the treaty his plenipotentiaries in Burgundy had accepted in his name, he sent off to the Duke another covey of envoys to begin all over again. No sooner had they gone than the English merchants raised an uproar against the flood of Burgundian imports pouring in. Warwick's friends lost no time in blaming the Queen for turning Edward against Louis and favouring Burgundy, though this was quite unjust. There were even suggestions that heads should roll.

A weaker king would have been intimidated by this fierce reaction, but Edward did not quail, suspecting—not without reason, perhaps—that Warwick was behind the agitation, or at least prepared to take advantage of it. He had not overlooked the Earl's continued absence from Court, and for once anger mastered his normal good humour. Warwick was too far off to be directly attacked, but he had a brother, George Neville, Archbishop of York, who had already been humiliated by losing his Great Seal. Now Edward spitefully inflicted yet another slight upon him.

The Archbishop had had high hopes of becoming a Cardinal, which aspiration Edward secretly opposed, not only because the Archbishop of Canterbury had, in his view, a better claim, but also because such a promotion would strengthen the Warwick faction. When, on the 18th September, 1467, the Pope by decree gave the coveted red hat to Thomas Bourchier, Archbishop of Canterbury, the King maliciously despatched the letter announcing this to George Neville. This mean action was designed not only to wound the Neville family, but also, perhaps to show them that the King had great influence with His Holiness, and could as easily obstruct the papal dispensation for Clarence's proposed marriage to Isobel of Warwick. The Archbishop of York would, he knew, convey the hint to his brother, the Earl. Incidentally, the coveted red hat did not reach Canterbury till the 31st May, 1473.

[5]

That little Lancastrian gadfly, the Castle of Harlech, was still stinging away. Lord Herbert, the latest commander attempting its capture, caught a man trying to pass through his lines to the beleaguered defenders with despatches from Queen Margaret of Anjou. The prisoner was promptly sent to London to be "interrogated" in the merciless fashion of the age. The unfortunate man revealed under torture the secret of the French Court, that a *rapprochement* between Warwick and Margaret of Anjou was being mooted. Coupled with this was the hint that Warwick was lingering in Middleham Castle solely to muster and equip his supporters in readiness for her return to England, while Jasper Tudor was assembling other Lancastrians in Wales.

It is impossible to determine whether these confessions were true or invented. The trouble with torture is that one can never be certain whether what is extorted from the victim is fiction, fact, or even mere rumour transformed under stress into direct accusation. At all events, Edward swallowed these disclosures "hook, line and sinker", since they confirmed his suspicions, stimulating not only his fear, but also his growing animosity towards that humourless authoritarian, Warwick.

He lost no time in telling the Earl that strange things were said of him, and ordered him to return to London at once to defend himself. Warwick replied flatly that he would do no such thing, even if given a safe-conduct. After some bickering by messenger, Edward allowed the Earl's accusers to be questioned by the Earl himself. Warwick vowed that he had neither encouraged nor made overtures to Margaret of Anjou, "the foreign woman", but would not return to Court while ever the Woodvilles—Lords Rivers, Herbert and Scales—were in attendance there.

An accusation once lodged in a suspicious mind—and a medieval king was a fool if he were not suspicious—is rarely removed by plain denial. Edward professed to believe his minister, but distrusting him, quietly strengthened his bodyguard by an extra 20 men, "strong varlets of the best archers", whom, after a stay of seven weeks in Windsor, he took to Coventry for the Christmas festivities. The primary motive for this visit was to see for himself the condition of the country. What he saw made him increasingly uneasy. The merchants and notables of London, becoming more prosperous daily, were his friends, but elsewhere his popularity had declined. Not only were there disturbances and outbreaks of violence at widely separated points throughout the realm, so that vandalism, pillage and the slaughter of game occurred, but also in Yorkshire a leader, known as "Robin of Redesdale", had raised a band of bowmen numbering some hundred, and had privately put them under Warwick's orders. Robin is believed to have been Sir John Conyers, a relation by marriage of the Earl of Northumberland. Warwick sent them away, saying they should be told when they were needed.

Whether the King knew this at the time of his Coventry visit is uncertain, but probably it had leaked out or been suspected in certain quarters, and brought to his notice.

There was also trouble in Ireland—when was there not? The Earl of Desmond, Clarence's deputy, had done well there, keeping that turbulent country quiet, but no successful man lacks enemies. The Bishop of Meath quarrelled with him and invented the story that Desmond wished Edward to rid himself of his Queen and marry a princess from overseas who would bring him a powerful alliance. Whether Desmond suggested this to Edward is not known, but something caused the King to replace him by Worcester, who had him executed at Drogheda in February, 1468, on a charge of aiding the Irish rebels. It is said that Queen Elizabeth, Edward's wife, stealing her husband's signet ring, used it to sign the order for Desmond's death.

The cruel Worcester had exceeded his powers, but the King, though he may in the silence of the night have regretted Desmond's death, took no action against the man responsible until the vindictive Earl by his ruthless methods made Ireland too hot to hold him. In the end Edward had to bring him home.

[6]

Louis, ever desirous of stirring up the English hive, and eager to know the latest news, now sent an envoy, Monypenny, to England, with secret instructions to support Warwick in his machinations. Monypenny saw many influential people in London during December, 1468, and did his best to frighten the Yorkists with talk of a coming alliance between France and the supporters of Henry of Windsor. From London he travelled to Coventry, where he was speedily granted an audience by the King.

Edward inquired whether he carried letters. Monypenny replied negatively. Edward then asked sharply: "Have you any for Warwick?" The envoy admitted he had, but denied knowledge of their contents, except that Louis was astonished that his last embassy had drawn no answer from England.

On New Year's Day, 1468, a mob attacked the home of Earl Rivers, doing considerable damage. Things then took a turn for the better, however, for the great baron, Warwick, suddenly changed his mind. Whether persuaded by his brother George, Archbishop of York, a mediator between two bold and stubborn men; whether afraid that Edward's presence at Coventry betokened a forthcoming attack upon him at Middleham; or whether he was disconcerted by the King's ability to govern serenely without him; it is difficult to decide. The fact is that he agreed at last to come to a Privy Council in Coventry called by the King.

This meeting took place during the second half of January, 1469. Edward, who had by now recovered his temper and was prepared to forgive, took Warwick's reappearance as a sign of regret for bad behaviour, and made him welcome. There was an insincere reconciliation between the Earl and the Woodville clan, but for all his deference to the King, Warwick was in no way appeased. He opposed the marriage of Margaret of York to Charles of Burgundy, suggesting that both Charles and the Duke of Brittany were fawning on the King merely to serve their own ends. When the

King audaciously asked him to lend Burgundy 100,000 marks to pay for 4,000 archers, he firmly refused. With much irritation and reluctance the King agreed that eventually another Council meeting should be held. This was fixed for a month later.

By now the growing intimacy between Warwick and Clarence had attracted the attention of watchful observers. Even the ambassador of the Duke of Milan knew of or suspected their alliance. It was probably the knowledge that he could count on both Louis and Clarence that made Warwick so stoutly oppose the King's pro-Burgundian policy. He was again secretly sounding the French king.

The Earl's reappearance and his reconciliations temporarily stunned and disconcerted his enemies, for Monypenny, returning to London on the 8th March, felt justified in reporting to his master, Louis, that things looked more hopeful, and that Warwick was highly popular in the country and exceptionally well-disposed towards France. Though the Council had still not definitely decided to accept a treaty, he fully expected to return shortly with the best possible news.

Five days later Edward followed Monypenny to London, and it was then announced that the contract of marriage between his sister and Charles of Burgundy had been signed. A new commercial treaty between the two countries had been drawn up and ratified, and Charles had undertaken to assist England if attacked.

The marriage settlement, a complicated legal document, amounted in effect to this:

1. The Pope's dispensation enabling Charles to marry Margaret was to be obtained by Charles at his own expense.

2. Edward was to give the Duke 200,000 gold crowns in instalments, paid at Bruges.

3. Margaret was to retain her rights of inheritance in England and elsewhere.

4. The payment to Charles was to be guaranteed by English and Italian merchants in Burgundy or elsewhere.

5. Edward was to cover all Margaret's "bottom drawer" expenses, and pay for her journey to Burgundy.

The other provisions need not detain us, but Charles had driven a hard, a terribly hard, bargain, as some considered it. Why did Edward agree? Obviously some strong compulsion drove him, for he would experience great difficulty in raising even the first instalment of his sister's dowry—50,000 gold crowns. The answer is twofold.

First, he feared that Louis of France, acquiring too much power for England's good, might one day combine with Burgundy against him, jealous though these two princes were of one another.

Secondly, he needed an ally against Margaret of Anjou if Louis for his own reasons should take up her cause and lend her a French army. At all costs he had to have the Burgundians on his own side. Moreover, to ensure that Charles should not be exposed to a countervailing league between Francis, Duke of Brittany, and the King of France, he negotiated with Francis a purely military pact, whereby England would send 300 archers to Cancale in Brittany if Brittany were attacked by the French. The proposed pact contained interesting provisos whereby any French territory overrun became Edward's property if captured by his own troops. The Duke agreed to these terms, and the pact was signed. Edward now had two kings to his bow.

In the spring of 1469, a rising in Yorkshire broke out, being led by Robin of Redesdale (p. 162). It was more significant than it seemed at the time, for there is reason to believe it was Warwick's first move in his forthcoming campaign against the King. The disturbance came to nothing, being easily put down by Northumberland, who was, nevertheless, unsuccessful in capturing the leader himself.

ELEVEN

1469

[1]

THE TIME WAS now ripe, Edward felt, to put pressure on Parliament. Coming before them on the 12th May after a brief adjournment, he revealed that he now had two first-rate allies against the perfidious French, was negotiating a similar pact with the Duke of Normandy, and had secured treaties ensuring peace and trade with Scotland, Denmark, Naples and Spain. He was hoping for similar treaties with the Germans and Aragon. The time had now come to ask Parliament for help in recovering her French territory, lost during the reign of Henry of Windsor. He undertook to take a mighty army to France, nipping in the bud any prospective French invasion of England. If his appeal were rejected, his new allies would lose all confidence in him, and protect themselves as best they could, leaving England to face invasion alone.

Edward was experienced enough to know that a war to recover territories lost through blunders by the previous régime would be popular. Paying no heed to Warwick, Parliament voted Edward all the money he needed, and did so with enthusiasm. The wily King had now to meet the Burgundian bill or the marriage would not take place and the alliance fall through.

Warwick, using his brother, the Archbishop of York, as his mouthpiece, and bitter at his political defeat, told the papal legate at Edward's Court what was planned, greatly alarming him, so that he sent the news to the Pope, who immediately raised difficulties regarding Margaret's marriage, postponing his dispensation. Edward, desperate, extracted from the city merchants a mere £10,300, which was not nearly enough. He therefore asked for and received a further £300, which they agreed to lend, but only if he pledged to them a proportion of the money Parliament had voted for the forthcoming war. To this the King was forced to agree, and as a result, he was able to hand over to the Duke of Burgundy on the 28th May, through intermediaries, the first instalment of his sister's dowry.

At this stage the King was virtually embezzling for his private ends monies granted to him by the nation for war, but the cementing of the Burgundian alliance was in his eyes as valuable as an army, and justified his action.

The secret service with which no medieval monarch could dispense, Edward least of all, was constantly on the watch, and at this very moment caused the arrest of a nobleman's servant, on whom were found letters from home and abroad indicating treason by two Lancastrian knights, both of whom were sent to the tower. Cornelius, the servant, when cruelly tortured—heated iron being applied to the soles of his feet—betrayed or accused many worthy men, including respectable and respected merchants, of correspondence with Margaret of Anjou, which was naturally assumed to be treasonable.

This, however, was less disturbing than his confession that Sir John Wenlock, his own master, was similarly involved. Wenlock's original attachment to the exiled Margaret had been forgiven, which made his renewed treachery unpardonable. Of all the accused, he alone was of particular distinction and authority.

However, for the time being Edward kept his knowledge to himself, anxious that nothing should interfere with his sister's marriage. Whatever his private emotions, he radiated jollity and goodwill, designing to put Wenlock off guard and get him out of the country, which was possibly the reason why he appointed him one of Margaret of York's escort. Scales was also deputed to accompany her and give her away on the King's behalf. At the head of the lovely women the Princess was to take with her was the Duchess of Norfolk, while Edward sent two of his jesters as well to beguile their journey.

Margaret's trousseau, provided by her royal brother, cost him £2,450 and included a bridal dress and clothing, two gilt pots, two basins with ewers, a gold spoon, carving knives, a dozen silver vessels, bedding, carpets, cushions, etc. For her food on the journey to Bruges she was allowed £200, another £900 being locked up in her treasure chest, while the Mayor, Richard Lee, a grocer, and the Aldermen of London, gave her two silver basins filled with gold coins to the value of £100. She was thus no beggar maid going to King Cophetua.

On the 19th June, the Princess left a house in Blackfriars belonging to the Government, known as the King's Wardrobe, which was a repository of royal costumes for great occasions. After attending a service at St. Paul's, she rode on Warwick's horse to a monastery at Strafford Langthorne, where she joined Edward and the Queen. Here she remained for a few days. Clarence and Gloucester, her nephews, came here to say their farewells. She then proceeded to Canterbury with these two young men and thirty lords and ladies, and sailed from Margate on the 23rd in the *New Ellen* with an accompanying fleet.

[2]

Her wedding, when it took place at the Stadhuis, Damme, was a splendid affair, the festivities lasting nine days. In procession through the streets of old Bruges, where she had been met on arrival by the Bishop of Utrecht, Charles's brother, came the ambassadors and envoys of England, and after them those of Burgundy wearing their richest garments and elaborately adorned. Next came the domestic officers of the Duke's household, his knights and chamberlains, princes and great lords, handsomely attired.

Behind these marched drummers, trumpeters, clarion players and minstrels, providing joyous music, while gorgeous in their wake came the numerous heralds and kings-at-arms, each wearing his brilliantly coloured and decorated uniform. Four sergeants-at-arms of the Burgundian household then came by, and at last the dark-eyed bride appeared, fair-haired, red-lipped, with arching eyebrows. She was seated on a litter of cloth of gold on crimson velvet, and wore a sleeveless dress of the same material in white, with white flounces, over which was a resplendent surcoat of Persian cloth of gold. From her shoulders hung a mantle of crimson cloth of gold, while from under her kerchief or headcloth her long hair flowed in a golden cascade, surmounted by a crown. Surrounding her litter, twelve knights in armour carried the Order of the Duke, the tallest among them keeping a firm grip on the Princess's conveyance.

After the bride rode her ten women on white horses with handsome trappings and elegant harness, followed by six carriages richly embellished, three covered with crimson cloth of gold, and three with vermilion cloth of wool. Finally came the chief traders of Bruges and other countries, including wealthy men from Florence, Genoa, Lombardy, Spain, Austria and England, in their costliest raiment.

The progress of the bride through the town was enlivened by entertainments and tableaux in the streets and at crossroads, where wild beasts were exhibited, some of which snuffed up wine, claret, hippocras or milk.

[3]

Margaret having departed, Edward could devote himself once more to affairs of state. The French King knew that his overtures had been in vain, and that his country was in great danger. Looking round for help, he decided to carry the war into the enemy's camp by means of a third party, the exiled Earl of Pembroke, Jasper Tudor, whose title had been revoked by Parliament on Edward's accession. Louis also took the exiled Margaret of Anjou, of whom Jasper was a loyal supporter, under his wing, invited her followers to join her at his Court, and sent a secret instruction to her friends in England to be ready to fight for her when circumstances made it possible.

Jasper Tudor was the second son of Owen Tudor, a Welsh knight, and Katharine, Owen's wife, formerly Katharine of France, widow of Henry V. There is no certainty that she was married to Owen, but we may give her the benefit of the doubt.

It was arranged that Jasper should land at once on the Welsh coast with an army. As the King's half-brother he would carry some weight; but the project was pitifully organized. Instead of a powerful escorting fleet of well-armed men-of-war, all Pembroke could extract from the miserly Louis was three small ships, while his total strength consisted of a mere fifty men. His available cash was equally scanty.

He sailed from Honfleur on the 24th June, while Margaret, the prospective Duchess of Burgundy, was herself sailing to Burgundy from Margate. The two expeditions do not appear to have sighted one another. Both enjoyed fair weather, and Jasper, without the formidable array of seasoned fighting men he had hoped to transport, landed in Wales at a point not far from the stubbornly-resisting Castle of Harlech, still encircled by Lord Herbert. Jasper was not nearly strong enough to cut through the English ring, and was compelled for a time to abandon hope of raising the siege and making the castle his headquarters. Instead, he marched against unprotected Denbigh, gathering up adherents as he went.

Taken completely by surprise, Denbigh offered no resistance. It was seized, and some of its wooden houses were soon ablaze. Here Jasper "held many sessions and assizes" in the name of King Henry.

Lord Herbert, learning of Jasper's return, quickly by urgent messenger brought his brother into the field. At the head of a pursuing army they engaged the Welshman, and had little difficulty in crushing his miserable handful of men. Expecting this defeat, Jasper had already laid his plans, and succeeded in escaping. Once more he went into hiding in the Welsh mountains, as he and so many of his people had done before. A few of his abandoned men got away, but most surrendered, twenty of them being executed without delay. His three little ships had already returned to France, one being captured, however, before she reached port.

This last defeat broke the spirit of the men of Harlech, whose commander, David Abenon or Ap Enyon, surrendered to Lord Herbert on the 14th August. The castle had held out with incredible pertinacity for seven years, receiving food and supplies from surrounding Lancastrian supporters. The tiny garrison of no more than fifty men included that young boy, the King's own nephew, Henry Tudor. Sir Richard Tunstall was also captured. As a reward for his triumph, such as it was, Herbert was given the Earldom of Pembroke, previously owned by Jasper Tudor, and guardianship of Henry Tudor. The prisoners were all carried to London by the new Earl, but only two were beheaded, by order of Earl Rivers. The most important were granted pardons, possibly because the

King, as a good soldier, admired the bravery with which they had defied his generals for so many years. Herbert presently conceived the notion of marrying the young Tudor to his own daughter, Maud, but this did not come to pass.

[4]

The commotion in Wales was paralleled by another in London. The revelations of Cornelius had seriously alarmed the King's party, and many of those accused by him were now tried at the Guildhall. Sir Thomas Coke or Cooke, a former Mayor of London (1462), was the principal person arraigned. He was known to be a rich man, and had played a dubious part in the rebellion of Jack Cade. There is good reason to believe he was innocent of these latest accusations, but he had to pay the King £8,000 for his pardon and also give the Queen 800 marks. The King, having an army to raise and more instalments of his debt to Charles of Burgundy to pay, was desperately short of money and borrowing where he could, even pledging some of his jewels. He was only too glad of chance windfalls such as Cooke provided.

Charles, as has been seen, had been in no great hurry to marry Edward's sister, whom he appears never to have seen until she arrived on his doorstep, but at the Castle of Utrecht, where she, her attendants and her committee of welcome, were residing, he was much impressed by her beauty, and for the first time displayed enthusiasm for the marriage. One wedding gift he could have brought her, however, was withheld—the withdrawal of his prohibition of English cloth. This caused Edward much annoyance.

According to Margaret's escort when they returned to England, the Burgundians showed them no more favour than if they had been Jews. They had had to pay, they said, extortionate prices for meat and drink, and one of them remarked that even his horse had slept more comfortably than the yeomen, for at least it stood in the stable, whereas at times those poor fellows had had to lie out in the street, no one being able to get a bed for less than 4d. a night.

Some disgruntled men—goldsmiths, tailors and other traders—decided to revenge themselves on the London Flemings by attack upon those of that nationality living and working in Southwark.

Meeting at Radcliffe, about a mile from Limehouse, they planned to take boats to Horsedown on the way to Rotherhithe and about half a mile from London Bridge, drag the foreigners from their beds before 6 a.m., and kill them, or if not that, "cut off their thumbs and hands" to stop them from plying their weaving trade.

For this, however, boats were needed to take them over the river. While bargaining with watermen for passage, they were overheard. Their evil purpose was reported in the right quarter, and they were promptly arrested, being held in jail for a considerable time.

[5]

Members of the Hanseatic League, a federation of the more important cities of North Germany, had had for generations special trading privileges in England, which they were anxious to retain. In the summer of 1468 friction arose between the League and the King, the League being accused of seizing four English ships. These had in fact been taken by the Danes in revenge for a raid by English fishermen on Icelandic villages. Edward, ignorant of this, promptly closed the Hanseatic warehouses in London, threw their merchants into jail, and fined them £20,000. This led to a serious quarrel. Neither side would budge, the League refusing to pay, and the King rejecting all requests to free their merchants, though one or two escaped. In the end, after Charles of Burgundy had pleaded for them, Edward, relenting reduced the fine to £4,000, and after meditation, restored their privileges pending a further conference.

This inglorious squabble, in which Edward was clearly in the wrong, even if he did not at first appreciate it, showed clearly his great need of ready money.

Louis of France, disturbed by the utter failure of Jasper Tudor's invasion of Wales, which meant that France was still in danger, determined by a bold stroke to sever at least one link of the chain the alliance had drawn round him. His armies attacked and defeated the Duke of Brittany before either Burgundy or England could come to his aid. Nevertheless, he did not, even now, give up hope of friendship with England. Taking a leaf out of Charles's book, he offered a daughter of his own as wife for the Duke of Clarence. Too astute to dismiss this proposal out of hand, Edward sent an ambassador to discuss with Louis this and other matters of dispute between them, while steadily going on with his military preparations.

Three hundred archers were to go to the Bretons in accordance with their treaty with England which was ratified by both parties on the 10th August. The Duke of Brittany was obliged to ratify it, having been severely mauled and driven back by the French.

Despite these ratifications, Edward, with perfidy typical of the period, sent his envoy on from Brittany to Noyon to discuss with Louis both the marriage of Clarence and a possible truce, but Louis cunningly marked time for some weeks, hoping that Brittany would be decisively beaten before Edward's archers took the field.

With a great show of decision, Edward appointed Scales Admiral of a fleet to carry his men under Lord Mountjoy to Brittany. This force was to comprise 300 archers as promised, as well as 1,100 marines, and to assemble at Portsmouth at the end of September, the ships being made ready at Gravesend and Sandwich. While Burgundy and England slowly responded to Francis's desperate appeals for help, yet never sent a soldier marching or a ship sailing, Louis achieved his objective. Francis was rapidly worn down by the powerful French army, and with a weakness and lack of courage which revealed him as irresolute and untrustworthy, laid down his arms without either consulting or notifying his allies. His ships, which had entered Plymouth harbour and were waiting to transport Edward's men, suddenly weighed anchor and silently, inexplicably, sailed away.

When Charles and Edward discovered he had surrendered, they were infuriated, but Edward was also displeased with Charles, who was still maintaining his embargo on English cloth, ignoring all attempts to have the matter discussed. Edward's envoy to France now came back empty-handed, for Louis no longer needed him, and was openly helping Margaret of Anjou to regain the throne for her husband.

[6]

Edward contemplated an invasion of France to recover the English province of Guienne, but a rumour that Margaret of Anjou was assembling a fleet at Harfleur led him to order Scales to intercept and engage her. However, the rumour was untrue. Scales sailed hither and thither in the Channel for some weeks, battling against rough seas, but without firing a gun. At the close of November his ships docked in the Isle of Wight having achieved nothing, and having cost their King another £18,000, which he could ill afford.

The King now sanctioned or promoted the arrest on a charge of treason of John de Vere, the new 13th Earl of Oxford, Warwick's brother-in-law, son of the former Earl, himself convicted of treason in 1462. Imprisoned in the Tower, Oxford, whether guilty or not, "talked", and his admissions caused two men of the Duchess of Norfolk's suite at Princess Margaret's wedding to be convicted and beheaded at Tower Hill. For these revelations, Oxford himself was pardoned and released on the 14th January, 1469, but without regaining royal favour.

During this period a new conspiracy was discovered by the capture of more letters from Margaret of Anjou to her supporters in England. Aldermen, merchants and others of greater importance were arrested, including Sir Thomas Hungerford, whose father had been executed after Hexham. Another was Henry Courtenay, son and heir of the Earl of Devon. Both were arrested in Wiltshire and jailed at Salisbury, being beheaded at near-by Bemerton. Edward attended their trial. Paston was also accused of causing riotous assemblies in Norfolk and summoned to Salisbury.

Edward's nerves were badly shaken by these disclosures, and his unforgiving pursuit of traitors continued. The year, which had been marked by a great hurricane lasting thirty-six hours, went out amid unrest, fear, suspicion and bloody punishment. The new year, 1469, brought new hope, however, for the Queen, pregnant again, was near the end of her time. All anticipated a son and heir, but were once more disappointed. On the 20th March she produced yet another daughter. Nevertheless the conventional rejoicings took place, the infant being named Cicely after her grandmother.

His immediate anxieties over, Edward felt free to rebuild the alliance broken by Brittany. Francis, seeking to repair his damaged reputation, was now making fresh overtures to the King, who, with his ready comprehension of human error and fallibility, welcomed the Breton ambassadors, and once more promised friendship and support. During the first week of April envoys came from Burgundy also to concert with him new measures for curbing the King of France. Decorations were exchanged, but there was no cancellation of the restrictions on the importation of English cloth. The Hanseatic League also took their revenge for unjust treatment by threatening to sever all trade relations unless their London agents were compensated for financial loss or their confiscated property was restored. Negotiations dragged on, but were eventually broken off. Thenceforward most English traders avoided the Hanse ports, and almost all the agents of the League left London .

[7]

A certain Robert Hillyard, calling himself "Robin of Holderness" now brought out the Yorkshire farmers, who resented the levying by St. Leonard's Hospital in York of tithes on corn, which the farmers had never been able to prevent. This corn, they asserted, was given not to the poor, as it should have been, but to the rich and the governors of the hospital. They advanced on York, and before the city walls demanded the removal not only of the tax, but also of the new Earl of Northumberland (Montagu) and the restoration of the Earldom to the Percy family.

The citizens hastily took in supplies, fearing a protracted siege, and were in doubt whether to sally forth and attack or stay behind their walls, but Northumberland himself, fresh from his victory over Robin of Redesdale, put them to flight after a fierce struggle, Robin of Holderness being caught and executed. When darkness fell, the Earl and his men retired into the city. The rebels, unsubdued, but having no siege guns with which to breach the walls, threatened to advance on London instead.

Robin of Redesdale was by no means finished with, either. Early in June he rose again, this time in Lancashire, and with a much more formidable army. The King, jealous, perhaps, of Northumberland's successes, and wishing to show that his own military prowess was unimpaired, received advance warning of this revolt, and decided to quell it himself, though first he had to raise an army. Expecting no difficulty, he left London on the 5th or 6th June with Richard of Gloucester and other peers and nobles. He first made a pilgrimage to the shrine of St. Edmund at Bury, and Our Lady at Walsingham. In the light of later events the absence of Clarence from this expedition is significant.

In his lazy, dilatory way, danger not being imminent, the King paused at the Moor (Moor Park), the Hertfordshire home of George Neville, who undertook to join him shortly with every man he could muster. The Moor was a great house of which the King was exceedingly fond, for there he could follow the chase under ideal conditions.

Edward passed through Norwich, Lynn and Wisbech, then came to Croyland in Lincolnshire, which he democratically inspected on foot, delighting the inhabitants with his favourable comments on their buildings and bridge. From Croyland he went down river to Fotheringay Castle in Northamptonshire, where the Queen was resting, and loitered for a week. His army was steadily growing, while guns and munitions poured in from the capital. At Stamford, Brandon tried to turn him against Paston, but Edward made answer: "Brandon, you can beguile the Duke of Norfolk and turn him about your thumb as you like, but I must tell you, you cannot do that to me, for I understand your false dealing well enough." Edward was evidently getting to know men.

On the 5th July he moved through Grantham and Newark to Nottingham, a wise change of course. His spies had brought news that made a further advance northwards dangerous. Redesdale's was no ill-prepared, unplanned rising, they reported, but a carefully-engineered and well-led revolt. The rebels were strong and well-equipped, and wherever they went, issued a proclamation, couched in terms no mere country squire could have formulated, accusing the King of choosing evil counsellors, debasing the currency, imposing excessive taxes and allowing his favourites to impeach good men, whose lives and property then lay at their mercy.

Edward discovered also that these rascals had had the effrontery to lay down conditions for his retention of the throne. He must live within his income, tax his subjects for essential purposes only, forbid his favourites to slip greedy hands into the people's pockets, and maintain the laws with justice and determination. He saw in this and the three successive northern risings the hidden hand of Warwick.

TWELVE

1469

[1]

THE SULLEN BEAR, Warwick, having witnessed these events, kept his
thoughts to himself, but his consternation was great. He went on
preparing a powerful naval force ostensibly to defend the country,
making a series of brief visits to Calais, Ardres in Burgundy, and
Aire, where he renewed acquaintance with Margaret of York, now
Duchess of Burgundy. He sought to convince all he met that he
was reconciled to the King, and indeed, one who encountered
him during this period was charmed by his friendly manner, and
had no suspicion of the schemes he was hatching.

When the Earl returned to England, Robin of Redesdale's first
rising had proved abortive and Robin of Holderness had been defeated. The time was not yet ripe, he saw, for an armed struggle
against the King, whom even Northumberland, Warwick's own
half-brother, supported. Perturbed, Warwick took the fleet, consisting of about thirty ships, to raid the French coast, coming
dangerously close to Bordeaux and Bayonne, but not disembarking
men there. His object was probably not so much to harm Louis as
to show he commanded a fleet loyal to him and fully capable of an
invasion, if the need for one arose.

Redesdale's second revolt suggested, however, that the time had
come to move, and quickly. Edward had made the great mistake of
leaving London stripped of armed men. The Earl had already told
Clarence of his plans and had summoned the Neville clan to hold
themselves ready. Many seniors of this house were dead and others
too old now for battle, but they had sturdy sons brought up in the
old traditions, and both able and willing to fight for their leader and

their former king. One was Thomas Neville, whose daughter, Alice, was the wife of Sir John Conyers.

As "Captain" or Governor of English Calais, Warwick had won great popularity with its garrison. If he re-established himself there, he would take over not only a valuable port, but also a body of tried and capable fighting men and an excellent fortress from which, should his plans prosper, he could threaten Burgundy's flank. Through his brother George, the Archbishop, he advised the Redesdale men that he and Clarence might join them at any moment.

Clarence, at Canterbury, made his way to the coast. The Archbishop of York, the Bishop of London and a prior from Canterbury followed, ostensibly to attend the blessing of a newly-built ship, the *Trinity*. This ceremony performed, Warwick joined Clarence, and the two of them returned to London, probably by water from Queenborough, near Rochester.

Still maintaining a pretence of loyalty to the King, Warwick now released one of his secrets, telling Coventry by letter on the 28th June that Clarence was betrothed to Isobel, and that after their wedding, he and his new son-in-law would march north to join the King. The city was instructed to gather up men for this purpose, but instead of moving north, Warwick, his wife and daughter, Clarence, the Archbishop of York and the Earl of Oxford, took ship to Calais. There, on the 11th July, in the church of the Virgin Mary, Clarence and Isobel were married, a special dispensation having after all been granted by the Pope. The ceremony was performed by the Archbishop. Clarence was now a rich man, for Isobel brought him as dowry her share of her mother's extensive estates. He saw himself as the future King of England.

This marriage, which Edward had forbidden and of which he was ignorant, was Clarence's first public defiance of his royal brother.

[2]

Warwick's absence had given the Queen and her favourites the upper hand at Court, and now some administrative blunders led to a decline in popular esteem for the Government. The commons grumbled that they were being bled by the hospitals, the abbeys and the barons. The ecclesiastics complained that the Woodvilles were appropriating church revenues for their own purposes. The high-born resented the promotion of men with neither good blood nor great qualities, who had contributed nothing, they considered, to the common weal.

Safe in the strong fortress of Calais, Warwick showed his cloven hoof, hidden for so long, by drawing up a document for circulation in England, stating that he and Clarence had learned of the harm being done by the Woodvilles and other seditious earls and lords about the King's person. They were therefore returning to petition the King for the removal of these covetous folk, and would arrive on the 16th July. As many "treue subjectes" as possible should assemble and join them. With this letter Warwick enclosed copies of the proclamation issued by Robin of Redesdale.

As Warden of the Cinque Ports, Admiral of the Fleet and provider of naval employment, the Earl was far more influential in Kent than the absent Edward, and beyond question many of that county shared their countrymen's detestation of the Woodvilles and the heavy taxation for which they were held responsible. Men and supplies were awaiting the two peers and the Archbishop when, after a landing at Sandwich, they came to Canterbury on the 19th. With men drawn from the Calais garrison, Clarence's levies and the men of Kent, they marched on London.

Led by a great Earl, respected, wealthy and powerful, this strong army overawed the city, which threw open her gates, some of the leading citizens even lending money. Warwick knew that he must reinforce the Lancashire insurgents without delay, and instead of lingering in the capital headed north, aiming to take Edward by surprise and attack his rear.

Edward had soon learned of Warwick's landing, and immediately called his Council together in Nottingham. Two of the "evil counsellors" named by Warwick were the new Earl of Pembroke (Lord Herbert), and the new Earl of Devon, Humphrey Stafford of Southwick, granted the title after the execution of Courtenay, the previous Earl. These two men received an urgent and unexpected summons to the King, to which they at once responded.

Edward felt like a man stepping over quicksands which may at any moment swallow him up, and ordered his Council to reveal whatever they knew of this new plot. Taken aback, the barons denied all knowledge of the Earl's intentions, but admitted knowing his dislike of Rivers and the Queen's family. Rivers suggested that Pembroke (Herbert), Devon and the loyal leaders in the west country should intercept Warwick. Having a large body of archers and Welsh footsoldiers, they should be able to hold and even defeat him. Accordingly, Edward ordered these two Earls to march, convinced that Warwick and Clarence were conspiring to rob him of his crown.

His own army comprised merely about 200 men with bows and a handful of footsoldiers, and he knew its weakness. After Pembroke and Devon had departed, he told Rivers that the mainspring of the proclamation by the two Earls was envy. Meanwhile he summoned Clarence and Warwick to him, hardly expecting them to comply. He told Warwick in his message that in view of the trust and affection he felt for him, he could hardly believe him so hostile to his King as rumour reported, and he would be perfectly welcome when he arrived. Lord Mountjoy (Walter Blount) remarked to Edward in effect: "It's not you they're after, but Rivers and his offspring. You would be well-advised to send them away."

Thinking this advice sound, Edward ordered Rivers and the minor Woodvilles to leave the Court for their own safety until he knew better what Warwick intended. Rivers was quite ready to do as his son-in-law suggested, being loth, he said, to cause strife between his King and Clarence over himself. However, he and his son, John, set off from Norfolk for Wales, lodging first at Chepstow Castle. Lord Scales, at Canterbury, and the Queen, were ordered to join the King, and then sent to Cambridge.

Robin of Redesdale (p. 149) was quick to see that any check to Warwick would endanger himself, especially if Northumberland marched upon him. Nevertheless, Northumberland (Montagu), so quick to suppress the previous risings, was dilatory on this occasion, and may have secretly been in league with his half-brother, Warwick, or else sitting on the fence. Robin was therefore emboldened to advance on Leicester, so placing himself between the King and his capital.

[3]

Pembroke with the spearmen of Wales, and Devon with a large body of archers, each heading his own contingent, lost no time. Soon, on their way towards Northampton, they approached the little town of Banbury, having come together at a point in the Cotswolds. Hastings and Mountjoy had advised the King not to leave Nottingham. There he remained, but had he known that Pembroke and Devon had moved so rapidly he could easily have linked up with them. A French chronicler suggests that this information was kept from him by treacherous commanders.

Meantime Robin and his men crept forward stealthily and are said to have reached Shrewsbury, at one point on the Severn being but two miles from the slowly advancing Earl of Northumberland, who throughout this second insurrection seems to have left them severely alone. When at last the King learned of Pembroke's movements, he moved from Nottingham towards Daventry meaning to join him and Devon. A strong scouting patrol of his ran into some of Redesdale's men, and a skirmish took place. Some blood was shed, after which both parties withdrew, no further fighting being attempted. Redesdale retreated towards Warwick town, perhaps to pick up anticipated reinforcements, but when threatened by the combined armies from the west, he turned back in the direction of Banbury.

A dispute now arose between Pembroke and Devon regarding where they should lodge for the night—though another account ascribes this quarrel to rivalry over a pretty girl they had met. At Banbury on the 25th, the dispute flared up into a stormy encounter. In a huff Devon took his archers away to a camp ten miles off, and stayed there. Pembroke, in surly obstinacy, unaware that Redesdale and his men were close at hand, refused to wait next day for Devon to rejoin him, and set off along the road from Banbury to Daventry.

The rebels under Henry Neville and Lord Willoughby had left the Daventry road, by-passing the town, and were approaching Thorpe Mandeville, about three miles from Banbury. Between Edgecote and Culworth in Northamptonshire lay a triangular piece of land, flat and belonging to a gentleman name Clarell. It was known as Danesmoor, and was surrounded by three hills of unequal height at varying distances from one another. It was Monday, the 26th July.

Pembroke at last detected them, and would have been well-advised to fall back and await the men under Devon, with their archers and the levies from the western counties. Instead, convinced by various prophecies and misinterpreted signs that the day would be his, he at once attacked. The rebels had quietly occupied the crests of the three hills, which gave them a great tactical advantage. Nevertheless, with immense enthusiasm and dash the Welshmen and men of the borderlands stormed and captured the hill to the west of Edgecote Lodge. Their next objective was the east hill at Culworth, from which a good road ran to Thorpe Mandeville. Perceptibly Pembroke was carrying out a "pincer movement". If it had succeeded, the remaining southern hill, whose slopes carried Thorpe Mandeville itself, would have been isolated, outflanked and cut off by a turning movement along the high road. But the east hill held fast.

Pembroke had already suffered heavy losses, and his lack of archers prevented him from dislodging the enemy, while exposing them to merciless markmanship from above. Their onrush was halted, and immediately Robin's men began their own outflanking movement against the west hill, recaptured it, and making full use of their bowmen, forced Pembroke off the slope and back on to the flat meadows of Danesmoor.

Rallying, the Welsh, no longer within bowshot from higher ground, were able to deploy and use their superior numbers. The rebels, having expended their arrows, were compelled to fight hand to hand. Pembroke and his brother, Sir Richard Herbert, showed great gallantry, and at the head of their men, wielding poleaxes, tore twice through the rebel line. Thrown into disorder, the northerners were compelled to retreat. At one stage they were on the verge of rout, but suddenly there appeared in the rear of Pembroke's forces a new and unexpected rebel reinforcement.

Down the green hillsides, carrying high a standard showing the white bear of Warwick, and making the hills ring with tremendous shouts of "A Warwick! A Warwick!" came not disciplined ex-perienced soldiers, but a mob of rapscallions from Northampton

and surrounding areas under John Clapham of Skipton, one of
Warwick's supporters, who had fought against Edward at Towton
field. Had Devon's men been there and attacked, these irregulars
would quickly have fled, but under the impression that Warwick's
entire army had come up behind him, the Earl of Pembroke gave
way. He and his men scattered, those who could escape did so, and
the battle was lost.

This decisive victory was gained not so much by the verve and
foresight of the rebel commanders as by the pettiness of two stupid,
bickering nobles. The entire battle was fought within an area not
exceeding three-sixteenths of a square mile. Both Pembroke and
his brother were captured, and it is estimated that the losses on
both sides included 168 knights, esquires and gentlemen of Wales
killed, with 2,000 of their troops, together with 1,500 Englishmen.
Two of the Neville clan—Henry, and Oliver Dudley—died.
Henry was a cousin of Warwick and Dudley the son of Lord Dudley. A younger Sir John Conyers died in this battle, being the son
of the Sir John believed to have been Robin of Redesdale.

Hardly had the battle been won when the Earl of Devon and his
men came up. Seeing the beaten Welsh stampeding and the white
bear of Warwick floating high over the field, Devon hastily retreated along the road by which he had come.

On the 27th, the prisoners, Pembroke and Herbert, were rushed
to Northampton, now Warwick's headquarters, where he and
Clarence had in the meantime arrived. One account says that hot
words passed between the prisoners and Warwick, who in revenge
had them stoned by the people of the town. At all events they were
put to death later.

Having thanked the levies from Kent for their help and courage,
Warwick now allowed them to return to their homes, for these
men had made themselves highly unpopular in London and Southwark, having robbed beerhouses and attacked the Flemings. The
victory at Danesmoor had placed Warwick in a commanding
position between the King and his capital, and had made his rear
safe. His men spent some time in hunting down fugitives wherever
they might be laying their heads.

[4]

The King, advancing towards London from the north, having left Nottingham towards the end of July, had reached a market town in Buckinghamshire, about twelve miles from Northampton, named Olney. It should be pointed out, however, that some historians consider a village called Honily, three miles north-west of Kenilworth, to have been the scene of the following events, while another suggests a now vanished village named Olneye, near Coventry. However this may be, the news of Pembroke's defeat was brought to him here. Distressed, and declaring that he had been betrayed, he gathered up from the surrounding area every loyal man he could, gave them arms, and determined to take his enemies by surprise and crush them by superior generalship, as so often in the past. However, the news of Danesmoor had reached the ears of his men also, and they deserted in hundreds, leaving their King with a mere posse.

Olney (if it was Olncy) was protected by only a loopholed wall and a massive gatehouse, and was not strongly fortified. Seeing his danger, and after an indecisive skirmish, the King made new overtures to Warwick, and receiving disarming replies, neglected his own security, staying where he was and not expecting attack. Warwick soon discovered his military weakness, and having taken up a position close by, sent his brother, the Archbishop, with a squadron of mounted men to Olney to seize him. Towards midnight, the Archbishop hammered on the door of the King's lodging. Questioned by the royal bodyguard, he demanded instant speech with their master, and given news of his arrival, Edward sent word that he was to come back next morning, as he himself needed sleep.

This brusque dismissal annoyed the Archbishop, who became peremptory. Scenting danger, the King at last gave him leave to enter his bedchamber. York at once ordered him to get up and dress. The King refused, saying he wished to finish his interrupted sleep.

'Get up at once, and come to my brother, Warwick, without further argument!" the Archbishop commanded.

The tone in which he spoke revealed to the King that resistance was useless. He dressed and was led quietly to Coventry, where he arrived on the 2nd August. On the 8th he was transferred to Warwick Castle, being treated throughout with all the respect his position warranted. Warwick received him courteously, declaring that he meant him no harm, and giving him leave to wander freely within a few miles radius of the Castle, but always with an escort of guards. The Earl had not yet thrown in his lot with the Lancastrians, and might possibly have allowed the King to retain his throne once the hated Woodvilles had been rooted out; but he made it perfectly clear that he was now, and meant to remain, the master. If he allowed Edward to continue his reign, it would be but an act of grace on his part, and at his discretion.

During the next few weeks the hunted Yorkists were one by one rounded up. Earl Rivers and John, his son, had left Chepstow, the populace of the town having risen against them, but were caught hiding in the Forest of Dean, taken to Kenilworth Castle, outside Coventry, and beheaded on the 12th August, at Gosford Green. Devon was surprised at Bridgwater in Somerset by the commons there, and on Warwick's orders his head, too, was cut off. Thomas Herbert was executed at Bristol. The Dowager Duchess of Bedford, the Queen's mother, arrested by the father of a soldier killed at Danesmoor, was accused by him of sorcery, but was found not guilty owing to lack of evidence. She was the only prisoner granted a trial. Scales, however, evading his pursuers, took sanctuary.

[5]

A unique situation now existed. England had two kings, both captives of the same baron, one in the Tower, the other in Warwick Castle. The Queen, after bidding her husband farewell at Fotheringay, returned to London and Warwick allowed her to occupy apartments in the Tower, but with little luxury. She was once more with child.

Possibly the ease with which he had regained power took Warwick by surprise. The royal ministers made no difficulties, being prepared, it seemed, since no technical disloyalty to the King was involved, to work under the new régime. To avoid fresh disturbances and the creation of new enemies, Warwick allowed them to keep their jobs. Nevertheless, sooner or later, unless he were to usurp the royal authority, he must obtain legal sanction for his acts. For this, however, the King's co-operation was essential, since he alone could summon Parliament.

Edward, giving no trouble, agreed that Parliament should meet in York on the 22nd September. As a precaution against rescue Warwick had him stealthily removed by night to Middleham Castle in Wensleydale, Yorkshire, inherited from his father. Edward arrived there about the middle of August and remained till the 25th August. The King was quietly making his own plans. No monarch of spirit, even one so tolerant and forgiving as he, could do other than resent the humiliations inflicted upon him by the Nevilles. Warwick should have realized this.

Knowing Henry VI's weakness, and despite the unquenchable ardour of Margaret of Anjou, Warwick saw little hope for England if the Lancastrian King were restored. Now that most of the Woodville leaders had been disposed of, it would be better to keep Edward as puppet king and rule through him rather than remove him altogether. He was confirmed in this opinion by the rising fury in London, which had at first received him with acclamation, his true intentions not being generally known. After Pembroke's defeat and execution and the imprisonment of Edward, however, the commons rose, looting and burning, declaring themselves his loyal subjects.

The Duke of Burgundy's envoys were in the capital, dealing with a minor matter, Edward having sent them back there when the Lancashire disturbances arose. From them their master heard the grave news of Edward's fall. To the London insurrectionaries the Duke now offered all aid if they remained loyal to his brother-in-law and kept good order, but he swore to punish them severely if they did not. When the Mayor read this letter to them, the commons were much encouraged. Warwick, alarmed, persuaded Edward to condemn the wanton damage and destruction, and to threaten severe punishment if further unruly outbreaks occurred.

The mob dispersed and London became quiet again. Hardly had this boil burst and been healed than another appeared, this time along the Scottish border, where Humphrey Neville of Brancepeth, who had been hiding beside the Derwent, brought his men out again to restore Henry and eliminate Edward. His brother Charles rode with him.

This was not at all what Warwick wanted, and although these hotheaded Lancastrians were led by one of his own clan, he had to keep the reins of power in his own hands or be swept away. It was difficult to raise men against Humphrey, for by this time the commons were convinced Warwick, the King's jailer, had designs on the throne. They accordingly refused to stir for him. Let him fight his battles himself! If Humphrey won, they would at least see a legitimate king assume the throne, not an upstart baron.

Warwick was in a dilemma. Unless he acted quickly, this northern pustule would become a spreading disease, virulent and uncontrollable. He and his brother, the Archbishop, took the only decision possible to prove that he was not the King's enemy. He opened the gates of Middleham Castle and brought Edward first to York, then to Pontefract, seemingly once more a free man. Here the King remained till at least the end of September. The commons, relieved and gratified, now mustered in response to Warwick's proclamations, and were led northwards, where they quickly disposed of the two Nevilles, both of whom were beheaded in York, where Edward was taken on the 29th September to witness the executions.

[6]

Warwick's successes had in no way improved the state of the north country, which was wretched in the extreme wherever fighting had taken place. Churches and houses, if not demolished, had suffered great damage. Marauding rebels had ridden and still rode over what had once been fair and fertile lands, now neglected and unproductive. Money was being poured into armour and weapons as each covetous baron or loyal clansmen prepared to attack his adversaries. Simple men had been slain in hundreds to further the ambitions or plans of their masters. Crops had been flattened by contending partisans. Many villages, even the poorer quarters of towns, yearned as ever for a strong King who should once and for all end their miseries.

Whatever his feelings, Edward gave every appearance of con-

tent with his scant measure of liberty, and seems to have reassured
Warwick and his brother, the Archbishop, who believed he was
quite willing to obey and be guided by them. When Warwick's
levies came back from the north, the King soon learned that it was
really for him they had fought, and that at his command they
would cheerfully rise again. The time, however, was not yet.

The whole country now clamoured for the King to occupy his
throne again, and there were signs that more riots might break out,
and the Duke of Burgundy even invade the country, unless he
were restored to his former dignities. Disturbed, Warwick told the
King that if he behaved himself, he would be taken to London,
could visit his Queen, be shown to the people, and honoured by
them as their sovereign.

This was precisely what Edward wished, and he promised
everything Warwick asked him to promise. The city was promptly
notified that the Archbishop of York was bringing Edward to
London—a free man—and he was to be welcomed with all ceremony. So, during the first week in October, he departed for his
capital.

A great company, including his brother, Gloucester, and the
nobles Hastings, Arundel, Northumberland, Essex, Mountjoy and
Buckingham, with a brilliant array of minor figures, came out to
meet him. Also present were the Mayor, his Aldermen, dressed in
scarlet, and the men of the crafts, dressed in blue. The procession
entered London by way of Cheapside. Accompanying the King
were about 1,000 mounted men, not all of them armed. He had
parted company with his escort, the Archbishop, at the Moor,
near Rickmansworth, the prelate's home. With the Archbishop
lodged also the Earl of Oxford, who had come out with the other
peers from London. The two of them set out next day to rejoin the
King at his lodging place, a room in the Tower of London with an
oriental carpet on the floor. They had gone but three miles when a
rider met them with a royal command to stay where they were,
and the King would send for them when he wanted them.

George Neville, the Archbishop, recognized in this curt message
a repayment for his own peremptory order to the King to rise
from his bed. His stomach went down, and he was assailed by a
vast unease. The King took up new quarters at the Palace of West-

minster after a brief intervening stay at the Palace of St. Paul's, on the 17th October, 1469.

Warwick's nervousness made him a bad general and also a statesman whose courage was liable to fail him in a crisis. He had not dared to ride with Edward to London, where he could keep an eye upon him and become his unchallenged chief minister, but had stayed away, uncertain, perhaps, of the reception he would get from the people, and uncertain also of his safety among the principal adherents of the King.

Edward himself was too keenly aware of his own immediate insecurity to display his true feelings. Since he owed his restoration to popular clamour rather than to Warwick, valour or ability, he decided to lavish eulogies on his brother, Clarence, who, like the great Earl, had kept out of London, but at the same time he flattered and pretended friendship with Warwick, the Archbishop of York, and the Earl of Oxford. His servants were, however, less enthusiastic, and there were many speculations as to the reason for his subservience. Nevertheless, circumspection was in his view essential.

THIRTEEN

1470

[1]

WARWICK'S ABSENCE MEANT that the Earl could not and did not now instal his supporters and clansmen as ministers. Men suspected that little patronage was to be had from him while ever he lay skulking in the provinces. Even the Great Seal of England remained in Stillington's possession, the Privy Seal being with the Bishop of Rochester, Thomas of Rotherham.

Meantime, Edward worked hard to re-establish himself, and gradually, showing his strength, brought back to Court men for whom he felt affection or liking. He allowed Lord Scales to emerge from sanctuary and take over his father's Earldom as Earl Rivers. His loyal brother, Gloucester, was made Constable of England and Chief Justice of North Wales. Langstruther, the Treasurer, was dismissed, and William Grey, Bishop of Ely, given his place.

New troubles arose in Wales, whose people objected to Gloucester's appointment, and had to be put down by force. Edward wisely decided that for the time being it would be advisable to bring both Warwick and Clarence to London, where they could be more effectively courted, cajoled, and watched. He therefore summoned a Grand Council of peers of the realm for November. Both Clarence and Warwick undertook to attend, and the Council met on the 6th of that month, but weeks went by without their reappearance. They were waiting to see, perhaps, how the King and his ministers conducted themselves, while secretly they got together a sufficiently impressive retinue to accompany them to the capital. That some fear of their intentions was felt by the citizens is indicated by the strict watch they kept during the night preceding the Earl's arrival.

When he did appear, Warwick sought to convince the assembly that he had returned to England merely to undo the evil wrought by Earl Rivers and his family, whom he accused of having pocketed money belonging to the state. This the King hotly denied. Nevertheless, not feeling strong enough as yet to overthrow the Earl, Edward proposed that all should bury the hatchet and work together for the good of their land.

Parliament compelled both factions to make concessions. Warwick had to acknowledge Edward as the rightful King and accept his rule. The King had to proclaim at the Kings Bench in Westminster, and later throughout the country, a general pardon, valid up to Christmas, for all who had risen against him. This meant that neither Warwick nor Clarence could now be arraigned as traitors. He had also to repay the grants of money extracted from Parliament in 1468, and to promise the hand of his four-year-old daughter, Elizabeth, to Montagu's eldest son, George, aged nine, and create him Duke of Bedford. Edward having no son, this George might some day inherit the crown.

As long as Warwick had to be placated, peace must be kept with France. Edward therefore offered to receive envoys from Louis, who, crafty and suspicious as ever, and uncertain what to make of the situation in England, assumed that Warwick had turned his coat and was once more in league with the English King, which boded ill for France. He held back his envoys, who had already been sent their permits to enter England, and made ready to meet a possible invasion by the Yorkist army.

In their turn Warwick and Clarence were suspicious of the King, but as long as the country remained disturbed, he could not, they conceived, dispense with them. They went on endeavouring by devious means to win supporters and work for a *rapprochement* with France. Both these quiet treacheries and the King's security were suddenly threatened by disputes between rival landowners in Norfolk and Lincolnshire.

[2]

The Pastons of Norfolk, who had been in hot water time and again, now quarrelled with the Duke of Norfolk so fiercely that in exasperation he attacked Caistor Castle. Then armed conflict broke out between the Countess of Shrewsbury and Lord Berkeley. These disputes were, however, far less important than a third, which by pure chance, as it seemed, but in reality by design, blew up into an open insurrection.

It all began with a trivial feud between a knight of Gainsborough, Sir Thomas Burgh, and Richard, the sixth Lord Welles and his son, both Lancastrians, which ended in the destruction of Burgh's house and its sacking. This storm might eventually have blown over but for one fact—Burgh was the King's Master of Horse, while Welles's brother-in-law was Sir Thomas Dymmock, the King's Champion and a supporter of Welles. The King's attention was at once drawn to this quarrel.

Summoning to him both Welles and Dymmock, he heard their complaints, after which he promised to leave their persons unharmed till he had investigated the matter impartially.

Probably Warwick and Clarence saw here a chance to weaken the King's position, for by trusted minions Warwick spread terrifying rumours that the King was coming with an army into Lincolnshire to crush with the utmost ferocity the people of the district. Their property and goods would be seized, and they would be executed in great numbers. Early in 1470, from Warwick Castle, the great Earl fomented a general rebellion, urging Lord Welles to muster his men, but not to march until Clarence gave the signal, by which time he himself would be free to join them.

The Welles's efforts in this direction were suspended, however, by a command from the King to put their case before him again in London. With some alarm they set off for Westminster, where they took fright and went into sanctuary in the Abbey. To Warwick's disgust they presently made their peace with the King, and were pardoned. Arising out of the false reports, however, open insurrection by the commons of Lincolnshire now broke out. Edward, who had been on another pilgrimage to Canterbury, ordered his levies to be at Grantham on the 12th March, meaning to lead them himself. Warwick also was ordered to meet him there.

The King was about to leave, when, hearing that Clarence was coming to London, he delayed his departure. The brothers came together behind the dark walls of Baynard's Castle, near Blackfriars Bridge, which was at that moment the home of Cicely, Duchess of York, their widowed mother. Clarence explained that he had come to see his wife, but in reality, if Sir Robert Welles, Lord Welles's son, is to be believed, his true motive was to plead the Welles's cause with the King, and to hold up the royal advance into Lincolnshire.

Overjoyed to see his brother again, Edward welcomed him fraternally. Together they mounted their horses and rode through the city to make their oblations at St. Paul's. Clarence was evidently unable to hinder the King, for soon afterwards Edward began his northward journey. He passed through Ware and reached Waltham Abbey on the 6th, staying overnight. Clarence pretended to be going westwards, but in reality met Welles and Langstruther, the Prior of St. John's, for a conference at the Priory, then went on to rejoin Warwick.

The King, now between Buntingford and Royston, had ordered both Clarence and Warwick to bring up their men, but suspended the order when intercepted letters disclosed that Sir Robert Welles was calling up men in the names of Clarence, Warwick and himself. Large numbers were assembling in Lincolnshire, Yorkshire and elsewhere. To Royston came, however, an ingratiating letter from Clarence, so cunningly and falsely written that the King allowed the original order to stand. Thanking Clarence for his promise to come with Warwick and prove there was no truth in the reports, he yet could not ignore that Robert Welles was now calling himself Grand Captain of the Commonalty of Lincoln. He therefore ordered Lord Welles and Dymmock, both still in London, to come at once and explain themselves. They caught up with him at Huntingdon, where Lord Welles admitted that he and Dymmock had instigated the rising, planned in Welles's own house, but he carefully concealed the part played by Warwick and Clarence, and their intention to make the Duke king. (It is only fair to point out, however, that Welles's admissions have been denied by some modern writers.)

Both men naïvely assumed that the pardons recently granted them covered these new revelations, but Edward arrested both, holding them responsible with their lives for any further revolt, and carrying them to Fotheringay. Welles, losing his nerve, sent news of his arrest by messenger to his son, who was then advancing on Leicester to link up, as pre-arranged, with Clarence and his father-in-law. Robert at once abandoned this advance, and on instructions received from his father before he departed to meet the King, hastened to Stamford to pluck Welles out of Edward's hands by a surprise night attack.

Edward was in Fotheringay Castle on the 11th, and next day in Stamford, where he halted to refresh himself and his men. New messages came from Clarence and Warwick, now in Coventry, saying they would join him that night in Leicester. Puzzled by the lack of news concerning Sir Robert Welles, who seemed to have vanished into thin air, the King was suddenly advised by his scouts that the rebel commander had reached Empingham, a mere five miles away, and was preparing to attack.

[3]

Lord Welles, the father, had been warned that if his son did not surrender, Dymmock and he would lose their heads. Without hesitation, therefore, the King now had both men executed. This done, he followed his normal procedure, and marching four and a half miles with great speed, flung his men straight at the insurgents. Taken unawares, they were thrown into confusion. Sir Robert and some of his officers, wearing the livery of the Duke of Clarence, shouted, "A Warwick! A Clarence!" but this failed utterly to inspire their men, who at the first roar of the King's cannon broke and fled in terror, being cut down as they ran, although they tore off their jackets the better to fly. Hence, this battle is known as that of "the Lose-coat field". Down to modern times the place of combat was termed the "Bloody Oaks" because of the many dead and wounded left lying among the trees.

Evading capture, Sir Robert followed his men. In the pursuit, however, some of his lieutenants were killed, together with one of Clarence's household. On this man were found documents revealing the plot to remove the King. Edward went back to Stamford, and convinced now that Clarence and Warwick were marching against rather than for him, ordered them to join him, bringing only their normal escort, and dismiss their armed men, since his victory had removed the need for their support.

From Coventry they replied that they would do as he wished, but instead, they moved on towards Burton-on-Trent. When the news of Welles's defeat came through, the original rising in Yorkshire faded away of its own accord, but the King learned of a further Lancastrian rising there, this time by Lord Scrope of Bolton, in that part of the country of Yorkshire known as Richmondshire and Holderness, where it was being said that since Lord Welles and Dymmock had both been executed. no royal pardons could be trusted, and all must resist the forthcoming assault on their lives and liberties. Edward marched north again, and from Grantham, where he lay on the 15th, instructed Northumberland (Montagu) to quell the Yorkshiremen.

By this time Sir Robert Welles and a lieutenant of his, Richard Warren, had been captured and brought in. Now from their own lips came the full, but diffuse and almost incoherent, confession that Warwick had not only been behind the Lincolnshire rising, but purposed to put Clarence on the throne. Outsiders advised the King that these two powerful nobles had not dispersed their men, but were advancing on Derby and Chesterfield, almost certainly to reinforce the rebels in Yorkshire. In fact, they themselves now proposed a meeting with the King at Retford, which, however, they had no intention of attending.

Edward consequently quickened his pace, coming to Newark on the 16th and Doncaster on the 18th. He now despatched Garter-King-at-Arms to Chesterfield with a stern order to the Earl and his brother to wait upon him at once, telling them he knew through Sir Robert Welles and from papers taken from a dead rebel, a servant of Clarence's, of their plot. Nevertheless, to Clarence he held out, even now, a promise of pardon if he would but humble himself before him, and resume his allegiance.

Warwick and the Duke, fighting for time, declared themselves quite prepared to do his bidding and come in all humility, but as their lives might be in danger from the Woodville faction about the King, they needed first a safe-conduct, secondly a free pardon, for themselves and all their associates. After consulting his Council, the King insisted on attendance by the 27th without prior conditons. On the 19th March he beheaded Sir Robert Welles in Doncaster, all his force being witnesses. Then, proclaiming Warwick and Clarence traitors, and riding out at 9 a.m. on the 20th, he made a forced march to Chesterfield at the head of "many goodly men . . . well arreiyed".

The mounted men reached Rotherham on the 21st, only to find that Clarence and Warwick, alarmed, had flown to Manchester, meaning to persuade Lord Stanley, one of Warwick's brothers-in-law, to join them, and also to gather up additional recruits. This done, they meant to enter York and confidently await the king, believing themselves powerful enough to defeat him.

A further royal Council decided it would be impracticable to follow them because of the difficulty of feeding the army, since the country through which they must pass could not support great numbers, while Warwick's army had almost certainly exhausted such supplies as would otherwise have been available. Warned by Edward's recovery of power, Montagu, still Earl of Northumberland, subdued the recalcitrant Yorkshiremen so successfully that their leaders, including Lord Scrope as well as Robin of Redesdale, came presently to York, vowing that the escaped Clarence and his father-in-law had been behind their revolt, and seeking forgiveness for their offences.

[4]

Edward decided to enter York and bar Warwick's path should he double back in that direction in hopes of being powerfully reinforced and persuading Northumberland to join him. If this were indeed Warwick's purpose, the Earl was disappointed. Stanley in Lancashire would have nothing to do with him. The Earl of Shrewsbury, on whom he had counted, also declared loyalty to the King. Northumberland remained quiet. Warwick saw then that the north was no longer of value to him, and his cause there lost. With Clarence he turned south, meaning to take ship for Calais, of whose men he was sure, and from there like a medieval

Sisyphus once more roll the heavy stone of treason to the summit of the hill of power.

The King, having spent the night in Pontefract Castle, marched into York on the 22nd, and on the following day was visited by Northumberland and the rebellious Robin. Convinced that Northumberland had not been wholehearted in supporting him, and unwilling to leave this clever Neville in a position of considerable power, he stripped him of his Earldom, giving him instead some additional income and the title of Marquis of Montagu, which was of little significance. This demotion deeply offended John Neville, now but a Marquis, who commented that the King had given him "but a pye's nest" with which to maintain his estates. The original Earl of Northumberland, Henry Percy, still languishing in the Tower and guarded by Lord Dudley, the Constable, was offered freedom and reinstatement in return for an oath of allegiance and £8,000. Percy at once agreed, and was restored to his earldom.

Edward now imposed the heavy hand of regal authority on his enemies. Clarence and Warwick were again declared rebels and traitors, and rewards were offered for their capture. Clarence was dismissed from the Lieutenancy of Ireland, and in his place John Tiptoft, the ruthless Earl of Worcester, Constable of England, was installed, with orders to repel any attempt by Warwick or Clarence to land in that country.

Five days were spent in resting and refreshing the army. The news now came that the fugitives were heading for Devonshire. The King despatched messengers urging the authorities in the western shires to call out their men and intercept them. At the same time he commanded Warwick and Clarence to be in York not later than the 28th, while he also sent to Wenlock, now Commander of Calais, an authorization to prevent the Duke and the Earl from entering that port.

[5]

Meanwhile, the two rebel peers, following the banks of the River Severn, had reached Devonshire without difficulty. When they did not arrive in York as ordered, the King set out in hot pursuit, following a less tedious course. He passed swiftly through Nottingham, Coventry and Burford, hoping to get to Exeter before them, but this time even his forced marches were not swift enough. Warwick and Clarence with Oxford and but a remnant of their forces had already left Exeter for Dartmouth, where they were joined by their wives. Edward for his part did not arrive there till the 14th April.

In that Devonshire port Warwick took over some small craft, and the entire party sailed for France. Warwick was always happier at sea than on land, and as his ships beat up the Channel, he turned in to Southampton, in whose harbour the refitted *Trinity*, one of the largest and best men-of-war of his former fleet, was lying. His intention was to capture it, but Anthony Woodville (Rivers), a poet in his spare time, was on guard. When Warwick's sails came drifting slowly up Southampton Water, he prepared the port to resist. Consequently the surprise failed, and after a short engagement, the *Trinity's* guns broke up Warwick's attack, killed some of his men, and left one or two of his ships disabled. These were seized by Woodville's men and towed in.

Warwick had no choice now but to make straight for Calais, where when he arrived his welcome was not what he had expected. His lieutenant, Wenlock, despite Edward's orders, would have let him tie up, but Wenlock's own deputy, Lord Duras, a Gascon, refused to allow it. In this he was backed up by Vaucler, commander of the port defences. Nevertheless, a hint was dropped in Warwick's ear that he might be luckier at a later date. The merchants and traders of Calais were also against allowing the Earl to enter, since they badly needed the favour of the English King for their ultimate prosperity. Since these men alone could provide the cash to pay the garrison, they were bound to have their way. As Warwick's diminished convoy displaying his pennants approached the harbour, they were met by gunfire, losing seven or eight men.

This was so contrary to the Earl's anticipations, for he firmly believed he had the garrison and the town entirely in his pocket, that he was convinced his vessels had not been recognized. For several days, therefore, he hung about the harbour just out of range of the guns, during which period the Duchess of Clarence gave birth to a son. Her difficulties were probably another reason why the ships did not put back to sea again, for advantage was taken of this event to seek admission a second time. Failing in this, for Duras had learned in the intervening period from Charles of Burgundy that he was willing to come to his aid within four days if required, Warwick gave up hope. The Duchess's son was still-born. In response to pathetic appeals, Vaucler allowed the infant's body to be taken into Calais and buried there. Wenlock had, indeed, smuggled a couple of flagons of wine into the Duchess's ship for her comfort, but with the wine he sent a letter urging Warwick to seek refuge elsewhere.

(Afterwards, Edward rewarded Duras by making him Deputy for Calais and giving him the Order of the Garter.)

Despite these rebuffs, Warwick had one important success. In charge of the English fleet was now Lord Howard, and under him, commanding a few men-of war, Thomas Neville, the Bastard of Falconberg. This member of the clan stole away to join Warwick, linked up with him outside Calais, and proceeded to make lightning raids on Breton and Burgundian shipping, carrying off fifteen or sixteen of their vessels. However, some were presently recaptured by Howard.

Warwick finally set sail for Honfleur in Normandy, arriving there on the 1st May. A chronicler relates that when he and Clarence first landed in France, a blazing star appeared in the west with a spear-like flame (obviously a comet) causing alarm among the King's household.

The Earl appealed at once to Louis of France for help and permission to remain. Louis hesitated. The Burgundians protested that this permission should be denied. Convinced, however, that his advantage lay in supporting the enemies of England, Louis thought this a heaven-sent opportunity to score off his old adversary, Edward of Rouen, and sent high officials to welcome the fugitives.

[6]

Edward, discomfited by the escape of the rebellious nobles, had stayed in York for a time to quieten the north, moved slowly towards Salisbury, and unaware of Wenlock's treachery, luckily forestalled by Duras and Vaucler, was deeply grateful to him for

expelling Warwick from Calais. The King consequently extended
Wenlock's powers and made other pleasant gestures towards the
men of Calais. When he learned the truth, however, he relieved
Wenlock of his command, promoting the young Anthony Woodville, now Earl Rivers, in his place. The Duke of Burgundy, however, less well-informed, perhaps, or from motives of policy, consoled the offender for his dismissal by offering him a thousand
crowns a year, which the deposed commander gleefully accepted,
undertaking to refrain in future from disloyalty to his king.

Edward now moved on with the Earl of Worcester to Southampton. Twenty-two of the senior officers and yeomen taken from
Warwick's ships were here beheaded or hanged, drawn and quartered without delay by Worcester's order. The bodies were
shamefully treated, being hanged by the legs and exposed on
stakes pointed at each end and thrust into their buttocks until they
protruded at the neck, whereupon the severed heads were impaled
upon them. As usual, excessive punishment produced everywhere a
strong reaction against the Earl, who was fiercely hated. Clapham
was executed and the Prior of St. John's, Langstruther, committed
to the Tower.

Although the King still bore a grudge against the Archbishop
of York, he had no certain proof that he was implicated in the
latest Warwick offence. He allowed him, therefore, to remain
under what would today be called "house arrest" at the Moor. A
number of the King's men were quartered on him, and he was told
to stay where he was until sent for.

The Earl of Oxford, having slipped through the wide meshes of
the Edwardian net, had reached France, but drastic punishment
was meted out to those rebels who remained in the King's power.
To this day Worcester, who was responsible, is known as "the
Butcher of England". The rest were pardoned, and the King, after
a short stay in Southampton, departed for Canterbury, where he
arrived during the first part of June, being met by the restored
Henry Percy, Earl of Northumberland, and his predecessor in that
title, the Marquis of Montagu. The Queen, with his new daughter,
and many peers and bishops, were also there.

A council was called, and as a result the coastal defences were
strengthened against possible invasion. The King inspected the

work at Dover and Sandwich, then returned to London, where he settled down once more to enjoy himself, confident that his enemies had been robbed of prestige and power, and that the crown was his for life. Although messages came to him from time to time that Warwick, Clarence and even Burgundy were plotting against him, he considered these reports alarmist, relying on his own spies to keep him informed, and on the strength of his shore and sea defences to keep him safe.

Nevertheless, Louis of France was a more formidable opponent than Edward appreciated. The French King placed no trust in Clarence, whose weak, shifty, envious and greedy character he speedily discerned, but was despite himself impressed by that resolute, eloquent, determined woman, Margaret of Anjou. He was also agreeably affected by Warwick's dignity and courage under adversity, and by the knowledge that he had still a great following in England. The Earl had never been beaten by Edward in the field, Edward having merely been lucky in defeating one minor leader before the Earl could reach the battlefield—or so Louis conceived. If these two, Warwick and Margaret, could be reconciled, they might prove an irresistible combination, pointing a double-barrelled pistol or its medieval equivalent at the English King's heart.

Louis was delighted to find that similar ideas were crystallizing out in Warwick's own mind. Presently Earl and King revealed their conclusions to one another. Warwick went even further than Louis. Once Henry was King again, he suggested, the combined weight of their two nations could destroy Burgundy.

As always, however, Louis was better in thought than action, being one of those who see the force of and accept an argument, but shrink from translating acceptance into action. No sooner did he learn that Warwick shared his views than he discovered difficulties in their execution. There were two great stumbling blocks, he pointed out. The first and greatest was Margaret herself. Proud, strong-willed, revengeful, the exiled Queen would not readily stomach an alliance with the very baron who had thrust her husband from the throne. There would have to be much open contrition, feigned or otherwise, much self-abnegation, much courtesy, flattery and cajolery, of this high-spirited mare by that old warhorse, the Earl. Above all, Warwick would have to convince her of both his courage and his loyalty. She might well doubt these until she had proof to the contrary. Warwick was, after all, a man with a price on his head, a refugee, deprived like herself of status and splendour. It was going to be difficult to convince her that a defeated, exiled man could still be a valuable ally. At present she must be exulting in his downfall.

The second stumbling block was Charles of Burgundy, Edward's brother-in-law, who, furious at the Bastard of Falconberg's attacks upon his shipping, was urging Louis to expel Warwick if he did not wish the treaty between them to be broken, with consequences that might be dangerous.

Notwithstanding his hesitations, Louis went on with his schemes while simultaneously protecting his own interests. Quietly he requested Margaret and her son, the Prince, still at René of Provence's house, to come to him at Angers. Warwick was advised to re-embark with Clarence at Honfleur and take his ships to the Channel Islands, leaving behind their two wives, who should be looked after as befitted their station. Louis could then notify Burgundy that they had departed, so preserving the threatened treaty. Once in the Channel Islands the Earl could find a pretext for returning in secret to a port in the Cotentin peninsula, such as Cherbourg or Granville, where they would be safe and not readily detected by Burgundian spies. Louis himself would go on pilgrimage to Mont St. Michael, near St. Malo, and arrange to hold a secret conference with the two of them at Granville.

Regarding this as a plot intended merely to get him out of the country, Warwick would have none of it, refusing to move his ships. What is more, he allowed the Bastard to go on burning, plundering and stealing Burgundian vessels. It was rumoured that in this way he acquired over 100,000 écus, and that he sold his prizes to French buyers. Naturally the Burgundians were outraged, but since Louis insisted that he had not broken the treaty between them and refused to accept responsibility for these attacks, they took the law into their own hands, making retaliatory raids on Warwick's ships in Norman ports, assisted by Earl Rivers and a squadron of the English fleet. When Louis in turn grumbled, Charles protested that no more than Louis had he broken their treaty.

FOURTEEN

1470

[1]

AT LONG LAST the French King met his two suppliants at Amboise in central France, doing them all possible honour. First, he received Warwick, who declared himself perfectly willing to meet Margaret of Anjou and ally himself with her, undertaking to raise a powerful fleet and fight in England for King Henry. Louis promised the expedition a handsome subsidy. Another scheme, previously mooted and now agreed upon, was the marriage of Warwick's younger daughter, Anne, to Margaret's son, the young Prince Edward. Louis was left to sound Margaret, and if he overcame her objections, to arrange a meeting between them.

At this period Louis was being plagued by the Burgundians, whose ships, with those of England, were despite his protests piratically raiding and plundering his shores. His own people were resentful, demanding action, and objecting also to both the protection he was giving to two scoundrels (Warwick and Clarence) who had betrayed their own king, and the heavy cost to the country of maintaining and supporting them. As a result, during June Louis's bearing towards the Englishmen changed. He offered the Duke of Burgundy a compromise to end this nebulous hostility between them, and told Warwick he would cut off all supplies of money unless he took his ships away.

Warwick's reply was to transfer his fleet to Barfleur. Possibly he and Louis had agreed that some such move was necessary to meet criticism. In any event the Earl's only hope lay, he saw, in winning over Margaret. With a woman of her calibre a fleet fully visible was worth two out of sight in the Channel Islands, and he was convinced she would never come to an understanding with him unless she could see with her own eyes that he still had power.

Margaret, in Tours, did not join Louis in Amboise till the last week in June. Almost before she could gather breath he plunged her straight into matters of high policy. First, since there was a good chance that her husband might regain the throne of England with—but not without—the help of France, he wanted a firm and lasting treaty of peace and friendship between their two countries. Agreed!

Next, the only man who could win and hold England safely for Henry of Windsor was—the Earl of Warwick. Would she accept him as friend and ally? Margaret was stunned, then furious. How could she place her trust and confide as a friend in a man with a queen's father's blood on his hands?

For that matter, Louis pointed out, Warwick had equal reason to repudiate her, for had she not had his father's head cut off and killed his uncle and cousin? Yet for his country's sake the Earl was ready and willing to forget all this. Was she less magnanimous? Could she not do the same?

The Queen retorted that Warwick had called her son either a bastard or a changeling. What mother could forgive that? Moreover, he had executed many of her dearest friends.

True, Louis replied, but at Coventry she had insisted that Warwick should be indicted as a traitor, which was not an easy thing for the Earl to overlook. It came to this, he went on, if she really wished her husband to be free and King of England again, she must be a Queen in truth and subdue her personal feelings for his sake and the sake of her people. Otherwise he was not prepared to support her.

With much reluctance Margaret at last conceded the point. She would meet the Earl, hear what he had to say, and defer her final decision until after their interview.

Louis was delighted, adding, however, that it was essential her son, Prince Edward, should sail with Warwick and land with him in England. This would inspire the people, who would see in him a young and handsome prince and future king, whom they could respect and love.

This was a blunder. Louis had unwittingly touched the Queen in her most sensitive spot—her tigerish mother love. Trust her darling to a perfidious baron? Place his precious life at the mercy of a pitiless turncoat? As soon leave a young lamb in the jaws of a wolf!

Nevertheless, having coaxed and bullied the Queen into conceding the major point—an alliance with Warwick—Louis was not going to yield to her maternal emotions. Day after day he hammered away at her until she became steadily more compliant. Finally, he decided it was safe to arrange the all-important meeting.

Warwick, already having difficulty with the obstinate, silly Clarence, had the sense to leave him behind, knowing he would produce no good impression on the sharp-eyed, unfriendly Queen. Instead he brought with him the Earl of Oxford, a much more personable and engaging former Lancastrian. They met at Angers on or about the 22nd July. Margaret, her rancour stimulated by sight of the man she had hated for years, was not readily won over. Warwick, a much more talented statesman, was quite prepared to let her strain at the gnat if he could swallow the she-camel. When led to the Queen by the King of France, he knelt in great humility before her, seeking pardon for his past offences, and undertaking to serve her and her husband loyally for the rest of his life. Vindictively, Margaret kept the Earl on his knees for fifteen minutes, and even then did not grant him pardon. Determined to show her regality, she treated him with stony hauteur, welcoming Oxford with much greater warmth.

The issue trembled in the feminine balance. Louis, fearing that at any moment Warwick might rise and walk out, threw his weight into the scales, undertaking to guarantee the Earl's fidelity. Now that the King had committed himself fully to her cause, Margaret gave way, pardoning the kneeling Warwick, and setting to work to drive the hardest of bargains. She was not a Frenchwoman for nothing. She insisted that the Earl must withdraw his offensive remarks about herself and her son. This presented no difficulty. When, however, it was suggested to her that an indissoluble link should be formed between these new allies by the marriage of Prince Edward to Warwick's daughter, she was once more pricked in a tender spot. This was absurd! What good could come of it for either herself or the Prince?

Louis replied, perhaps, that this union would give Warwick a personal interest in regaining the throne for Henry. Consequently he would guard his young son-in-law with his life, knowing that some day his own daughter would be Queen of England.

Margaret replied that she had had the offer of King Edward's daughter, Elizabeth, for her son (a story probably invented on the spur of the moment), so why should she accept this proposal?

Now, however, through his representative, her father himself urged her to agree, and in the end she bowed to the inevitable.

At once Louis applied to the Pope for a dispensation. It was arranged that the young couple should be married in France. King Henry was to be restored to his throne, and the Prince should succeed him on his death, acting meantime as Regent, his father being incapable of effective governance. If the Prince died childless, Clarence and his heirs were to inherit the kingdom. The exiled Lancastrian peers would return to England, resuming all their estates and offices.

This agreed, Warwick and Louis on the 4th August vowed with solemn oaths before the high altar of the Cathedral of Angers to aid and support each other, Margaret contenting herself with a vow to regard the Earl as a loyal subject and overlook his former offences.

[2]

All this, when made known to him, affronted Clarence, who had leagued himself with Warwick believing the Earl would put him on the throne. Now he saw himself fobbed off with the remote possibility that his heirs might reign, but not he. This treacherous, self-seeking man began to consider turning his coat again. So Warwich had betrayed him! Very well! He in turn might some day betray Warwick!

The newly-allied trio began the serious work of planning the invasion of England. Louis was to provide money, ships and men, and to maintain the Queen, her son, and Warwick's daughters, Ann and Isobel, as long as they remained in France. If by mischance they had to return to France, he would again maintain them. Margaret still refused to let young Edward participate in the invasion, but won for Clarence a promise of the Dukedom of York.

Losing no time, the Earl journeyed with Margaret to Honfleur to

prepare the invasion fleet, but Burgundian ships had posted themselves at the mouth of the Seine, blockading virtually the entire
Normandy coast. There they remained all summer, so that no
French ships could safely put to sea. Warwick's sailors, having
received no pay, became mutinous, so that Louis had once more to
come to the rescue with ready cash. Warwick proposed that the
French fleet should attack the Burgundians and break the blockade,
but Louis was unwilling to denounce his treaty with Charles,
arguing that it was Warwick's task, his men having now been
paid, to fight his way out.

It is said that Margaret of Burgundy sent a messenger to France
nominally to bring proposals for peace to the Duchess of Clarence,
but in reality conveying a fraternal message from her brother
Edward to Clarence pleading secretly with him not meekly to let
Warwick supplant him, so destroying his own blood. The Duke
replied that if he came to England with the Earl, he might abandon
him and rejoin the King—so, at least, it has been claimed.

During July, Warwick seized an opportunity, raised anchor, and
sailing out of Honfleur, cruised along the Normandy coast, probably
to keep his men in training and test the alertness of his enemy. De-
tecting his movements, the Burgundian Admiral made towards
him, whereupon the Earl retired into a strongly fortified port.
Louis ordered his own fleet to drive off the Burgundians. Warwick
sailed out to join them, but was repulsed with the loss of eighteen or
twenty men. However, the French when they arrived were too
powerful for the Admiral, who withdrew without a fight.
Throughout the following weeks, however, he kept up his short,
sharp raids on French shipping and on the villages of the coast, relentlessly burning them to the ground.

Louis and his people were greatly irritated. They wanted the
English to get out of France, and Louis therefore hurried to Normandy to quicken their departure. By the end of August Warwick
had prepared and concentrated his invasion force. Suddenly, out at
sea storm clouds massed, a fierce wind blew, and soon the waves
were tossing the blockading Burgundian ships wildly hither and
thither, so that they scattered, beating their way as best they could
back into harbour. Some were driven ashore in Scotland and
Holland, and by the time the rest limped into port, they were short

of food. Much valuable time was lost in re-provisioning, and now, the hostile fleet being out of the way, Warwick gave the signal to depart. On the 9th September he left La Hogue, with the Bastard of Falconberg, Oxford, and Jasper Tudor, the much-travelled original Earl of Pembroke.

When the storm died down, sixty ships under a French admiral crossed the Channel. Two separate landings were made, at Dartmouth and Plymouth, where they arrived on the 13th. The French fleet, having done its work, lost no time in returning to France.

[3]

Edward did not know he was in peril. Warwick had assiduously despatched emissaries with manifestoes, promises and instructions to all his English friends, and almost certainly Margaret had urged her supporters to rise when the Earl landed. Towards the end of July or early in August impatient Yorkshiremen rose again under Lord Fitzhugh, Warwick's brother-in-law. The King relied on the Marquis of Montagu to deal with these hotheads, but Montagu, though he could easily have advanced from the northern borders, could not or would not do so.

A good, cool, careful soldier, Montagu was fonder of defence than attack, preferring, like Warwick, not to engage in hand to hand combat himself, but to survey the battle from above and control its course. Polite to men of his own rank, he was amiable with inferiors without descending to their level. A keen student of men, dignified in bearing when not in his cups—he was a hard drinker on occasion—he was subtle in action and thought. With handsome features he combined a love of dress, being fond of velvets, furs and cloth of gold encrusted with costly jewels.

As day followed day with no news that the rising had been put down, Edward, suspecting treason, made another lightning dash, meaning to smash Fitzhugh himself and castigate Montagu for his dilatoriness. He knew that Warwick was gathering an invasion fleet. Indeed, the Duke of Burgundy had already told him where the Earl proposed to land, but disbelieving him, Edward had wasted time in hunting which would have been better spent in making his ports ready for defence. Instead, he merely strengthened the Tower by bringing up big guns from Bristol and increasing the stock of bows and arrows. The Queen, pregnant again, with her children around her, was lodged in the Tower.

This done, Edward went north.

As usual he moved with extreme rapidity, taking only a small force—all he could muster in the brief period available. Passing through Leicester, Doncaster and York, he reached Ripon, only to learn that on hearing of his approach, Fitzhugh had withdrawn to the border. With his companions Rivers, Gloucester, Hastings and Worcester, Edward returned, therefore, to York, having heard perhaps of Warwick's manœuvres at sea and the manifestoes he was scattering. If the Earl were to land, he himself might be trapped as once before, away from his capital.

Had Edward marched at once from York and regained London, Warwick might have found it much more difficult to establish himself, but Edward lingered in York, and was still there on the 7th September, as Paston reported. The King had found the city turbulent; Fitzhugh undefeated and lurking in the background; Montagu not actively hostile, but at least an enigmatic, able presence in command of a fine army. Paston wrote on the 5th August that the Courtenays had risen in Devonshire—they were as hot-headed and untrustworthy as the Percies—and that Warwick and Clarence were expected to land at any moment.

Reluctant to leave the north unpacified and simmering, Edward, convinced that Warwick would repeat himself and land in Kent, urged his Kentish supporters to resist, or if this proved impracticable, to retire on London, where he would shortly join them. By the time these messages were received, however, Warwick was already in England.

[4]

At Dartmouth Warwick was reinforced by some thousands of men whom his adherents had gathered together in anticipation of his arrival. The Earl now formally proclaimed Henry of Windsor "Henry VI, King of England", stigmatizing Edward as "usurper, oppressor and destroyer", and calling on all men to join him lest they regret it. He laid strict injunctions on his own men to avoid pillage, brawls, rape and other unpopular offences. At Exeter he raised his standard, and while Jasper Tudor went off to Wales to recruit more men, Warwick and Clarence at the head of 40,000 men (if this is not an exaggeration) marched into Somerset, being joined this time by the Earl of Shrewbury and Lord Stanley with a large body of armed men.

Warwick had earlier written to his brother, the Archbishop of York, a letter of which the following is a paraphrase.

"It is with no easy mind—far from it, indeed—that I now make a settled judgment of King Henry and King Edward. Henry is a most holy man, loving his friends deeply, and thankful for any benefit. His son, Edward, born to great renown, bountifulness and liberality, from whom every man may expect a great reward, is concerned only to relieve his father in this calamity.

"On the other side, you have a man ready to offer injury, ungrateful, given up entirely to sensuality, and already reluctant to take exercise. He insists on paying more attention to new upstart gentlemen than to the ancient nobility, so that the nobility must either destroy him or he will destroy them. But we in particular who are most affected must not ignore the situation. I believe you know how, the moment he occupied the throne, he at first secretly, then openly, envied our house, and in one way or another tried every day to lessen our honour, as if he had given it to us, and we had not raised him to royal power and authority."

The Earl was much encouraged by the way in which the areas through which he marched sent men to join his ranks and came forward with gifts of money and supplies. His objective was to reach the capital before Edward, release Henry from the Tower, have him crowned again, and dethrone the Yorkist "usurper".

Eventually Edward learned that Warwick had landed in an unexpected quarter and was moving across country on London with a formidable array of men. With a haste that would have been better displayed earlier, he at once offered Fitzhugh and his followers an amnesty, hurried from York with his faithful brother Gloucester, Hastings and the rest, and summoned Montagu to meet him at a point farther south. By this time the sluggish Montagu with about 6,000 men had reached the Castle at Pontefract, and was apparently remaining loyal.

Edward also urged Charles of Burgundy to intercept Warwick's ships if he should be driven from England and once more take flight by sea. When the Duke read this message, he remarked dryly: "He would have done better to keep him out altogether."

Edward censured Warwick and Clarence by letter for issuing proclamations which made no mention of himself, ordering them to come to him "humbly and measurably accompanied". As stated, however, Warwick responded by commanding all men from 16 to 60 to join him, and proclaiming Henry of Windsor King.

The King arrived in Doncaster, determined that if Montagu, in whom he now had little trust, did not join him as instructed, he would push straight on next day, and deal with him later. Montagu was, in fact, secretly exchanging letters with Warwick, and preparing to change sides. The injustice of Edward in taking away his earldom still rankled with him, so that he now nursed as great a hatred for his sovereign as formerly he had felt affection. Thus, there came about the strange situation that on each side a powerful lieutenant was preparing to betray his leader. However, the Marquis of Montagu, deciding to appear loyal until he could do Edward the maximum injury or until he could see clearly which way the struggle was going, marched out of Pontefract and took the road to Nottingham. His secret design was probably to capture the King, many of whose force would, he believed, desert and join his ranks, while the rest would offer little resistance.

He did indeed come within nine miles of the royal army, and explaining how he had been robbed of his title, revealed to his men that he proposed to change masters. They promptly replied with cheers for King Henry.

Edward and his staff spent the night in Doncaster at a fortified house protected by a drawbridge, his troops being quartered in nearby hamlets. Either while he was at dinner or when in his bed-chamber, Alexander Carlisle, his leading minstrel (or according to another account, one of Montagu's men) rushed in, crying that Montagu had declared for Henry, and with a strong force of cavalry was hastening to capture him, being but six or seven miles away. Incredulous at first, then convinced by spies despatched to ascertain the truth, the King armed himself, posting guards at the drawbridge of his lodging. His Council advised him to fly, for with so small a force he could not long withstand Montagu, while the

Archbishop of York with 4,000 men was reported to be but a day's march away, and eager to support his half-brother.

Without hesitation the King accepted this advice, and "feigning to make his water" departed on a good horse for Bishop's Lynn, a little fishing village on the Norfolk coast, about seventy miles from London, but in crossing the Wash, some of his men lost their lives by drowning, the King himself having a narrow escape from the same fate.

Arriving on Michaelmas Day, the 3rd October, 1470, he found there a few ships, one well-stocked with food, and two others about to carry merchandise to Holland. Commandeering one of these he sailed for Alkmaar with about 800 men. These had no clothing other than their armour, and no notion of what they would do when they landed. The rest of the Yorkist force was disbanded by Hastings, who was left behind. For the time these men were to submit, he told them, until one day the King returned.

Edward's journey was disturbed by gales and by a number of Hanseatic League ships, which chased him to the very entrance of the port. He could not dock because it was ebb tide. However, his pursuers were also held up, being of greater draught, and drawing as close as they dared, dropped their anchors, waiting till the tide flooded them in and they could board his ship. Before this happened, however, news of his arrival was brought to de Gruthuyse, now Governor of Holland, who came to his rescue. Sending away the Hanseatic fleet, he came aboard the King's ship, escorted her by way of the Helder into the placid Zuyder Zee and so to the town of Alkmaar. It was the 11th October.

Edward gave his only worth-while possession, a robe lined with martens' fur, to the skipper of his ship, promising not to forget him when he recovered his kingdom. Without haggle or fuss de Gruthuyse, remembering his own warm reception by the King in London, provided him and his company with cash, clothing and friendship, then conducted them to the Hague.

[5]

So, in little more than a week from landing, Warwick was once more master of England. Luck and Edward's miscalculations had greatly assisted him. The combination of Lancastrians and Nevilles had placed him in a strong position, for these two bodies constituted by far the greatest body of armed men in England. The rest—manufacturers, farmers, merchants, traders, craftsmen, labourers, ecclesiastics—had to maintain neutrality, their secret motto being doubtless "A plague on both your houses!" These wanted peace above all, but neither the incapable Henry, his overbearing, arrogant, foreign Queen, the grim aristocrat, Warwick, the treacherous, selfish Clarence, nor the luxury-loving, amorous Edward, seemed willing or able to give it them. They had to swim with the current, going on quietly with their work and letting kings and barons fight among themselves.

In Calais, where Warwick had always been a favourite, forty-five minutes had scarcely gone by after Henry's restoration when the burghers of this English possession took Edward's favour from their caps and replaced it with the ragged staff of Warwick, in gold for the well-to-do, in gold embroidery on cloth for the less affluent. Nevertheless, even here some retained the white rose of York.

In London, the Mayor, Richard Lee, a grocer, was at the Guildhall in his great leather-padded chair under a pall of velvet when the news came to him and the Council, brought by men who had ridden their horses hard, that the Earl of Warwick was advancing on the city.

Broadly, however, the administrators of the English towns and cities, like the traders, secretly preferred Edward, not only because he had tried to get them a fair share of the market in the Low Countries, but also because he was again seriously in their debt, and their only chance of getting their money back was by his return to the throne.

Warwick would have been well-advised to occupy London in person, as was expected, as quickly as possible, but once again, uncertain, perhaps, of the reception he would get, he decided first to discover what support he would receive in the rural areas.

Meantime, one of his friends in the capital, Dr. William Goddard, a celebrated preacher, delivered on Sunday, the 30th September, a sermon in which he maintained Henry's right to the crown. On the following day, Sir Geoffrey Gate, another of Warwick's party, was rash enough to throw open the Southwark and other jails, releasing all who supported the Earl, while at the same time every rogue and vagabond in sanctuary was allowed to come back into circulation and roam the streets of the city.

These men, virtually destitute, made the most of their freedom. They tore into the shops and alehouses, grabbing whatever they desired, and surged in a drunken, howling mob towards the gates of the city, which were promptly shut in their faces. Seeing their chance in this uproar, the drunken Kentishmen turned savagely on their old enemies, the Flemings in Southwark, Limehouse, Radcliff and Whitechapel, doing them great injury. The Queen, terrified by this tumult, left the Tower with her daughters and her women, and went under cover of darkness into a sanctuary church in Westminster which had rooms over it, three of the most commodious of which she occupied. The Bishop of Ely, Treasurer of England, and other prelates, did the same at St. Martin's-le-Grand.

Elizabeth now pleaded with the Mayor to occupy the Tower and hold it against the mob, but although the civic authorities put armed men on twenty-four-hour guard, they hesitated to provoke the marauders by an attack upon them without a powerful military leader at their head. In the end, they allowed Gate to retain control of the armed forces in the Tower, but shared the administrative control with him, for which purpose they entered its precincts on the 3rd October.

FIFTEEN

1470 - 1471

[1]

HENRY VI WAS still in the Tower, where he occupied a gloomy room, octagonal in shape and looking out on the Thames through a window with long spiked bars of iron. On the walls, Scriptural incidents had been painted, and an arch gave access to a tiny antechamber. As one came in, the royal bed, of curiously carved wood, lay on the right, enclosed by damask curtains. Henry's oratory was in a corner, and contained a cross, a bound copy of the Mass and some relics in receptacles of crystal and gold. The poor prisoner's sole companions were a dog and a caged starling in a window. On a table were globes, telescopes and other scientific instruments.

Two days later the Archbishop of York, riding in with a considerable force, entered the Tower as Warwick's representative. By agreement with the Earl and Clarence, the Mayor, Richard Lee, and his aldermen, led by the Bishop of Winchester—went in search of Henry. Dismissing his guards, they transferred him to the well-furnished rooms just vacated by Queen Elizabeth. He was "not worshipfully arrayed as a prince, and not so cleanly kept as such a Prince should be".

On the 6th, Warwick himself, with the Bastard of Falconberg, Shrewsbury, Stanley and the Prior of St. John's, came into London through Newgate. Met by the Archbishop, they proceeded in state. All shops and booths were shut, but from the upper windows of houses lining the thoroughfares hung streamers of silk, cloth of gold and arras. The balconies were packed with sightseers, who, when the leaders came into sight, shouted, "A Warwick! A

Clarence!" From every alley the populace swarmed out to see the men-at-arms and their commanders.

The first to appear were the trumpeters, drummers and gorgeously arrayed heralds. The shrill notes of the instruments, the thumping of the drums, stirred the blood of those who waited to set eyes on the great Warwick in his armour of Milan steel. On a splendid horse, he was followed by an esquire of his household bearing his helmet. After him rode Oxford, Fitzhugh, Shrewsbury and Stanley. Other nobles, knights and esquires came after, and finally, to the delight of all, the men-at-arms appeared, announced by heavy, rhythmical tread and the clank of steel. Even Warwick's humbler retainers wore crimson coats with his emblem, the ragged staff, on front and back. A large crowd trailed after them, some cheering, others silent from fear.

By contrast with the Earl, Clarence looked surly, pallid, and peevish, with a drooping mouth. His unimpressive appearance was mitigated by a short cloak of fine crimson velvet with white hose of cloth, secured by gold laces, and short, equestrian boots of tooled Spanish leather, exquisitely embroidered and of inordinate length. His gilt spurs and the gems of his cap, with its overlong plume, sparkled in the sunlight. Over his white horse pearl-studded saddle-cloths of gold were thrown. Above him streamed his banner borne by a herald.

As was expected and correct, the Earl knelt in token of allegiance to Henry when he came to him in the Tower. The feeble King was brought out and led on horseback through Cheapside to St. Paul's. Clothed for the occasion, Henry wore a long gown of blue velvet, originally Edward's. If not strictly an imbecile, he was no more than a shambling simpleton, with small features and a humble, amiable, submissive expression. Long confinement had made him flabby and robbed his skin of tone. He looked pale and unhealthy. His hands were veined, small and soft, and his wandering blue eyes lacked concentration. When he walked, it was slackly, with slow, ponderous steps, his shoulders somewhat bowed. His voice was low. Part of his time in captivity had been spent in writing verse of no poetic value.

Whenever he attended Privy Council meetings, he did not—indeed, could not—answer questions, and the proceedings over, he had to be escorted by two attendants from the chamber. Cries of "God save the King!" came from the crowd lining the streets, and after offering at St. Paul's, Henry was taken to the Bishop of London's house as a temporary measure, for the Westminster Palace was under repair. Warwick was his companion. Clarence occupied the palace of the Earl of Salisbury, and Oxford the house of Lord Hastings. In the villages great bonfires were kindled and the church bells pealed, as clergymen and troopers reported that Edward had flown.

[2]

The Earl soon quelled the rioters, and a week later, gathered up that poor, poor pawn, Henry VI, variously described as "like a sack of wool", "as mute as a crowned calf", "a shadow on the wall", and led him to St. Paul's again. This procession resembled a puppet show rather than a royal parade designed to win for the King the love and confidence of his people.

True, Warwick held his train and Oxford went before him bearing the sword of state, but when seated on his throne and re-crowned, Henry showed himself "the mere shadow and pretence of a king". The helpless monarch was now taken back to the partly repaired Palace of Westminster, whose walls had so recently rung with Edward's laughter, and there, day after day, came the crowding sycophants and hangers-on to pretend a reverence they did not feel, and partake of meals for which they had not paid and would never be expected to pay.

Who now governed England? Warwick! But even Warwick dared not appoint himself Regent. He restored his brother, the Archbishop of York, to the Chancellorship, dismissed the Bishop of Ely, made Langstruther, Prior of St. John's, Treasurer again, gave Jasper Tudor the Lord Lieutenancy of Wales and restored him to his earldom. He himself resumed the titles of Grand Chamberlain and Lord High Admiral, and once more took command of Calais. He trusted his half-brother, Montagu, no more than Edward had, telling him bluntly to stay in the north and keep the border. Hales, Bishop of Coventry, was given the Privy Seal.

And Clarence?

Not unnaturally the Duke looked for his reward, but instead of being made at least Joint-Regent with Warwick, he had to be content with the Lord Lieutenancy of Ireland again, even that being grudgingly awarded. (Warwick had to remember Queen Margaret and the claims of Prince Edward, her son.) These open slights confirmed the Duke in his decision to break with Warwick when the chance came.

Pembroke (Jasper Tudor) came back from Wales early in November, bringing with him young Henry Tudor, his nephew, about 14 years old, who had been well cared for by Lady Herbert. Jasper was now his official guardian. There is a pleasant fable that when Henry VI saw him, he stared at the boy for a long time, then said: "Lo, this is he to whom both we and our adversary, leaving the possession of all things, shall hereafter give room and place."

[3]

It is generally agreed that throughout this period Warwick behaved with sense and tact, except that he made small concession to Clarence's ambition. (Even Richard of Gloucester always respected the Earl!) One man, however, he could not tolerate—John Tiptoft, Earl of Worcester, "Butcher of England", translator of Cicero and Caesar, author of works in Latin and English. The people of England would be behind him, he knew, if this man were severely punished. Worcester had been caught hiding at the top of a tree in a wood at Weybridge. On taking over the capital, Warwick had him thrown into the Tower. He was impeached on the 15th before a court presided over by the Earl of Oxford, whose father and brother he had condemned, and he was sentenced to death by execution on Tower Hill.

A ferocious mob gathered in the streets before the 17th, the day appointed, and would have torn him to pieces had the sheriffs not hidden him overnight in the Fleet prison. Next day he was taken on foot under strong armed guard and beheaded on the scaffold at Tower Hill with *three* strokes of the axe, one for each member of the Trinity, at his own request. He was buried in Blackfriars church chpael

Worcester, whose death caused great rejoicing, was an educated, literate man, whose writings had been printed by William Caxton. The printer wrote of him: "In his time he flowered in virtue and cunning none like him, among the lords of the temporality in science and moral virtue. . . . The axe (that slew him) at one blow cut off more learning than was left in the heads of all surviving nobility". His widow hastened to take a new husband in Sir William Stanley.

On the 26th November, Henry through Warwick summoned Parliament to meet at Westminster. The Archbishop of York opened the proceedings with Jeremiah's words: "Return, O backsliding children, saith the Lord, for I am married unto you!" Edward was declared a usurper, Gloucester and his other friends were impeached. Montagu was officially pardoned, and Warwick appointed Lord Protector of the King.

[4]

Edward's sole hope of regaining his throne lay with Burgundy, where he had the staunchest possibly ally in de Gruthuyse, but Duke Charles was given to second thoughts. Though bound to the Englishman by ties of marriage, he was also bound to Henry VI by ties of blood. Somerset, Exeter and other Lancastrian lords were attending his Court. Moreover, Edward's power seemed to be broken, whereas that of Warwick, Margaret of Anjou and Louis combined was great enough to be frightening. He would possibly have shed mere crocodile tears had Edward been drowned on the way over. Nevertheless, he remembered that Edward had been a prisoner before, and despite this had returned to power. Might he not do so again? It would be good policy to keep him as a rod in pickle, so to speak, in case Warwick, Louis or both should unite against him.

He played, therefore, the old Janus game, with on one side a smiling face for the unhappy Edward, and on the other, a wary one for the triple alliance. While allowing Edward 500 crowns a month to keep him going, he at the same time spoke soft words through his envoys to Warwick. Comines, Charles's envoy, on reaching Calais received no official welcome, and noted that Warwick's livery was worn everywhere. On the gate of his own lodging more than 100 crosses and rings were painted, indicating that Louis and the Earl were now allies. Outwardly, at least, Edward had no supporters in the town.

Warwick, ever mindful of Charles's previous cold shoulder, ever cherishing his determination to ally England once and for all with France, strongly reinforced Calais against any potential Burgundian attack, and suspended his own plan for a direct advance on Burgundy, only because strongly opposed in this by the lobby of the wool merchants.

Edward, whose temperament prevented him from slothfully waiting to be assisted, became impatient. After kicking his heels for some time in hopes of military and naval aid on a large scale from his brother-in-law, which he did not get, he tried to meet Charles face to face and bring him to a decision. Charles, however, kept him waiting on the doorstep, and but for alarming news from England might have left the deposed King to eat his heart out at the Hague.

The news that disturbed him was that Louis's ambassadors to England had returned to the French capital, Paris, on the 28th November, and sealed there a treaty binding the two countries to make war on Burgundy. The young Prince Edward, Henry's son, had officially accepted this treaty as his father's representative. Charles at once prepared to receive King Edward, who left the Hague on the 26th December, and on the 2nd January, 1471, met Charles at Aire, where they held a two-day conference, after which Charles went away. The Duchess, Edward's sister, also came to Aire to meet her brother, whom she had not seen for some time.

Edward then proceeded to St. Pol as guest of Jacques of Luxembourg, met Charles for a second time, and at a nocturnal conference renewed his plea for massive aid. From St. Pol, on the 9th Edward wrote to Francis II, Duke of Brittany, begging his help in recovering the kingdom from which he had been expelled "by the great treason which was compassed towards me". The letter, signed "voster cousyn, Edward R." by the King himself, is in the British Museum. Somerset and Exeter did their best to thwart him, but Charles, still pretending neutrality though knowing Warwick's plans, went quietly ahead with preparations to help his royal guest, carefully concealing his intentions from Somerset and Exeter. These two returned to England believing there was no hostility at

Charles's Court, but rather amity and good will towards the English government.

[5]

Louis moved too quickly, however, and by suddenly resuming active war against Burgundy compelled Charles to take sides. The Duke gave the handsome sum of 50,000 guilders "with the cross of St. Andrew" to the English King, and secretly prepared three or four ships to carry him from La Vere in the island of Walcheren in Zeeland to his own shores. He also hired fourteen Hanseatic ships to go to England with him, see him safely landed, and return within fifteen days.

Warwick had tried in February, 1470, to persuade Queen Margaret and the Prince to return to England, declaring that Henry wished them to come, but once more she refused. Neither she nor her supporters placed full confidence in the Earl, and the Queen had no intention of handing over her precious son as a hostage to Warwick. For his part the Earl distrusted Somerset, Exeter, Pembroke and the more ambitious and influential Lancastrians. Although he restored these nobles to their estates and possessions, and allowed a Parliament to annul their proscriptions as traitors, he did not believe their reports of Charles's friendly attitude.

It is to his credit that he made no attempt to harm or humiliate Edward's Queen. In fact, throughout this period of his greatest power he left her in peace, and even showed her small kindnesses. She was pregnant again, attended by Mother Cobb or Coff, who was sheltering under the same roof. Her protector, Abbot Mylling, sent her various items "for her comfort", while a benevolent butcher let her have "half a beef and two muttons every week" for herself and her attendants. Nevertheless, she was in comparative poverty, abandoned by her former sycophantic companions. Warwick appointed Lady Scrope to serve her when her time came.

Henry's feebleness was more than balanced by Warwick's force and authority, and the Earl's powerful hand kept firm control of the country. Nevertheless, such popularity as the new régime had won rapidly faded as the weeks went by. There was no genuine royal focus for veneration and love. Had Margaret had the courage and prescience to come to England with her son when her husband

The picture of Edward the 5, who at the age of 13 yeares
was deposed, and cruelly murdered, by the procurement of Richard
Duke of Gloucester his vnnaturall vnkle, when he had raigned
2 moneths and 11 dayes, and obscurely buried in the Tower.

Edward V, 1470–1483, eldest son of Edward IV. The lines are believed
to have been written by Sir Thomas More

Richard III, 1452–1485. A sixteenth-century painting in the National
Portrait Gallery (artist unknown)

was recrowned, and shown the Prince to her people, she might have been carried forward on a great wave of popular rejoicing and reassurance. Instead, she lingered in France while the year 1470 dragged to its close.

Secondly, Warwick himself never came close enough to the common people to understand their distrust of the French, and their reluctance to be embroiled in another war, even if thereby they might win parts of the Low Countries. That a formal treaty had been signed with the French, and that ships and men were being thrust into an already overflowing Calais in readiness for a spring offensive against Burgundy, offended those moneyed interests seeking to maintain trade with the Netherlands.

Thirdly, the conscience of kindly folk was pricked by the knowledge that their one-time Queen, Elizabeth, was bearing a child in fear and poverty, and was to all intents and purposes a prisoner, dependent on charity.

And lastly, there was always the uncertainty. How long would it be before Warwick was challenged, if not by Edward, by Clarence, Gloucester, or some other with aspirations to the throne, and the country plunged once more into internal strife and all the evils that came with it?

Moreover, Edward was highly popular with the ladies of his capital, especially the wives of knights, esquires, aldermen and merchants, many of whom had granted him their favours and had a soft spot for him in their hearts. The aloof patrician Warwick made no such appeal. These ladies steadily worked upon their husbands and friends to ensure their support for the King in exile if ever he should return to claim his crown.

There was also that matter of the outstanding, unpaid royal debts earlier mentioned, which made the goldsmiths, drapers, vintners and victuallers to whom they were owing long to have him back. But perhaps stronger than all these motives was the discovery that the longed-for relief from taxation and the distresses of war was proving illusory. Indeed, if this projected new war were embarked upon, taxes and sorrow would be even greater than before.

On the 2nd November, Queen Elizabeth gave birth in affliction —to a son! Heir to the throne, if ever his father regained it, the infant was christened "Prince Edward of England", and baptized

14

"like a poor man's child", except that the Duchess of Bedford and Lady Scrope became his godmothers and the Abbot his godfather. In so christening her child, Elizabeth defied Margaret of Anjou, an act of some courage in her circumstances.

Sir Thomas More wrote of her as sitting "alow in her rushes". Everywhere, however, in those homes still loyal to Edward, the child's arrival was regarded as a good omen. The Duke of Buckingham and the Archbishop of York persuaded Elizabeth to entrust him in due time to his uncle, Richard of Gloucester, a curious fact which can be interpreted in various ways.

[6]

Although the official reasons given for Queen Margaret's return to England are the treaty signed in Paris and the persuasions of Louis, it seems more likely that she was spurred on by the news that a son and heir had been born to Edward. The wave of popular goodwill towards this new-born child made the public appearance of her own son essential. Leaving Amboise on the 14th December, she came in state to Paris with Prince Edward, Warwick's wife and daughter, and all her retinue. Shortly afterwards she departed for the handsome old city of Rouen, a stage nearer England.

Advised of her impending arrival, Warwick planned to escort her from France, but was short of cash, and loth to leave England. The city of London was dunning him for repayment of earlier loans. Reports were circulating that Edward would soon be in England again. Clarence was showing a marked lack of enthusiasm for the French alliance and the attack on Burgundy. Consequently, the Earl did not leave the capital until the 27th February, when he proceeded to Dover, hoping the Queen would arrive, but upset by the news that he was not coming to France to escort her, Margaret had refused to leave Rouen till she knew he had sailed into a French port.

Chance now took a hand in the game. Great storms swept the Channel, and she could not put to sea. Warwick waited vainly for her at Dover, just as she waited vainly at Rouen for him, until unable to wait longer, Warwick, dispirited and full of foreboding, returned to London.

[7]

The French in their opening attack on Burgundy had taken St. Quentin. Charles created a diversion by launching Edward against their English ally. The 900-strong force to accompany the English King mustered at Bruges, where Edward was living at the house of de Gruthuyse. They included 300 Flemish mercenaries armed with the new hand guns, and when all had come in, numbered about 1200. Merchants of Flanders and Calais lent him money, and on the 19th February he left Bruges and walked in procession to Damme, five miles north-east of Bruges, solely to give the people a sight of him—a mark of affability.

On the 2nd March he boarded the *Antony*, which, with other ships, was sheltering in the creeks of Walcheren. They were held up for nine days by the gales that had delayed both Margaret and Warwick, but at last, on the 11th March, 1471, they left Flushing, Edward accompanied by Gloucester, Earl Rivers, Lords Hastings and Say, with other lieutenants and knights. The force of the wind was such that within twenty-four hours they sighted the coast of Norfolk, having lost only one ship, which carried horses. They would have landed that night at Cromer, but Warwick had already sent Oxford's brother there, Thomas de Vere, to imprison all Yorkists suspected of readiness to help the King, and to take charge of the defences. As soon as his ships anchored, Edward realized that they would be opposed by a force of commons, greater than he had expected. To test the local feeling, however, he had a boat lowered containing two knights, Sir Robert Chamberlain and Sir Gilbert Debenham, who were to land and see what they could do to obtain approval of his entry. These men soon discerned that the inhabitants were too terrified to join the Yorkists or give them permission to camp. In fact, Warwick had ordered every man on the eastern shores to resist with all his might any landing by the exiled King. They were consequently in arms and ready, and could not be persuaded to change sides.

The ships put out to sea again, and for two days were blown northwards by heavy winds, until they had to seek the first possible landing place for fear of shipwreck.

In December Warwick had taken what should have been ade-

quate precautions against invasion. He had ordered Montagu to
raise every man he could in the north, and his commissioners were
all over the provinces summoning the sheriffs to come to them and
receive instructions. His ships under Falconberg were shadowing
the Burgundian vessels, and might very well have intercepted and
destroyed Edward's small convoy had not the great gales driven
them to shelter. As on so many occasions in his life, Edward was
lucky. He had chanced his fortunes on speed and surprise, and by
putting to sea without waiting for complete calm, once more defeated his enemy's well-laid plans.

The invasion fleet was badly scattered by the continued storms,
but on the 14th the *Antony* approached Spurn Head and a small
fishing village, known as Ravenspur, on the northern shore of the
Humber estuary. It has since been eaten away by encroaching
seas and no longer exists. In an earlier day Henry IV had landed
here after exile. The men of the *Antony* went ashore, and at once
Edward knelt to offer thanks to God for his survival. By good fortune this part of the coast was undefended. Five hundred men
landed with the King, who feared that the rest had foundered, but
the following night Gloucester came ashore with 300 more at a
point four leagues off. On the 15th the remainder of the force
came in, Rivers, with 200, having beached at Powle, thirteen miles
away, and the others wherever they could.

The gentry of Holderness were in no way pleased to see this
royal army land on their coast, and despite the sneaking regard the
commons had for Edward, the power and authority of their
superiors prevented either encouragement, reinforcement or welcome of the invaders. The fishing villages alone gave them hospitality and a few men. Indeed, a ballad of the period records:

"Lord, the unkyndnes was shewid to Kynge Edward that day!
    At his londynge in Holdyrnes he had grett payne:
His subjectes and people wolde not hym obey,
    Off hym and his people thay had grett disdayne,
There shewid him unkyndnes, and answerid him playne,
    As for kynge he shulde not londe there for wele ne wood.
Yett londed that gentill prynce, the will of God was soo."

SIXTEEN

1471

[1]

EDWARD AND HIS Council decided to march directly on York
rather than move south, which would mean crossing the Humber
with seasick and weary men, and then meeting strong opposition.
Denied leave to shelter and rest in the walled city of Kingston-on-
Hull, he moved off, and promptly encountered a token resistance
farther east, where an assembly of some size under a priest, "Martin de la Mere", whose real name was John Westerdale, came out
to oppose him. However, by fair words and some bribery he persuaded these men, despite Westerdale's objections, to let him pass.
Some of the muster even joined his ranks.

The King showed his mastery of the political game by declaring
everywhere that he came only to claim his dukedom of York and
to support the King as a faithful subject. By these means, together
with much flattery and a little judicious distribution of promises
and cash, he proceeded unhindered on his way.

So, on the 18th, having rested in and passed through the friendly
little town of Beverley, Edward came to the gates of York. Before
he arrived, while still three miles away he had been warned by
Thomas Conyers, Recorder of the City, that entry was dangerous
for him, but having ignored the warning, was delighted to learn
outside the gates from two of York's citizens that if he undertook
not to aspire to the throne again, the city might, for the sake of his
beloved father, admit him.

A second formal warning against entry failed to deter him, for
the same two men offered to open the gates to him as long as his
men stayed outside the walls, where they could not terrorize the

inhabitants. With his habitual courage, Edward, risking imprisonment, rode in with a handful of his followers just as priests were
saying Mass at the gates. He wore a Prince of Wales feather in his
cap, and he and his men shouted, "Vive Henry and Prince Edward!" as they advanced.

No sooner was he inside than the gates closed ominously behind
him. At the first crossroads to which he came a large body of
armed men were waiting. His officers were alarmed, but the King,
holding up his hand for silence, rode forward alone, and addressed
these men with such charm and subtlety that by the time he had
finished, those who hated Warwick were shouting, "Long live the
noble Duke of York!"

Repeating to the Mayor and aldermen that he had no other purpose than to resume his estates and dukedom, he so charmed them
that when dusk came they reopened the gates, allowing Gloucester,
his archers, and all the rest of the army to come in. According to
one account it was agreed that their stay should not exceed twelve
hours. However, Westerdale, still hostile, protested to the Mayor
when, at noon next day, Edward still remained in his city lodging,
but was partly appeased when the ex-King undertook to keep his
promise and go.

Westerdale now suggested that before being allowed to depart
he should take an oath in the Minster not to claim the crown. The
King cunningly inquired: "Where are the nobles before whom I
must swear? Unless you send for the Earl of Northumberland,
who invited me here, as this letter bearing his seal shows, and send
also for other nobles of the county, I cannot in honour take the
oath. You will then have to keep me here another two or three
days till they arrive." It seems evident from this that there was
some correspondence between Edward and the Earl.

Privately Gloucester and the other lords proposed the assassination of Westerdale, whereupon the Duke and his archers would
seize and open the city gate. Edward rejected this plan. Nevertheless, although Gloucester went away, he returned fully armed, and
going to Edward's room cried: "To horse!" Afraid that they
would be overpowered and held in the city against their will,
he had had his brother's horse brought to the door of the lodging.
Mounting, the King ordered his trumpets to sound, and with all his

company rode out through the gates, encountering no opposition.

Edward was nervous of Montagu, lying with his army in Ponte-fract. To deceive the Marquis, in case he meditated an attack, he did not take the direct route to London, but marched through Tad-caster, Wakefield, Doncaster and Sandal, a Yorkist possession. Then, joining the direct road again, he came to Nottingham. Nothing had occurred to alarm him.

[2]

Warwick had ordered Montagu by messenger to engage Edward, but it is said the message was never received. It is also said that Clarence had instructed him to let the King pass. However this may be, Montagu did not move until Edward had left his area, being always two days' march behind. His motives are not difficult to conceive. He was probably playing for time again. Secretly he liked and admired the Yorkist King, against whom his resentment had now cooled. In keeping the Marquis out of London and not at once restoring him to his earldom, Warwick had made another of his many mistakes. Edward had given him the slip and was now in Neville territory. Let Warwick and Edward fight it out between them, Montagu may have thought: the result would decide his course for him. We must also consider the possibility that Montagu may not have felt strong enough to attack. Nevertheless, con-sidering the small size of the royal army, this is difficult to believe.

So, unmolested, Edward advanced. Percy, Earl of Northumber-land again, remained quiet, and his people would not have dared to meddle with the King without their Earl's direct orders.

As Edward moved south his force steadily increased. Sir William Parry and Sir James Harington brought him 600 men. Sir William Stanley came in with another 3,000, while from Hastings's estates flocked in hundreds of yeomen and commoners. Gratified and heartened by these accessions, the King flung off all pretence, openly proclaiming himself the rightful King of England and France. His spies now reported that a body of some thousands under Exeter, Oxford and Beaumont had reached Newark, and were at that moment on the way to intercept him.

Without delay the King sounded the advance, and sped forward to destroy this force before it had had time to take up a good tactical position. His boldness and speed succeeded as before against opponents once again caught unprepared. The Lancastrian leaders shook in their shoes when they learned to their amazement that he was a mere three miles away and rapidly approaching them. At 2 a.m. they bolted. Edward occupied both Newark and Leicester unopposed. Here another 3,000 men joined him. All he had had to do was cut down a few stragglers.

[3]

Warwick had left London to muster his own supporters, putting his brother, the Archbishop, in charge of the capital. At the same time he summoned the inglorious Oxford and Somerset also to join him at a point below Nottingham. As has been seen, however, Oxford had fled, but the Earl believed that Clarence and Montagu would soon be with him. From Leicester he arrived in Warwick with the intention of intercepting the King, but when he learned that Oxford had abandoned his post without a struggle and was rushing for shelter to Coventry, he assumed that his adversary was in overwhelming force, and leaving Warwick Castle, himself moved to Coventry, where he shut himself up, afraid to stir. Clarence, who had gone into Gloucestershire and Wiltshire to raise men, advised the Earl to await his arrival before bringing Edward to battle.

On the 30th March, to Warwick's probable dismay, who should appear before the gates of the town, long before he was expected, but the King himself and his army, numerous, audacious, confident enough to send a herald challenging the Earl to come out and fight. Edward probably knew by now that Clarence intended to leave Warwick in the lurch, and may have wished to defeat the Earl without aid from his brother.

Warwick made no attempt to accept the challenge. He was under great stress and full of misgiving. How had Edward eluded Montagu? Was that lukewarm general convinced that his half-brother was on the losing side? The Earl sent messengers urging Clarence to hurry, but Clarence was still busy calling up men in the name of King Henry, and they were coming in with their coats showing the collar of Lancaster. He was not yet ready. In Wells on the 16th when he heard that Edward had landed, he had perhaps decided craftily, like Montagu, to mark time until he knew how his brother fared.

By the 2nd April he had come as far as Burford. Edward waited three days in the hope that Warwick would be goaded into leaving the town of Coventry and attacking him, and one account relates that he even offered Warwick a pardon. The Earl, however, demanded a good appointment in his government as well, which Edward was not willing to concede. Seeing that the Earl would not be tempted, he entered the town of Warwick, deserted and defenceless, and was received with acclamation as King.

Clarence was now but a few miles away, advancing with an army of some 4,000 men. After dinner on the 4th, the King marched three miles along the Banbury road until the Duke's soldiers could be seen a mile away. Halting, he, Gloucester, Rivers, Hastings and the rest rode forward another half mile, where Clarence and his staff came to meet them. It was a dramatic and exciting moment. Both armies were drawn up in good order, facing one another, and at any moment a hasty move might have led to a bloody struggle. However, Gloucester, going forward as intermediary, took the Duke first, then his royal brother, aside alternately. In this indirect way they talked until agreement was reached. Clarence knelt to the King, who raised him, whereupon the brothers embraced many times in sight of their armies, speaking with great affection to one another. To the sound of trumpets, peace between them was declared.

The combatants-to-be discarded all armour and weapons for the time being. So unexpected was Clarence's change-over that his men had hastily to put Yorkshire white roses on their collars. At his order they shouted for the King. Minstrels struck up jovial songs, and the two armies fraternized, happy not to be shedding each other's blood. Clarence's men respected the King as a great soldier, and going over to them, he addressed them with kindness, making many promises, then escorted the Dukes to his own royal lodging in Warwick. The armies followed, taking up quarters in and around the town.

Clarence had not only been disappointed with his treatment by

Warwick, but was also convinced that Queen Margaret regarded him as a danger to her beloved son, being ready to deprive him of the succession the moment her weakling husband was out of the way. He had begun to fear for his life, and had welcomed his sister's and mother's offers to sound Edward regarding a reunion. Others who had facilitated the secret negotiations between them were the Duchess of Suffolk and the Archbishop of Canterbury.

Edward now proclaimed a general pardon for the Duke and all his men. Swearing a solemn oath of fidelity to each other, they now conferred, and Clarence denounced his treaty with Queen Margaret and the Prince, her son, doing his best to persuade Warwick to join them against her. but the Earl, an honourable man, spurned these approaches. He thanked God, he said, that he was himself and "not that traitor Duke", and remained obstinately loyal to his pledged word. Challenged again to come out and fight, he sensibly stayed behind the stout walls of Coventry. The combined armies of the brothers were now running short of food, but with Warwick safely locked up in the midland city, London lay wide open. The King determined to take it before he could be prevented. With desperate haste he plunged forward, reaching Daventry on the Sunday. Here, in the church of St. Anne, a "miracle" is said to have occurred.

The royal procession, entering the church, paused and knelt before the crucifix. On a pillar hung a small, painted wooden casket which, as the custom was, had been closed until Easter by means of an iron bolt. Inside it was a little alabaster figure or image of St. Anne herself. When the King knelt, the casket suddenly flew open of its own accord with a great crack, breaking the bolt, so that the image could be seen. It then closed as it had opened.

Edward remembered having vowed, when in danger of shipwreck, to pray and offer before the first representation of the Saint he should see. This vow he now fulfilled, both he and his followers regarding the "miracle" as an excellent omen. From Daventry he drove through Northampton to Dunstable. He had not yet set eyes on his infant son, and even if tactics had not impelled him to hasten his advance, paternal desire to hold this precious infant in his arms would have done so. From Dunstable, therefore, he sent word of his coming, warning the city fathers that before many days he would be among them again, ready to pay all his debts, or if he did not actually say this, it was certainly implied.

Leaving behind a rearguard of spearmen and archers, he received in St. Albans a valuable increase in strength from the eastern counties, and later, from the north. He was now on the fringes of the capital.

[4]

Warwick stirred himself. Joined at last by Oxford and Montagu, he took a leaf out of Edward's book, leaving Coventry at the head of a considerable force to take the King by surprise. Arriving in Northampton, in his wake, he sent messengers riding fast through the night to his brother, the Archbishop of York, and to Sir John Stockton, a mercer, the new Mayor of London, ordering them to defend the capital against Edward. He moved fast but did not overtake the swiftly-moving King, being always a day behind.

In London things happened with great speed. The Archbishop told the city fathers to raise men at once and throw back the approaching Yorkists, promising that Warwick would be at their gates withinin forty-eight hours. The citizens were in a quandary, and a council meeting was called. They knew that Queen Margaret was waiting to cross the Channel, and might set foot in England within hours. Indeed, two days previously Somerset and Devon, with Dorset, had left London to raise every man they could muster, and in all probability would join her after they had put themselves out of Edward's reach. What were they to do?

The new Mayor avoided a painful and dangerous decision by taking to his bed with a diplomatic illness. His deputy, Sir Thomas Cooke, solved the problem thus thrust upon him by leaving the country altogether. Unhappily for him, his ship was seized by the Burgundians, and he underwent a long imprisonment in Flanders. Ralph Verney, a former mayor (1465), took control on the 9th.

Meantime, York harangued the people in St. Paul's, but only a few would take up arms for Warwick. Even when he brought Henry out of the Bishop's Palace with a cluster of accompanying peers and made him ride on horseback in procession through

Cheapside and Walbrook to the great cathedral, the poor monarch cut such a sorry figure that he discouraged rather than patriotically stimulated his subjects. "It pleasured the citizens as a fire painted on the wall warmed the old woman." Seeing this, the terrified Archbishop sent his secretary to Edward to plead for pardon.

Verney and his councillors were not strong enough to with-stand the King, and were in any event well-disposed towards him, all the more now that Clarence had deserted Warwick, whom they considered no match for Edward as a general, and who was still a good way off. They decided to allow the King bloodless entry into the city, and smuggled out a message to this effect, which he received at St. Albans. On the night of the 10th, unaware of York's craven offer of surrender, they and the commons rose, surprised and overpowered the guards, and seized the Tower so that the guns should not blast the Yorkist army when it arrived. They also seized Aldersgate, whose guards were equally unprepared, and held it for the King.

On Thursday morning "in dyner tyme" Edward marched in with his brothers and the loyal lords. Though a few banners show-ing Warwick's ragged staff could be seen here and there in the streets, there was no resistance. Once again he had won a great city without a battle.

Having been received by Verney and the councillors, he went straight to St. Paul's, impatient though he was to see his wife and son, for protocol had to be observed. He was offered the rood at the north door, and then proceeded to the Bishop's Palace, where the Archbishop-Chancellor, quivering with apprehension, humbled himself, took a solemn oath of allegiance, set the crown once more on the King's head, and begging for mercy, was carried to custody in the Tower, as were the miserable, pathetic Henry, still wearing his long blue velvet gown, and other residents of the Palace. Henry is said to have embraced his supplanter, saying: "Cousin of York, you are very welcome. I know I am in no danger from you." Ed-ward assured him he need have no fear.

This done, the King prayed in Westminster Abbey, and imme-diately thereafter was reunited to the Queen in Westminster Palace, to which she had been conducted. The scene between them was commemorated in a delightful verse:

"The King comforted the Queen and other ladies eke.
His sweet baby full tenderly he did kiss.
The young prince he beheld and in his arms did bear.
Thus his bale turned him to bliss.
After sorrow joy, by the course of the world is.
The sight of his babies released part of his woe.
Thus the will of God in everything is do."

Nervous of Westminster, where Warwick still had friends and
followers, and eager to see his mother, the King took the Queen
and his son to Cicely's residence, Baynard's Castle, to the west of
the city, and here they and Clarence lodged for the night. It was
Holy Thursday, and divine service was held.

[5]

The following day, Good Friday, Edward's supporters in London,
led by Thomas Bourchier, Archbishop of Canterbury, the Earl of
Essex and others, having mustered their men the day before,
brought them in, armed and ready, to strengthen the combined
armies, the Kentishmen prominent and numerous among them.
It is estimated that the King now had 7,000 men under his command. He took good care to see that all were fed and rested, for by
now two important items of news had come to him: first, that
Warwick was marching rapidly on London; secondly, more exciting even than this, that Burgundy and France had made peace
at last, on learning which Warwick snarled that Louis was treacherous and a perjurer.

As usual, the King was ready for battle much sooner than his
adversary expected. On the Saturday, his tall commanding figure,
armed and handsome, rode into St. John's Field, where the people
had originally acclaimed him as their chosen sovereign. Here the
army had assembled, and with them a great mass of commoners,
whom he now praised for their loyalty, while at the same time
pardoning all who had been constrained under threat or by necessity to support his enemies. This wholesale clemency won him
many friends.

As bold and determined as ever, Edward had brought Henry

from the Tower with him, partly, perhaps, to show the flaccid, foolish King-that-was slumped in his saddle as a contrast to his own erect and virile self, and partly to remove him from Margaret's grasp if she should land and thrust for London while he was grappling with Warwick. He had now sent Queen Elizabeth and her children, his mother the Duchess of York, the Archbishop of Canterbury and the Bishop of Bath, to comfortable lodgings in the Tower for safety.

In the afternoon, at 4 p.m., the entire army marched northwards to meet the great Earl, rumoured falsely to command 20,000 men, and advancing from St. Albans with Montagu, Exeter, Oxford and all their glittering retinue.

[6]

Warwick, now at the height of his powers, was admired for his courage, his soldiers in particular respecting him for his readiness to meet the same dangers and endure the same miseries as themselves. He had the reputation of being genial to the humblest, reserving his aloofness for the knights, esquires and men of rank. His munificence, lavish entertainments and hospitality were famous, but no man dared insult him or take unseemly liberties, knowing that he would swiftly avenge himself.

Perceiving that Edward would be in London before him, and that the capital had neither the fortifications, men nor supplies to hold up a resolute attacker, he halted at St. Albans for rest and to feed his army, which had corrugated the mud of many roads with hooves and feet and the rumbling wheels of gun carriages. Then, on the 13th April, he moved to Hadley—not the present Hadley Green—a village halfway between St. Albans and London, a few miles from Barnet. They arrived at noon.

That night he camped on the level brow of a hill a mile and a half north-west of Barnet. Here a flat field, Gladsmoor Heath, commanded a good view of the surrounding country, and afforded space. The point is now known as Hadley Green, and the position he chose for his tents lay along a high road on the western side, where a hedge sheltered his men from observation. Its exact position is believed to have been between Wrotham Park, which lay behind him, and the Windmill. Before settling down for the night, he sent out scouts to discover if Edward had moved out of London.

Soon after their departure, these men passed through Barnet, and pushing on southwards, encountered at Hornsey Park Edward's advance guards, who at once attacked, driving them helter-skelter back to Barnet. Elated, the King's men pursued, and the scouts, as well as a small detachment left behind to guard Barnet, taking fright, fled back to the camp.

[7]

It is not easy to trace the course of the battle. The modern road pattern differs in important respects from that of Edward's day. In 1471 the present Barnet–St. Albans road did not exist. The land at that period was open and unencumbered, forming part of Enfield Chase. The road now known as the A.1000 ran due north from Barnet across Hadley Green and towards the monument commemorating the battle, and then turned somewhat to the northwest before running on to St. Albans. The present road to Potters Bar was probably but a mere foot-track. In effect, one military road alone ran north across Hadley Green, which extended well to the east of the village of Monken Hadley and into Hadley Common. The village itself probably stood in the very centre of the Green. The records suggest that Warwick's right wing rested on Monken Hadley, occupying the crest of a steep slope, with rough broken ground below, difficult for an attacking army to cover, and making it impossible for Edward to advance unchallenged along the road.

If he attacked the centre, Edward would be faced with a steep climb of over 100 ft., in approaching which he would have to ford several streams. He could have spent the night under roofs in Barnet, but true to his practice, preferred to creep as close as possible to Warwick's position so as to make a surprise attack at dawn. He therefore moved stealthily forward in the darkness.

Examining his line of advance, we must remember that the old road into Barnet took a much less direct route than the modern main road, swinging in fact to the west up the valley of the Dollis Brook. Having found an easy way up on to the plateau, Edward came into Monken Hadley from the *west*, not the south. Thus, he avoided the stiff climb, which his medieval transport vehicles could in any event not have negotiated, and his advance guards arrived in Barnet by the long route, while his main force was still a mile behind by road, but in fact less than a mile as the crow flies from Warwick's camp. In other words, when the Earl learned that Edward's *scouts* were in Barnet, he was seriously misled, because by that time the whole of the royal army was within striking distance of his position. Edward probably had a much clearer notion of the enemy's whereabouts, for he could see the long, curving road into Barnet, and could estimate with some accuracy Warwick's probable camp site.

Warwick, having moved from the north, would be less familiar with the character of the Barnet approach road, and it is an interesting point whether he imagined Edward to be entering Barnet from the west. Most of the ridge on which he camped is now occupied by buildings and a golf course, and it is difficult to study the ground properly. The existing commemorative obelisk known as Hadley Highstone stands within the boundary of the ancient parish of South Mymms, and was erected in 1740 by Sir Jeremy Sambrook of North Mymms. It originally stood opposite "The Two Brewers" but was moved thirty-two yards farther north in 1842, probably because the new position more accurately represented the site of the main battle.

When Edward's scouts reported to him, he halted his men along the road, faced them to the right, and during the evening advanced up to or even across the little stream that ran along the foot of the slope. The two armies then spent the night but a few hundred yards apart, though it was too dark for anything to be clearly seen. The King's army probably never entered Monken Hadley village at all, but cut across the corner, as it were, ready to attack from the valley at dawn. At this point the King drew his line eastwards along the uneven low ground, from which, at his signal, they would charge in a great moving arc up to and along the plateau.

So the two armies lay facing one another, each awaiting the dawn and shrouded by the comforting darkness. This was the moment before battle, when hearts beat violently and minds probe into futurity with what strength they possess, striving to draw some trifle of comfort and a reassurance that on the morrow all will be well.

Richard Neville, Earl of Warwick, 1428–1471, "The Kingmaker"

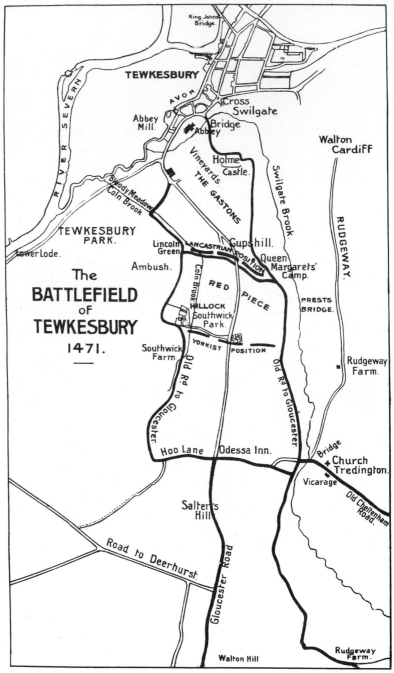

A plan of the battlefield at Tewkesbury showing the Yorkist and Lancastrian positions

SEVENTEEN

1471

[1]

TO SHAKE THE nerve of the King's men and do them grave injury
Warwick ordered an all-night bombardment with his big guns, the
only effective battery of its size in England at that period. During
the night, however, the King's right wing had filtered well to the
east, overlapping the Earl's left, while the Earl's right similarly
overlapped Edward's left. Neither commander appreciated this,
so that dawn on the 14th, Easter morning, found both under
serious misconceptions as to their respective positions. Warwick
having believed the Yorkists farther off than they were, his gunners shot harmlessly over the heads of their adversaries, the balls
probably falling in Barnet or the road up to it. Edward's cannon,
relatively few in number, made no reply, the King not wishing to
disclose his position, which he saw Warwick had misjudged.

During the night none of the soldiers discarded their armour
while resting in their tents. They could hear each other's distant
and muted movements—the clatter of steel, the whinnying of
tethered horses, the calls of sentinels. Sleep was difficult. As
dawn approached, Warwick urged his men to fight hard, show
courage, and remember they were united for freedom against a
usurper. Edward spurred on his, too, by a royal oration. They
were, he said, waging war against men who, thriving on dissension, grew fat on the slaughter of their own countrymen and the
utter ruin of their native land.

His forward ranks had dug themselves in, throwing up earthworks and palisades. Now luck came once more to their aid. When
the sun came blindly over the brow of the hills, an unexpected

ally was present for the Yorkists. Out of the low ground had issued a dense mist, rising and coiling, which filled the whole valley in which Edward's men lay with a level white sea of cottonwool. Superstition later ascribed this to the machinations of a certain Friar Bungay.

To the watchers on the crest of the ridge the Yorkists below were invisible, while the Yorkists could see nothing of those above them. The King had placed himself in the centre with Clarence, who he suspected might change sides again without warning if the battle went against him, and whom he determined, therefore, not to let out of his sight. It is fair to say that Edward liked Clarence, but did not trust him, whereas he trusted Gloucester, but did not like him.

Hastings was given command of the Yorkist left wing, Gloucester of the right. Up on the hilltop Oxford and Montagu with men of the east and north had charge of Warwick's wings, while the Earl himself commanded the centre, directing operations as usual from the rear.

[2]

At between 5 and 6 a.m. the alarm was sounded in Edward's camp, and the battle began, lasting for five hours. Despite rumours Warwick had no more men than, if as many as, the King. The mist was thicker than ever, and his booming guns, still firing at unseen targets, were now answered in a minor key by Edward's, neither cannonade affecting the result. Moreover, on neither side could the archers take proper aim with "God's instrument", the bow, so that in essence the blind were attacking the blind.

Edward's trumpeters sounding the advance, his men climbed the slope with great energy, and to Warwick's consternation their heads came suddenly out of the mist like a bristling thorny hedge, in a howling, terrifying charge. He had not suspected they were so close. This onset of shrouded spectres, half-hidden in white vapour, did not daunt the Lancastrians, as English as their foes. They fought with all the fury and courage of their breed. Death was soon roaming the battlefield like a bald vulture, and the field itself became a roofless charnel house.

The shape of the struggle was governed by the unusual, unforeseen overlapping of the two armies. While Edward's men were reaching Hadley Common, Warwick's right wing around Monken Hadley was scarcely in the battle at all, so that when they heard fighting to their left, they were free to wheel on the flat Green and attack the King's left. Some of Hastings's forward troops here were driven back through Barnet and trapped on the hill where the modern road runs—the shortest route to London, but the most difficult for men running for their lives. These men, panicking, did not stop running till they reached London itself, where they startled and terrified the citizens by shouting that all was lost, Edward defeated, Clarence and Gloucester slain.

Over-excited by this success, Oxford swept after them in pursuit, his men picking their way through the steep ravine known as Dead Man's Bottom, hampered still by the mist, which hid the fugitives. Stupidly, some paused as at Towton to loot the Yorkist tents instead of continuing the chase. Seeing that further pursuit was useless, the commander turned back to the battle, still raging, but he and his men completely lost themselves in the mist, a mischance which was to have a terrible sequel.

Warwick's weakest and most vulnerable point was unquestionably his right, where he was forced to fight on level ground. He had probably expected the main attack to come along the Barnet road, and at this point he possibly posted his best men behind the hedge for protection. When, instead, the attack came up the slope out of the mist it took him by surprise, while the reckless chase of Oxford and his men on the right after a beaten enemy exposed possibly inferior troops on the ridge to Edward's picked men.

Seeing that Gloucester was crumpling up his left, the Earl reinforced them with a squadron of light horse, checking the Duke, who had to draw back. What with the blanketing mist, the heat and confusion of the battle, Edward was unaware that his left had disintegrated. He strengthened Gloucester's harassed force, and noon approached without an end to the bloodshed. Not surprisingly, the two armies had gradually pivoted round, until what had been Edward's rear was now, by reason of their respective advances and withdrawals, partly Warwick's, and vice versa.

Consequently, when Oxford returned from the rout of Hastings, he and his men did not take Edward in the rear, as they hoped, but advanced unknowingly towards their own force. The thick mist caused their badge—a silver mullet or star with streaming rays on both back and front of their surcoats—so closely to resemble the King's that Warwick's archers, posted to protect his rear, believed they were being attacked by the Yorkists, and fired volley after volley of arrows into the approaching men. Not without excuse, Oxford assumed that the Earl's bowmen had gone over to the King. Shouting, "Treason! Treason!" he and 800 men fled from the battle, and he himself did not pause till he reached safety far away.

Weary and badly weakened by their losses, Warwick's men slowly fell back. The Earl himself rode among them, shouting encouragement, then urged them once more to the charge, driving his horse towards the Yorkist ranks, or, according to another account, was forced by Montagu to dismount and fight shoulder to shoulder with his men. He carved his way into the core of Edward's force, and for a moment it seemed as if his skill would bring victory, but his men were now spent, and the Yorkists, closing in behind, severed him and his immediate followers from the rest and advanced to cut him down.

Montagu, knowing that all was lost, is said to have withdrawn his own men in readiness to go over to the King, putting on the royal livery, but Warwick, divining his intention, ordered his men to slay him, which was done. An alternative account suggests that a single soldier killed the Marquis on his own initiative, but this is doubtful, and in all probability he was killed in the battle.

With Montagu dead and Oxford gone, the battle was over. Warwick had dismounted for the last effort, tethering his horse to some trees near the existing obelisk, it is claimed. Hurrying to regain his horse, he leaped on to its back and galloped off into a wood. Unfortunately this was a blind alley, and he could make no progress. Edward's men, pursuing, caught up with and killed him, stripped him of all his clothing, and left him lying beneath green leaves and nesting birds. There, presently, the King saw him, bloody and naked. He is said to have deeply deplored the murder of his former friend, having neither ordered nor observed it.

The loss of their leaders, combined with fatigue and heavy casualties, took the heart out of the Lancastrians, who were now methodically destroyed by the well-trained, hardy men of Calais, loyal to the King. Edward's own bodyguard, who also fought passionately, helped on the victory. Finally the enemy line broke, and the beaten Lancastrians fled in a *sauve qui peut*. All Warwick's guns were captured. Somerset, galloping away, followed the fleeing Oxford. The two of them thought of escaping to Scotland, but learning that Jasper Tudor had raised an army in Wales to support Margaret, they turned their horses westwards.

The battle having been largely hand-to-hand, the number of dead was disproportionately large. It has been estimated that between 1,000 and 3,000 lay lifeless on the field, while more than 10,000 arrows were picked up. Edward, it is said, usually ordered his men to "save the people and kill the nobles", believing that after victory no Englishman should kill the common soldiers, so turning the people against him. At Barnet, however, this order was not given, so that the great majority of the dead were ordinary men.

Nevertheless, the mighty had not gone unscathed. Gloucester and Rivers both showed wounds. Early in the battle Exeter had been felled, stripped by the rough soldiery, and left for dead. One of his own men, finding him still alive, carried him to a cottage near-by, where a leech was procured for him. When at 3 p.m. he was fit to travel, this same man attended him all the way to London, where he sought sanctuary at Westminster, and being allowed by the King to remain there, was even granted half a mark towards his keep.

Through his wife, Anne, Edward's sister, Exeter sought a pardon, but failed, and later Anne divorced him to marry Sir Thomas St. Leger. Soon afterwards the unfortunate Exeter's body was found naked on the seashore near Dover, he having either been assassinated or drowned in an endeavour to fly the country.

The Yorkists, too, had shed much blood. The Earl of Essex, Lords Say and Barnes, had all three lost their eldest sons. Lord Berners and Sir Humphrey Bourchier had been killed. There was much grief that week under both ancient and humble roofs. The dead were presently buried in the field on the crest of the hill, a chapel being later erected to their memory. Such memories soon lose permanence, however, and eventually the chapel became a habitation, lived in for a time, then it vanished. Now only the obelisk remains to mark the battle and the dead.

The bodies of Warwick and his half-brother, Montagu, were transferred to a cart, and as the Yorkist army, after a pause for rest and sleep in Barnet, marched back to London, singing triumphantly, the creaking and groaning of the springless carriage bearing the two dead nobles made a subdued and dreary accompaniment.

[3]

When the gates of London opened to receive them, the cart was drawn to St. Paul's, where the two peers, cold in death, bloody and dishevelled, wearing only loin cloths, were set down in coffins on the pavement so that all could see them and know that their power had been broken for ever. There they lay for three or four days, then were taken for burial to Bisham Abbey, where the family vault of the Montagus was situated. Like so many memorials of the period, this, too, has disappeared, with its contents, but the brass matrix of Warwick's seal, taken from his body after his death, is now in the British Museum.

Back with the army came also that King who would never again sit on a throne—Henry of Windsor. He had been kept out of harm's way during the battle, and had suffered no injury. At one time, taking fright, he had tried to escape, and had ridden towards St. Albans, but was speedily recaptured and brought back to London with the returning troops. He still wore his blue velvet gown, much too big and long for him, and after being led by way of Cheapside to Westminster, was once more immured in the Tower.

Edward had preceded his troops, and outside the gates of London was warmly received by the city fathers and a great concourse of spectators. His victory was recognized as decisive by all who mattered, and not a single voice was raised against him. Londoners had by now grown accustomed to bowing and scraping first to this King-baron, then to that. To the city the affray at Barnet was but one more gang-battle, for which they would presently have to pay. The romantic name—"The Wars of the Roses"—hides, in actuality, a sordid struggle between rival landowners and warlords for power and possessions. Warwick was the last, and perhaps the greatest, of these. Had their strength not been shattered by Edward, they would have brought their country to a state of anarchy as great as that of China within living memory, when opposing war-lords forced her to her knees.

Edward's strength lay in that he did not batten on the producers and traders more than he was forced, but encouraged them, believing that a King powerful and in sole command was better for them and for England than one striving to please all and sundry, and at the mercy of his most powerful subjects. Nevertheless, he sought often to win over his enemies by generous treatment. It was not altogether his fault that, time after time, turning on him, they tried to stab him in the back.

The encouragement he gave to the merchants, manufacturers and traders was just the stimulus needed to promote the growth of a new force in English politics. Just as the discovery of gunpowder made it easier for a vigorous monarch to overcome recalcitrant nobles by his greater command of expensive cannon and shot, so Edward's encouragement of trade led to the rise and increasing predominance of civic and Parliamentary power. He was himself one of the greatest of the nation's traders, transporting in his own vessels his own commodities. He could talk to the men of commerce in their own language, and bargain with them as skilfully as if one of themselves. His open, happy sociability with men of low rank made him generally beloved, but all the same, he was no clown. He demanded respect, but a respect that could be given without servility.

He was quick to repair to St. Paul's, where he was received at the rood of the north door by the Lord Cardinal, the Archbishop of Canterbury, the lords spiritual and temporal and their assistants. Thanks were given to God for the great victory and two arrow-pierced banners offered. Bishop Waynflete bought his pardon for the sum of £1,333, and lived till 1486.

[4]

Margaret of Anjou had been held up in Honfleur for seventeen days and nights, awaiting favourable weather, and having been blown back several times. At long last, on the 24th March, she sailed in a ship belonging to John Langstruther, Prior of St. John's, who had been sent to escort her by Warwick with £2,000 to cover all expenses, and had been waiting for weeks while she dallied in Paris and Rouen. With the Queen sailed the young Prince and his new wife, as well as a body of knights, including Sir John Fortescue, esquires and soldiers. She landed after some difficulty in Weymouth on the 19th April, 1471. The Countess of Warwick, who had sailed in a faster ship, came ashore at Portsmouth, and took another ship, meaning to rejoin Margaret at Weymouth, but being blown back by renewed storms, she landed instead at Southampton, hoping to intercept the Queen on her way to London. Learning at Southampton of the dreadful calamities, and perceiving that without Warwick and Clarence her mistress had no hope of success, she abandoned her without shame, and crossing the river by Hampton Water, made her way through the New Forest to Beaulieu Abbey, founded by King John, where she claimed sanctuary. Margaret rode to Cerne Abbey with Wenlock, Langstruther and her son, thence to Exeter, where on the Monday she was received by a committee of welcome. The Duke of Somerset, the Earl of Devon, and Somerset's brother, Lord John, had met her at Cerne and bore the bitter tidings of Barnet. From their lips she learned of Edward's landing, the defeat and death of Warwick and Montagu, the renewed incarceration of her husband, and the defection of "false, fleeting, perjured Clarence".

"When she heard all these miserable chances, so suddenly, one in another's neck, to have taken effect, she like a woman all dismayed for fear fell to the ground, her heart was pierced with sorrow, her speech was in a manner gone, all her spirits were tormented with melancholy," the chronicler relates. "Right heavy and sore", another wrote of her.

Bewailing her misfortunes, which came after so much wasted effort and misery, Margaret foresaw terrible suffering for her son and herself. She conferred with her advisers, suggesting that the best course was for her to return with Prince Edward to France. The general view was, however, that her cause was far from lost. Somerset in particular urged her to stay and fight. Henry was still alive, and if a final attempt was to be made, it must be now, before Edward had consolidated his position. Barnet had cost him dear, many of his youngest, best and bravest soldiers having fallen. It would be weeks, months, perhaps, before he could raise another

army. Even if he succeeded, his troops would be raw and inexperienced. At Barnet luck had favoured him in many ways. Such
luck did not come twice. Moreover, Jasper Tudor was up in Wales
with a new and unbroken force. He, Somerset and Devon would
at once reinforce the men left to her after Barnet, and draw levies
from Cornwall, Devon and the west country, where the nobles
and knights were mostly loyal to King Henry, and Lancastrian
power remained intact. Once they had a strong army in the field,
others would rally round the young Prince and his mother, which
would not be the case if she took him back to France. Her immediate action must be to make a royal progress, showing her son to
the people and rallying them to his side. Moreover, that bold and
successful naval commander, the Bastard of Falconberg, would,
the moment they took the field, take control of a great fleet, raid
the Cinque Ports, harry and even occupy Kent, and make Edward
more than ever afraid to leave his capital.

Heartened by these arguments, the Queen, dearly longing to see
her son on his father's throne, gave way, not without foreboding.
She would like the notion better, she said, if her own life alone
were involved, but she shrank from endangering her son's. Could
he not be sent to France and out of harm's way till all was over,
or the struggle be deferred?

Somerset rejected both suggestions. Proclamations were therefore drawn up and circulated throughout Cornwall, Devon, Wiltshire and Somerset. The Queen and the Prince summoned all their
loyal supporters to come to them, and were joined in Exeter by
Sir John Arundel and Sir Hugh Courtenay of Boconnock in Cornwall, a well-known local knight of considerable wealth and
property, master of a fine body of men. Her numbers rapidly increased, but were not yet great enough for a march on London. It
was decided, therefore, to move in the direction of Wales and
rendezvous with Pembroke and the men of the north.

The Queen began her progress, the stages of which were kept
strictly secret, showing herself and Prince Edward first at Glaston-
bury, Taunton and then Wells, where she was told to wait. She
agreed, saying, "I pray God speed us well." Here, her foot-soldiers
pillaged the residence of the Bishop, and freed prisoners from the
town jail. From Wells she moved to Bath. More and more men

came in, and after Bath Margaret advanced to Bristol, designing to follow the banks of the Severn and take Gloucester, then held for King Edward. Meantime, commanders spread false reports that she was marching east to capture the capital.

[5]

Edward had been busy making sure that all the men who had fought at Barnet were being properly cared for if ill or wounded, either in the country if they could not travel, or in London if they could. He now summoned men from every district, and on the 19th April, having pardoned the Archbishop of York, kept the feast of St. George at Windsor, where his new force was assembling. Knowing by now that Margaret had landed, he was deceived by the rumours she had put about that she was advancing on London, either through Salisbury or along the Sussex coast into Kent. To support these rumours, Somerset sent a small body of men into Shaftesbury. Edward had sent out riders of his own, who while not locating her main body, did observe Somerset's Shaftesbury patrols and realize that they were merely a feint.

Once again the King's tactics were sound. Wasting no time, he set off from London on the 23rd, meaning to intercept the Queen, and by one of his swift, unexpected marches, which so often caught his enemies on the wrong foot, so to speak, bring her to battle before she was ready. If, however, the feint towards Shaftesbury meant that she was aiming to take Gloucester and link up with Jasper Tudor, he would follow and attack.

On the day of his departure, windows and roofs were peppered with those who had chosen good vantage points from which to see the army pass. Every thoroughfare swarmed with newly-arrived recruits. As the King appeared at the head of his men, his sword, axe and spear carried before him, guns were discharged and the onlookers howled passionately: "For York! For York!" Leaping into the saddle, Edward pivoted round kissing his hand in farewell to his female admirers, whose handkerchiefs fluttered in reply. He wore a golden helmet with a plume of black feathers, gilded spurs, and a handsomely figured sword in its scabbard. On one arm he carried a shield, and his consecrated banner of purple velvet bore his armorial device, a gold sun with rays under a white rose, embroidered on it in silver.

Every soldier displayed a torch flaming at the end of a pole, and as they marched out of the city, chanting priests with great crosses and long slender tapers burning went with them, being left behind only when the outskirts were reached. The advance guards then moved forward, showing white roses in their helmets and on their surcoats. The first halt was at Windsor.

[6]

Somerset had despatched a second small force through Yeovil and Bruton towards Reading, hoping the King would believe Margaret to be advancing through Berkshire and Oxford. Edward camped for the night at Abingdon but resumed his advance next day, reaching Cirencester by the Icknield Way. Learning that men of Margaret's army were in Chipping Sodbury, he summoned all the able men of Cirencester to join him, and at 3 a.m. pushed on at top speed to Malmesbury, eager to give battle, but he was disappointed. Margaret had moved to Bristol, and must therefore be making for the Cotswolds to join Pembroke. Gloucester city alone barred her way. Edward sent riders at express speed to the commander, Richard Beauchamp, Justice of South Wales, ordering him to hold up her progress at all costs, so that she could not cross the Severn by the bridge at the west gate of the city until he had come up to engage her.

At this stage Edward had no precise idea where Margaret was. The chronicler wrote: "The King, not having any certainty of his enemies, sent his scourers all about the country, trusting by them to have wist where they had been. About that place was a great and fair large plain, called a wold, and doubtful it was for to pass further, so till he might hear somewhat of them, supposing that they were right near, as so they might well have been if they had kept forth the way they took out of Bristol."

In fact, Margaret had already by-passed Sodbury when at midday he arrived there, and it was not till one of his scouts came posting to the top of Sodbury hill to tell him how near he was to her that, after resting the night, he ordered his men to go forward.

[6]

At Bristol Margaret was enthusiastically received, and there she picked up more guns, provisions and cash, while many of the populace joined her army. On the 2nd May, after a rest, she thought of giving battle at Chipping Sodbury, around which was a wold or plain of some size, and had even taken up position on Little Sodbury hill, nine miles from Bristol. Edward was then but a mile away. Learning this, the Queen's advisers decided it would be better not to risk their entire force. In Chipping Sodbury scouts of her army, forming part of the vanguard, came upon some of Edward's men seeking quarters, each for his own commander, and after a skirmish, took a number of them prisoner; it was in this way she learned how near she was to the King. At 1 a.m., leaving Chipping Sodbury on her left, she went by Patchway and Ridgeway to Berkeley Castle on the Severn, where the unfortunate Richard II had died. At that moment she was twelve miles ahead of Edward in the direction of the river crossing.

The following night, hearing that Edward was hard on her heels, she marched in darkness along a track leading north-westwards, out-distancing the King and presenting herself at the gates of Gloucester at 10 a.m. on the Friday. Her men had covered a total distance of thirty-six miles, an astonishing feat over such evil ground, all stones and narrow lanes, and with little food and drink.

She and Somerset had reckoned on being able to pass quickly through Gloucester, and cross the bridge over the Severn, so shortening the route, but they were disconcerted to find the gates firmly closed against them, arrows being loosed at their scouts as soon as they appeared. It was known that she had many sympathizers within the city, and Somerset, angered by Beauchamp's firm refusal to admit them, was for breaching the walls and taking the town by force, but the majority were against him, pointing out that Edward might catch up with them before they had overcome all resistance.

The Lancastrians had now a wholesome respect for his lightning attacks, and knew he was not far behind. They decided, therefore, to make a détour through the fields of Tredworth village, crossing the Portway, until they reached the East Gate of Tewkesbury, and if they could not use the ferry there, a mile to the south, move along the highway towards Upton-on-Severn, where another bridge crossed the river. In this way they would keep Edward safely behind them and link up with Jasper Tudor unhindered. It was essential to get there before the King, who would soon discern their goal and strive to prevent its attainment. Accordingly, Margaret drove her weary men, who had already marched twenty-four miles in fifteen hours, towards the little town.

Two roads ran between Gloucester and Tewkesbury. The Queen's men took that known as the Upper Way, which ran through Elmstone, Hardwick and Tredington, where it crossed a stream known as the Swillgate by way of a footbridge, which at that time had probably decayed and fallen into disuse, as many such bridges did because no one would spend time and money in putting them in order. Then striking the highway, they entered Tewkesbury town through what is now a park and a housing estate, and by way of Gander Lane, north of the Abbey Grounds, now a walled pathway.

The army arrived between 4 and 5 p.m. Since leaving Berkeley Castle, they had covered tens of miles, and the foot-soldiers, spent, tired and hungry, could do no more. Somerset had no option but to halt, or his horsemen would have been separated from the infantry. Some of his guns, lagging behind, had already been captured by a sortie from Gloucester.

A naturally strong position was chosen on the site of a former Roman camp, past which ran the ancient Ackerman Street. The Swillgate stream ran on their left, and the River Avon swirled half a mile away to the right, beside the town. The army camped in some fields known as the Gastons, on the southern slopes of an amiable hill, the town and the abbey being directly behind them. On both sides ran deep ditches following narrow, winding lanes between high hawthorn hedges. Everywhere the ground was broken and difficult, while away to their right the wide Severn flowed, unbridged at this point and virtually impossible to ford. Gupshill farm, a half-timbered house, now a row of cottages, also lay behind them, but outside the town. Their position commanded the approach road to Tewkesbury.

The soldiers slept, but the Queen's council had earlier learned, to their dismay, that the King was moving as fast and furiously as themselves, and was little more than three miles behind. Two choices lay open to them—to break camp at the earliest possible moment and continue their march, or to stand and fight.

A night march with weary, jaded men might cause discontent in the ranks. Moreover, the Avon bridge was narrow, and if they were detected, an attack would do them grave damage, and possibly end in massacre. Pembroke and his men, confidently awaiting them, would be exposed to a surprise Yorkist assault, Tewkesbury with all its supplies would fall to the enemy, and this alone would cause a great loss of prestige. They would henceforward be regarded as fugitives rather than an effective army.

Somerset, though opposed by some officers, recommended staying where they were. They had a splendid, almost impregnable position. Edward's men, he argued, must be as weary as their own. All the advantages were theirs. Let them, therefore, fight, if the King attacked. They need not fear the result.

According to some historians, as soon as his men had had sufficient sleep, the Duke ordered them to fortify the camp. They constructed earthworks and a stockade, and did all they could in the short space of time available. (This statement is, however, denied by Lt.-Col. Burne on military grounds.) He then drew them up in order of battle, and awaited the day with confidence and high hopes.

EIGHTEEN

1471

[1]

EDWARD, COMING IN hot pursuit over the Cotswold hills, received authentic news at last of the Queen's route when he came at 5 p.m. through Birdlip and Leckhampton to the little village of Cheltenham. Taking the shortest route, he had come over the level plains through Swindon and Stole Orchard, via Badminton and the Portway, his vanguard close enough to the Lancastrians to pick up their stragglers. He did not loiter, but hurried his men forward another five miles until they, too, had covered about thirty-six miles in the day, a magnificent feat in view of the difficult going and the lack of food and drink, for they had stayed long enough only to consume what little they carried with them. His men had been unable to find enough extra provender for either themselves or their horses, and had met with only one stream, the Froom in the valley of Stroud, which was soon so badly muddied and fouled by the horses of the vanguard and the wheels of the gun carriages as they crossed it that the main body and the rearguard found it unfit to drink, and could only moisten their lips.

His objective was to engage Margaret at once, and although, like her, he had to halt for the night to rest his men, he chose his camp carefully, placing himself so that she should not cross the Avon ahead of him. When after marching down the Ridgeway he came to Tredington, he was separated from her by only a few miles. High summer was still far off, but the weather had turned unusually warm.

Edward slept at the Old Parsonage in Tredington, a village still an unspoiled gem of the Gloucestershire countryside despite the buses that daily rumble through it. Where this Parsonage stood is now but a small cluster of cottages. The following day, Saturday, dawned clear and fine. It was the 4th May. At 4.5 a.m. Edward, who had celebrated his thirtieth birthday on the 28th April, sounded the alarm and drew up his men, numbering about 5,000, 3,000 of them foot-soldiers, in order of battle. Gloucester was on his left, Clarence in the centre, Hastings and the King's stepson, Dorset, on the right and to the rear. So the two royal pavilions faced one another, one showing a shield with a red cross on a white ground, with gilded banners waving above.

Before sounding the advance, the King sent 200 spearmen wide of his left wing to a point about a mile away where they were well-hidden by the trees of Tewkesbury Park. His aim was twofold: to set up an ambush guarding Gloucester against any outflanking attack, such as that led by Oxford at Barnet, and secondly, if the ambush were not needed, to intervene in the main battle by taking the enemy in flank or rear.

This done, he let the trumpets sound, and having offered up prayers to God, the Virgin Mary and St. George, gave the order to march. So swiftly did he attack that Queen Margaret and her ladies, who had slept at Gupshill farm, were surprised, and had to scuttle for safety, even as guns were roaring and arrows flying, to a small religious house behind the lines. There is an old mansion— Payne's Place—in the lovely village of Bushley which tradition claims to be that place of refuge. It is now a farm, commanding a beautiful view of surrounding fields and cottages.

[2]

Somerset had trusted his left wing, resting on the Swillgate, commanding the highroad to Tewkesbury, and forming his rearguard, to the Earl of Devon. Prince Edward, Wenlock and Langstruther held the centre. The Duke himself with Oxford was in command of the right, constituting the vanguard.

His trumpets ringing out, his banners sunning themselves in the mild air, Edward moved forward. To reach Somerset's position he could have crossed a deep stream, the Coln Brook, in full view of the enemy, by means of a narrow, wooden footbridge not 500

yards from the Lancastrian camp, which would have been bad
tactics. Instead, therefore, he probably crossed the Swillgate at
Tredington village. At this juncture the Swillgate was no placid
brook, but a rough, surging torrent, swollen with water from the
surrounding hills. He then came to a large field known today as
the Red Piece, about half a mile from Gupshill. Somerset should
have occupied this with a portion of his rearguard, but neglected
to do so, with the result that at this point he was dangerously
exposed.

Nevertheless, to an attacker the position was daunting. The
soldiers would have to struggle through ditches, hedges and outworks under a rain of stone shot and well-aimed arrows, risking
tremendous losses. Edward decided to begin the battle at a distance.
His gunners and archers, probably by now the most skilled and
accurate in all England, poured their missiles upon the exposed
right wing of Somerset's army. Somerset, replying, badly missed
the guns taken from him outside Gloucester.

It has been recorded in these pages that as a general, Edward was
blessed by luck. It was so on this occasion, for a strange thing happened. Somerset flung away his advantage of position by a
manœuvre, his reasons for which have been the subject of much
conjecture. Edward's fire may have been too heavy for Oxford,
who appealed to his chief for help, or Somerset himself may have
thought to catch the Yorkists flat-footed on the low ground by a
surprise attack. On the other hand, he may, with the vanity of an
inferior general, have sought to show that he, too, could be as
bold, reckless, tactically brilliant and lucky, as the King.

Whatever the explanation, having reconnoitred the ground, he
decided to take advantage of the trees screening his right and endeavour to outflank the royal left wing. By secret paths unknown
to the Yorkists, he and his men passed undetected by the spearmen waiting in the wood, and came into the Red Piece, from which
field he debouched close to the Yorkist centre, between Gupshill
and Southwick Park, where, however, a great hollow hampered
his advance.

This sudden, fierce onslaught did succeed in taking Edward by
surprise, and heavy hand-to-hand fighting ensued. The Yorkists
were driven back, but rallying, swept their attackers with skill and

16

gallantry over a ditch, caught them on the wrong side of a hedge, and with murderous energy flung them towards the Duke of Gloucester, whose men assailed them as they gave ground. They were in this unhappy position, between two ruthless enemy armies, when Edward's hidden spearmen, aware now of what was happening, left their place of concealment and took Somerset in the flank. This was too much for the Lancastrians, who broke and ran into the woods and closes, the lanes and ditches, striving only to save themselves.

Many were captured, wounded or killed as they endeavoured to reach Malvern Chase by crossing over the Swillgate. Somerset, however, wounded in several places, rode back up the hill to his original position. The battle was not yet over.

What orders the Duke had given to his left and centre we do not know, but it is certain that Wenlock, the turncoat, had made not the slightest attempt to come to his aid, staying inactive at the top of the hill, whereas it must have been clear to him that his task was to follow up Somerset's first successes and reinforce him at critical moments. One chronicler claims that when the Duke rejoined his men, he cursed Wenlock as traitor and coward, and smote him dead with his battle-axe.

Whatever the truth of this story, the rout of their right wing left the Lancastrians confused and dismayed. Seizing their advantage, Edward and Gloucester advanced swiftly up the hill, cutting down or bursting through hedges, leaping over or striding through ditches, until they could storm unhampered the hitherto unassailed position at the top.

Resistance was at first surprisingly weak. Then Somerset, though outnumbered and his troops falling on all sides, rallied the survivors to their standards in a compact mass. The struggle continued until the worn-out Lancastrians either died, fell to the ground bleeding, to be there battered and maimed, or fled. The entire force was pushed back towards the Swillgate. Cut off from the Severn by the Yorkist left wing, they were slaughtered at the bridges, at the fords, in the Red Piece, in the fields near the Abbey mill, and among the trees of Southwick Park. Some were drowned in the mill dam or in the swollen streams. Others flung away their weapons, and ran through the Gastons and the Vineyards, past the ruins of Holme Castle, now marked by a small stone monument, into Tewkesbury, where they sought sanctuary in the Abbey. Others again hid in houses that were willing to open their doors and admit them.

The Earl of Devon, Lord John Somerset, Langstruther, Prior of St. John's, and Sir Edmund Hampden, were among those who took refuge in the Abbey with the Duke of Somerset and many others. The victorious King came presently to the Abbey church to thank God for his triumph. As he advanced in state to the high altar, his eyes fell on those—and they were many—who had taken refuge there. It so happens that the Abbey church was not an authorized sanctuary, for treason at all events. Nevertheless, the King, who could legally have had them arrested and beheaded, granted them a free pardon, and they remained gratefully where they lay.

Once the King's back was turned, however, Gloucester and the Duke of Norfolk had them seized the following day, with a dozen others, led to a scaffold hastily erected by the cross in the town square, and beheaded, but not hanged or quartered. By this act Gloucester demonstrated his ruthlessness and self-will. That the King connived at this vengeful deed is nowhere authoritatively stated or implied. Sir John Fortescue, though made prisoner, was pardoned, probably because of his scholarship.

The fate of young Prince Edward, Margaret of Anjou's son, has been the subject of much controversy, but it seems reasonably certain that he was killed on the battlefield during the Lancastrian collapse, and is said to have cried vainly to the Duke of Clarence for help as he was about to be struck down. There is, on the other hand, an alternative story, totally unconfirmed, that he was captured and brought to the King, who, irritated by the Prince's bold replies to his queries, struck him across the face with his gauntlet, whereupon he was slain on the spot by Gloucester and Clarence.

The young Prince was lean, robust, with dark brown hair, dark eyes and a broad brow. He wore a short purple cloak edged with ermine, and embroidered with a swan in silver, the emblem of his grandfather. On his breast he wore the badge of St. George and a single ostrich plume, as became the "Prince of Wales". Edward ordered his body to be buried, with the bodies of the dead and executed, either in the Abbey or elsewhere. According to tradition, the Prince was interred in the Abbey choir. An inscription engraved on a brass plate was placed in position during the eighteenth century to mark the supposed spot, but this has now vanished. On the Abbey wall inside is today a more modern brass plate bearing an inscription in Latin. Somerset was buried before the image of St. James near the altar of St. Mary Magdalen, and with him his brother, the Earl of Devon.

Over 1,000 dead are said to have been strewn over the battlefield and its surroundings. Rich booty was taken, as well as many fine, foreign-bred horses. Great savagery was shown, soldiers who had fled into churches or churchyards being pursued and slain out of hand. For example, inside the parish church of Didbrook, near Winchcomb, some Lancastrians, sheltering, were mercilessly butchered despite the appeals of the clergy. The Abbot of Hayles was so appalled by this barbarity that he had the desecrated church pulled down and rebuilt at his own expense. This was not the only hallowed place to be defiled. Several other churches, having witnessed similar scenes, were also re-dedicated.

[3]

On Tuesday, the 7th May, 1471, the King left Tewkesbury for Worcester. Margaret waited at Payne's Place with Anne Neville, widow of Prince Edward, to learn how the battle had gone. The room they are believed to have used still exists. After the news of the Prince's death, they fled on the Sunday either to Little Malvern Priory, below Hereford Beacon, or to some other poor sanctuary which has long since disappeared. There they were found, and the King, told of her capture, hastened to assure Margaret that she would be treated with all respect. Sir William Stanley escorted her to Coventry, where Edward had arrived on the 12th, and here they remained for three days.

The King was joined by the Earl of Northumberland, and aimed to move north to crush once and for all the restive Lancastrians in the areas beyond the Trent, but Northumberland bore good tidings. The north had already submitted and sought pardon. Oxford, having escaped from Tewkesbury field, had taken refuge in Scotland.

Edward sent news of his victory to all the neighbouring counties, on whose loyalty he proclaimed his reliance. He hoped they
would send him men to fill the gaps in his ranks left by the battle.
About 500 of his force were sent back to London, and Northumberland was made responsible for maintaining order in the north
country. To Edward came alarming news, however, from the
Mayor of London and others.

The Bastard of Falconberg had not been idle. Pirate that he was,
he had been harassing Portuguese ships and stealing their cargoes,
his fleet being manned by a cut-throat mob of refugees, escaped
criminals, robbers, men made desperate by injustice, real or fancied,
and bold, brutal sailors. He was, the Mayor reported, daily increasing in strength and numbers, and having sailed from Calais,
had landed at Sandwich with a large force, and was gathering together there all who saw opportunity or profit in joining him,
meaning to pillage, burn and destroy the capital. The Kentishmen
were flocking to him—at least such as were eager for loot and rape
—and by threats of violence were compelling more peaceable
men to enter their ranks. The unfit, the incapable and the aged
were being bullied into supplying arms, providing armed men or
money. Altogether the Bastard had assembled about 15,000
men.

Gathering together in Coventry the remnants of his army from
Tewkesbury together with his new recruits, Edward marched to
London, Queen Margaret with him, and camped there. Alderman
Ralph Jocelyn, put in charge of the defences, had done his work extremely well. The drawbridge of London Bridge, raised and held
fast by stout ropes, had been pierced by three large holes to give
the guns behind them room to fire. Bags of stone and wool had
been hauled from Leadenhall to protect the defenders against
arrows and shot. Great spreads of canvas saturated with vinegar
were placed over the drawbridge to keep off that inflammable sub-
stance known as "wildfire", which could be readily ignited and
flung against timber constructions to set them burning. Guns with
their gunners were brought up from the Guildhall, while bows and
arrows in ample supply were also provided. Basins of water were
arranged at convenient points to put out fires, and at night, candle
lanterns were lighted so that the watch might see. All the cost was

borne by Bridge House, who also paid the bodies of liverymen who defended the bridge.

[4 [

The Bastard dashed through Kent, determined to capture London. This was no more than a piratical raid, an insolent challenge without forethought or statesmanship. Having passed through Sittingbourne, he appeared in Blackheath on the outskirts of London on the 12th May, and mustered his men in St. George's Field, Southwark. From there he summoned the city to admit him so that he might snatch King Henry from the Tower, promising to do no harm and merely pass through to meet Edward.

Lord Scales, guarding the capital with a local force, and having learned of the outcome of Tewkesbury, joined with the Mayor, William Edward, a grocer, and the city fathers in refusing him entry, though as usual many malcontents and rogues would gladly have given him passage in the hope of creeping from their hovels and alleyways to sack the houses and shops of the rich, as in Jack Cade's day.

Furious at this resistance to his will, Falconberg took guns out of his ships, ranged them along the south bank of the Thames, and bombarded both the city and the Southwark end of London Bridge in the hope of smashing a way through. At the same time he sailed his ships with 2,000 men up river to St. Katherine's Wharf. After the vessels had moored, half of his force attacked Aldgate, and half Bishopsgate. His guns, however, were soon silenced by the better aim and greater power of those from the Tower, the bridge, and elsewhere, and although at Bishopsgate the cannonfire and furious shooting of arrows caused much execution among the citizens, he could not break in.

Queen Elizabeth had taken refuge, the Prince and the Court nobles with her, in the Tower. Falconberg had set fire to the newly-rebuilt Southwark great gate of London Bridge, burning thirteen houses near the drawbridge. This turned even the neutrals against him, and brought him no advantage. He succeeded in carrying the outworks of the city for a time, some of his men pouring through Aldgate, only to find guns in the street directed straight at them at point-blank range. Had they advanced, they would have been mercilessly cut down. Daunted, they stopped, and at that moment the portcullis of Aldgate gatehouse came down behind them, cutting them off from their friends outside. The guns of the defenders roared, the citizens, yelling, charged forward, and the raiders were massacred where they stood.

Although he had threatened to destroy Westminster and outer London, Falconberg and part of his remaining troops on the southern bank of the river now withdrew towards Kingston-on-Thames, and marched westwards to meet the King. No sooner had they gone than Alderman Robert Bassett of Aldgate and Thomas Urswick, the Recorder, both in armour, got together a resolute body of men "commanded in the name of God", had the portcullis raised again, and sallied out. Attacking the men Falconberg had left behind to keep up the attack on the city, they charged with fierce cries, taking the enemy by surprise. The fury of angry citizens and yeomen drove the invaders back with heavy loss beyond Radcliff and Blackwall. Over 700 are said by one chronicler to have been killed in this fight.

The remainder, forced back to the waterfront, took refuge in their ships, cast off, and sailed back to the other side of the Thames. Some of those who did not get on board in time were chased all the way to Mile End. Many were taken and executed on the spot. Others, French by birth, were later ransomed. For this exploit the citizens were awarded two tuns of red wine for their refreshment. Scales now sent barges full of armed men up river, and prevented Falconberg from crossing at Kingston in pursuance of his plan.

It is possible that if the Bastard, instead of attacking London, had landed in England earlier at some western port, and moved swiftly towards Margaret before she was brought to battle at Tewkesbury, they might together have overcome the King, whose numbers might not have sufficed to defeat the well-armed, well-led and rapidly increasing armies of Somerset and Falconberg in combination. Indeed, enemies of the Yorkists had already attached themselves to the Bastard. The defeat of his rearguard, however, and the royal victory at Tewkesbury, disturbed him. His army was now split, some on one side of the river and some on the other, so that if the Londoners cut the bridges behind him, he would be in serious trouble. Accordingly, he checked his march, came back from

Kingston, and withdrew slowly first to St. George's Field, then to his camp on Shooter's Hill, Blackheath, three miles from London, where he paused for three to four days.

On the 18th May he heard that Edward, victorious, with a new army, was hurrying to London to relieve the capital. He had no stomach for another pitched battle. Nicholas Faunt, Mayor of Canterbury, a friend of Warwick's, persuaded him to abandon his enterprise. With 600 mounted men he slipped away from his army, galloped to Rochester, and from there to Sandwich, meaning to set sail for France. But the sailors from Calais had deserted him as he had deserted his army, and gone back home. The Kentishmen dispersed after a day and a night of doubt and discussion. Falconberg, an unhappy refugee, offered to surrender if granted pardon, but pending the result of his appeal, fortified Sandwich and seized all the ships in the harbour—forty-seven in all.

[5]

The King's work had thus been done for him before he re-entered the capital. Falconberg's career exemplifies, as did Wyatt's rebellion in the following century, the tactical weakness of operating without a unified command. Had Warwick, Margaret and Falconberg concerted their plans and moved as one disciplined force against the King, even his generalship might not have prevailed. As it was, they attacked singly at different times, being engaged and defeated piecemeal.

When, on the 21st May, Edward rode into London with thousands of horsemen and foot-soldiers, the swarthy Margaret of Anjou in a litter behind him, he came as an acclaimed conqueror. The Frenchwoman, so loyal, resolute and defiant, so tireless and proud, who had faced misfortune with courage and despair with resolution, was now a captive, humiliated in her own eyes if in no other. Stones and mud were flung at her as she went by, and coarse abuse was shouted. She had now been deprived of her last hope, and worst of all, that son for whom she had fought, and on whom she had lavished her love, was dead. With him she had lost all she held dear. One possession only remained to her—her husband, and even him she was soon, heart-broken, to lose.

Edward came bravely in at the head of the procession, followed by the two Dukes, his brothers, and all his nobles. Trumpets shrilled, banners streamed, horses clattered, rows of shouldered pikes bristled and gleamed, gun carriages rumbled on roughly cobbled ways. Between Islington and Shoreditch he was met by Earl Rivers and the Mayor, whom he knighted, as well as Urswick, Bassett, Verney, Lee, Young and Taylor, aldermen and councillors who had fought well against the rebels.

This time Henry's supporters were missing from the streets, afraid to show themselves. Red roses had vanished from sight. Tewkesbury, the retreat of Falconberg and the capture of Margaret, had made it plain that the Lancastrian cause was lost. Now, for good or ill, a Yorkist king was on the throne, with none to challenge him. Although Henry still lived, his son and heir was dead and he had no other descendant. The only remaining members of the Beaufort line were the Countess of Richmond and her young son, Henry Tudor, Earl of Richmond.

That night a death occurred whose cause no man knows. Henry of Windsor, the imprisoned ex-King, was found lying cold and still in the Tower where he was immured. One account says he was stricken by paralysis as a result of "pure displeasure and melancholy" after receiving the news of Tewkesbury, but this may be a Yorkist gloss. The consensus of opinion is that he was stabbed with a dagger near to midnight while at his devotions in the oratory of the Wakefield (some say the Lantern) Tower. Whether or not the Duke of Gloucester was responsible it is difficult to decide. It seems to have been established that the Duke was in the Tower that night, but so were others. Although it is unlikely that the assassination could have been carried out without Gloucester's knowledge, that his hand held the dagger cannot be asserted. There were plenty of hard brutal men ready to do a master's bidding. The murder of the unfortunate Henry, if murder it was, may even have been decided upon by the Council of State as "cruel, yet necessary" for the safety of the King "and the publicke quiet".

That Henry was sometimes ill-treated in captivity appears evident from his reported exclamation on one occasion: "For sooth and forsooth ye do foully to smite a king anointed so." From ill-treatment it is no far cry to murder.

On the 22nd May, Ascension Day, Henry's body was irreverently carried to St. Paul's. It is recorded that both here and at Blackfriars his face was exposed for a whole day, so that all might see him, and that on both occasions much blood gushed from the corpse's nose. This was held to signify that he had been barbarously murdered, a perfect *non sequitur*. The people, who had not set eyes upon him since before the battle of Barnet, saw a tall, thin, not ill-looking man, suggesting in death a final benevolence and peace.

Henry had been, one conceives, an innocent, simple, devout, unworldly and gentle prince from childhood upwards. Too gentle to master his nobles, he had a wife too arrogant to appease the commons. He himself ascribed his misfortunes to the sins of his ancestors, revered his religion and his God, was grateful for kindness and friendship, and loved learning and the learned. He was responsible for founding both Eton College and King's College, Cambridge. His authority was diminished, however, by the weakness of his claim to the crown. His mind became unhinged more than once, and he could never have made a firm and competent ruler. Warwick said of him that he was stupid, "one who does not rule, but is ruled". What he lacked in this respect, however, his Queen— "that scolding woman", as the Duke of York called her during his lifetime—supplied.

For many years Henry was regarded as a saint and a martyr. Margaret made desperate attempts to obtain possession of his body, but failed. About his coffin were "more swords and staves than torches". On the day of burial, the body was treated with the utmost reverence. He was carried by water in an unlighted barge, "without singing or saying", to the Abbey at Chertsey which he had always loved. Gliding past Runnymede and the little island on which Magna Charta was signed, the barge followed the serpentine course of the Thames to its destination. At Chertsey Abbey the coffin was guarded by soldiers from Calais, which, as one historian admits, was somewhat odd, since this French port alternately supported and was claimed by both York and Lancaster. More than £15 was spent on wax, linen and spices for the first interment. The second took place at a later date in the Lady Chapel of St. George at Windsor, the body being removed from Chertsey by order of Richard III.

His childless widow, the wretched Margaret of Anjou, survivor of this final tragedy, was at first lodged in the Tower, but did not long remain there, being held at the house of Lady Audley in London, then at Windsor, and finally in various places regarded as secure, mostly fortified castles, for four years, coming to rest at the Wallingford home of the Duchess of Suffolk, her former friend. An adequate income was granted to her, and she had fifteen well-born men and women as her attendants.

Towards the end of her captivity, she returned at her own request to the Tower, being supplied regularly with woollen cloth and velvet for her dresses. By the Treaty of Picquigny (p. 273) Edward eventually agreed to her being ransomed for the sum of £50,000, on condition that she surrendered to Louis of France all claim to her father's possessions in Anjou, Provence and Lorraine, and to the throne of England. She was then allowed to return via Dieppe and Rouen to her former residence in France. In the Château of Dampierre on the 25th April, 1482, at the age of 52, she died, being buried in the Cathedral of Angers.

NINETEEN

1471 - 1472

[1]

AFTER HENRY'S DEATH, the King, Gloucester and the army
marched once more out of London, this time to Canterbury, arriving on the 26th May. Here, as Henry himself had done twenty
years before, the King and his magistrates, wearing white roses,
inquired into the Kentish insurrection, arresting many, including
the already-mentioned Mayor Faunt, Warwick's supporter. Most
of them were hanged, drawn and quartered. From Canterbury
Gloucester rode to Sandwich, where he interviewed the Bastard
of Falconberg, who gave himself up, craved pardon, surrendered
his ships, and eventually went back with the King to London.

Edward appointed a Commission in Kent, headed by Lord Den-
ham and Sir John Fogg, to try the men of other districts and counties suspected of complicity in the rising. Heavy fines were inflicted
on those who did not suffer execution, even the poorest victims being mulcted in seven shillings, more than some of them had in the
world, so that they had to sell their spare clothing for what it would
fetch, and borrow the rest. The Sussex leader of the attack on Aldgate, Captain Spysing, was hanged and his head set up on that very
gate. Essex also met his death at the same time. Edward, back in the
capital and highly satisfied, now issued a general pardon.

On the 4th June, the Archbishop of York, Warwick's brother,
was given leave to depart from the Tower, and twelve days later
the King pardoned Falconberg, probably because, as in previous
instances, he admired the courage and military ability of that old
rascal. He placed him in the care of Gloucester, who travelled with
him to Malling in Kent.

The impetuous Falconberg, however, could not restrain himself for long. Left unbound, he slipped away, tried to recapture his fleet, was caught and taken to Southampton, then imprisoned in Middleham Castle, which Gloucester was using as his country residence, and executed in September, 1471. His head was set on London Bridge, looking towards Kent.

There still remained one irritant particle of rebellion in the oyster of Edward's restoration. This he determined to remove. Just before the battle of Tewkesbury, the former Earl of Pembroke, Jasper Tudor, deprived of his title, had marched along one bank of the Severn to join Margaret. The King now sent Herbert, Earl of Pembroke, Ferris and Roger Vaughan, a bold, courageous soldier, to capture him, but the Welshman, who had shut himself up in Chepstow Castle, surprised Vaughan by a sortie into the town, defeated and beheaded him. Chepstow, however, was too close to Edward's army for comfort, so Jasper retired once more into Pembrokeshire, pursued by a fresh force under Morgan Thomas, who finally located him in Pembroke Castle. Digging dyke and trench, he encircled this fortress, meaning to starve Jasper out. To the rescue, however, came Morgan's own brother, David, who, loyal to Jasper, helped him to escape.

The Welshman fled to the little port of Tenby, where a Breton ship awaited him, and he sailed away with his ward and nephew, Henry Tudor, Earl of Richmond, and a party of friends and supporters, arriving safely on the shore of Brittany, whose Duke received him with great kindness. There for fourteen years he remained, an exile, in great poverty, his movements watched and restricted. With his departure peace reigned in England.

Oxford also fled to France, where he took up residence at the Court of Louis as his pensioner. To all appearance he was finished with.

Edward deputed the Archbishop of Canterbury, Clarence, Gloucester and Rivers to supervise the education and care of the Prince of Wales, and to manage his household and estates until he was 14.

[2]

Now the unchallenged King of England, Edward was, like his people, weary of civil war, the condition of his country being much like that of Spain after the civil war of 1936. Free from military preoccupations, he could give his mind to government, and particularly to good government. He had seen many of his subjects brought to a sorry state, physically, morally and mentally, by decades of strife, and perceived that for his reign to last he must hold down the great baronial houses with an iron hand, while giving peasant, manufacturer, trader and merchant a chance to breathe and build up again the wealth unprofitably wasted.

He began with his administration. Sussex became Treasurer. The Bishop of Bath as Chancellor took over the Great Seal, and the Bishop of Rochester acquired the Privy Seal. Knowing that his popularity would be increased if he imposed no fresh taxes on his people, he made up his mind to live on the income from his own estates, which he could do now that he need no longer keep large armies in the field. To his private income was added also the money derived from the confiscated property of those executed for their part in the civil wars, and the sums paid for their pardons and ransoms by those who had been allowed to keep their heads.

In addition, some religious houses made him, voluntarily, handsome gifts of cash. Finally, he made much profit as a trader in his own right, selling through agents and sub-agents thousands of yards of broadcloth and hundreds of bags of wool from his estates. He was not alone in this. The Abbot of St. Albans, for example, did a good trade in Yarmouth bloaters. The Cistercian monks sold large quantities of wool. Skelton, the poet, summed up the King somewhat harshly in the following lines:

> "I stored my coffers and also my chest
> With takseys takynge of the comonealte,
> I toke ther treasure, but
> Of ther prayers maist
> I had ynough. I held me not content."

Anxious to prevent affliction and bitterness among the defeated, he pardoned in July John Paston of Norfolk, and took back into royal favour the Hanseatic traders whom previously he had harassed and punished. When it was proved to him that they were not at fault over the interception of the ships of Lynn by the Danes, he recompensed them in full for the losses they had sustained, and made a new treaty with them.

In September, he and the Queen made yet another pilgrimage to Canterbury, and it is said that on this occasion the number of pilgrims exceeded anything previously known.

[3]

So winter came, and Westminster was gay. At the Palace, Christmas was celebrated with songs, dances, enormous banquets, dramatic performances and masques, as well as a solemn Mass. The fertile Queen Elizabeth was pregnant again. Both Edward and she wore their crowns. On the opening day of the new year, 1472, she and her husband went in procession, he crowned, she uncrowned because of her condition.

Prince Edward's widow, the Lady Anne Neville, was by now heartily tired of her menial role. After Tewkesbury she had come to London by stealth, and taken work as a kitchenmaid. Clarence had helped her to escape. Gloucester had earlier caught sight of and admired her, and had expressed a wish to marry her, but the jealous Clarence, realizing that the marriage would bring half her estates to his younger brother, violently opposed the union. Gloucester sought in vain for Anne, until he found her in London, whereupon he placed her in sanctuary, and asked the King for leave to marry her.

Gloucester had dark brown hair and a fixity of attention such that his eyes seemed to bore into the mind of his companion. He could be smooth and gentle in speech and manner, and rewarded those who pleased him by their skill in music. Hasty in temper, he was subject to uncontrollable outbreaks of fury. His voice was agreeable and he had an engaging smile but essentially he was of nervous temperament, nibbling his lower lip when irritated. His features could at any moment contract, he would blink rapidly, and his hand would play with the knife at its side lifting it partly out of its sheath and dropping it again.

His head was small, and his pale face, oval and short, was marred by deep hollows. He resembled his father, the Duke of York, more than Clarence or the King. Sturdy and well-knit, with a short, thick neck, a withered arm and one shoulder higher than the other, he was said to be a hunchback. Loyal, but unforgiving, he probably resented that Clarence should be back in Edward's favour.

Clarence was annoyed by his request for Anne's hand, and a quarrel broke out between the Dukes, both of whom were living temporarily at Sheen. Clarence declared that having suspected Gloucester of designs on Anne, he had himself carried her off to London.

Despite Clarence's protests, the King, grateful for Richard's unbroken fidelity, granted his request, and Anne became the Duchess of Gloucester. Gloucester was in such haste to marry that he did not pause to obtain a papal dispensation.

Edward's two brothers had served him loyally since his return. He therefore gave Clarence the greater part of the estates and possessions of Warwick lest he should feel discontented, the remainder falling to Gloucester. Nevertheless, Clarence's outcries against the marriage continued, and all the King's tact was required to appease him. Notwithstanding this, the breach between the King's brothers reopened, and for years to come they harboured a grudge against each other.

In the spring the royal pair went to Windsor, and on the 4th April the Queen gave Edward yet another daughter, Margaret, who lived but a few months. The King spent Easter in Northampton, then hunted merrily in Leicestershire, lodging in Leicester town. For a time there was danger of war with the Scots, and he prepared to move north, but this came to nothing.

Seemingly still fond of the Archbishop of York, Edward had left him at his manor, "The Moor". On the 23rd April he went hunting with him at Windsor. It was said of the King that whenever in summer he followed the chase, numerous pavilions were erected to which he could retire with the lady or ladies of his choice. Before the Archbishop returned home, Edward promised to hunt with him next day in the Archbishop's own park. Overjoyed that the sun of royal favour had reappeared and was shining upon him again, the prelate dug out of their hiding places all his silver, his plate, and his richest possessions, which he had not dared to use since Tewkesbury. He even sent round to his friends to borrow whatever he lacked, so that he could receive the King in style, restocked his cellars with wine and his pantry with food, put on his most elegant garments, and sat waiting.

The King never came. Instead, a messenger rode up with a strict command that the Archbishop should go immediately to Windsor. He obeyed, and on arrival was seized and conveyed by night first to the Tower, then to a distant and impregnable fortress, and finally shipped off to Hamme Castle, near Calais, an exile. This dramatic change of heart by the King was caused by the resurgence of the Earl of Oxford, who, secretly encouraged by Louis, was making forays against Calais and the adjoining territory. Edward believed the Archbishop of York to be in league with him, but this has never been proved. Although pardoned, the Archbishop was unhappy in exile, and on being allowed to return to England, died at Blyth on the 8th June, 1476.

[4]

No sooner was the Archbishop gone than the King sent Sir William Parr and Sir Thomas Vaughan to confiscate all his treasures, which he presented to his infant son, the Prince of Wales. From the gem-encrusted archiepiscopal mitre he had a crown fashioned for himself. Moor Park passed by his favour into the possession of the Marquis of Westminster.

Edward was well aware that young Henry Tudor, Earl of Richmond, was the one surviving threat to the young Prince, his son, and the last male of the blood royal. He asked the Duke of Brittany to return him to England, saying he meant to marry him to Elizabeth his daughter. The Duke was willing, and envoys were sent to St. Malo to escort the young man, but Henry or his advisers, under no illusions, was convinced he would be murdered if he returned. He therefore feigned to be ill, or was. The Duke, meantime, warned that Henry's death was intended, sent his Treasurer to St. Malo, who arriving before the English, placed the young man in sanctuary, and so preserved a King for England.

Unable to maintain his royal dignity and his increasingly sensual

17

enjoyments on his own income and such windfalls as came his way, the King was again financially embarrassed by the autumn of 1472. He hastened, therefore, to recall Parliament, hoping he might be given a grant. Stillington, Bishop of Bath, was seriously ill, so Alcock, Bishop of Rochester, summoned the members, who met at Westminster on the 8th day after Michaelmas. The King strode in at 10 a.m., dressed in his robes and with a cap of maintenance on his head, this cap being an emblem of great majesty and honour, usually carried by kings and nobles. He took his seat on the throne, with the lords spiritual and temporal before him. The Speaker, William Allington, was in charge of the proceedings. The main business before them was money. The King made it plain he wanted a great deal. He had made up his mind, he said, to rid the country of the ever-present fear of invasion by the French, as well as of such gadflies as Oxford, aided as they were by French money. In consequence, he intended to muster the greatest army England had ever seen, transport it to Calais, and with it beat Louis of France to his knees. He proposed that this war should begin in the following year (1473), and he would lead the army himself.

Parliament on this occasion recognized Edward of York as the rightful King of England, formally restoring to him all his estates and possessions. His accession to the crown was thus legitimized. Although the proposed war with France was by no means popular—people had had enough of war—there is little doubt that much of the early unpopularity of the Lancastrian régime had arisen from the recapture by the French of such English possessions as Normandy, Gascony and Guienne. Their recovery appealed to patriotism and pocket alike. Edward suggested a grant of pay and rations for at least 13,000 archers for a year at 6d. a day each, apart from other requirements in supply and provisions.

He was not refused. A generous subsidy was offered, to be raised by a ten per cent deduction from newly-valued property and revenues. This sum was however, to be set aside, Parliament insisted, in a special army account and not embodied in the normal budget. In fact, if the war had not started by Michaelmas, 1474, it was to be returned to those from whom it had been extracted.

Edward was content with the result of his appeal, and as the tax commissioners got to work on the new assessments, he prepared to receive his old comrade and friend, de Gruthuyse, who was coming to Windsor in September on a visit to the monarch he had helped when in need. It had been a fevered summer, intensely hot, so that cattle died, while during the harvest period men and women collapsed, and did not always recover. In Canterbury in the previous year the King had thanked the chief men of Bruges for their generosity and kindness, announcing his great victories. Now he could repay one of his benefactors.

The occasion is of special interest because de Gruthuyse reported in considerable detail his reception at the English court, and so has given us a vivid picture, rare in the medieval records, of a royal occasion.

[5]

Taken to Windsor by Hastings, the Lord Chamberlain, and other peers, de Gruthuyse was at once formally presented to the King and Queen. They had set aside for him three large, carpeted rooms. The first of these, in which the Dutchman supped, was furnished with "beds of estate", of down covered with ermine-trimmed cloth of gold and a fine soft silk cloth. The second chamber held a feather bed, and was draped in white. It contained a massive cupboard. The last of the three rooms was a bathroom, the baths of which were shrouded in white cloth. All these rooms were "richly hanged with cloth of Arras" of white silk and linen.

The Queen had her own apartment, of course, to which the guest was taken by the King after he had supped. Elizabeth was engaged in playing "closheys", ninepins (or possibly an indoor form of croquet), with her ladies, using ivory pins, of which the central or "crowned" pin was known as "the king of the closheys". The evening was spent agreeably in dancing to the sound of instruments played by minstrels, many, if not most, of whom were gipsies. The King danced with his daughter, Elizabeth, and before the party broke up, he and his Dutch friend swallowed a final cup of mixed wine, sugar and spices.

The following morning, Mass was celebrated in the Royal Chapel, and the King gave de Gruthuyse a golden cup with a lid or cover of the same metal, studded with gems. He also presented him, as an unusual decoration, with a piece of the horn of a "unicorn", seven inches long. The Prince of Wales was presented to him by the Master Chamberlain, and the King and his guest then went a morning ride in the "little park", Edward insisting that the Dutchman should use his own fine horse as his mount. They slew a doe, which was bestowed on the visiting servants. The hunting lodge was their dining hall.

Dinner over, the rest of the afternoon was spent in wantonly slaughtering animals. Deer near the castle were hunted with greyhounds and buckhounds till they fell, spent and helpless, when they were killed and handed to the Dutchman as a perquisite. Edward also gave his companion a handsome crossbow in a velvet case bearing the King's colours stamped with the royal arms and emblems.

As dusk prevented further sport, the King rounded off the day by conducting his guest through the pleasure gardens and the vineyard. The company then returned to the castle, where evensong was heard. Here a magnificent banquet had been spread, this time in the Queen's chambers. De Gruthuyse and his son were given places of honour at the royal table, raised above the rest. The table below was graced by the ladies of the Court. De Gruthuyse's principal attendants were seated at a third table set in the outer chamber, the Queen's gentlewomen facing them.

The meal over, the banqueting tables, all of trestle type, were dismantled and stacked away so that dancing could begin. The guests retired to their respective chambers at 9 p.m. Hastings then took de Gruthuyse to his bathroom, saw him properly attended at his undressing, undressed himself, and both took a warm bath. Before going to bed, they consumed green ginger, sweetmeats, hippocras and sweet syrups.

At the meeting of Parliament, before the Dutchman returned to his own country, Edward created him on the 13th October Earl of Winchester. A concluding banquet was held in his honour in London. At all these royal feasts it was the custom for Garter-King-at-Arms to cry at the end, "Largesse! Largesse!", an open appeal for a tip from the satisfied guests. In benevolent mood after feasting well they usually showered gold upon him. Unfortunately, on this occasion the official in question had an impediment in his speech, and could not get the words out quickly enough. Before he could find his tongue, all the diners had trooped out, so that he never received his reward!

The last event of de Gruthuyse's visit was a procession to Westminster Abbey, headed by the King in a robe of cloth of gold with a lining of scarlet satin.

Hastings, referred to above and elsewhere, was one of the King's boon companions. A good soldier and an accomplished courtier, he had courage and discretion, having been Edward's confidant for many years. Master of the Mint and Chamberlain of the royal household, he seems to have had at one time an unhappy love affair (see pp. 303, 304), after which he lost his original sobriety, becoming the King's pander and drinking partner. Loyal to his master and at one time admired and even adored by Richard of Gloucester, he was inclined to be rash in action and openly ambitious. With the Queen, however, he was no favourite. Whatever the King thought of him, in her eyes he was the chief participator in and encourager of her husband's licentious behaviour. Her family also hated him because he had been made, in addition to his other offices, Captain of Calais, which post, Earl Rivers maintained, had been promised to himself. There was great jealousy among all the Woodvilles of the many favours Hastings received.

[6]

Knowing the intention of the English King to invade his territory, the King of France paid greater heed to Oxford's continual appeals for help than he would normally have done. Without great belief in the Earl's chances and solely as a pinprick for Edward, he gave the refugee noble a handful of ships and a little money for a raid on England. With these inadequate resources and with the recklessness of a fishing vessel firing on a battleship, the Earl set sail. Aided by calm spring weather, he landed at St. Osyth in Essex on the 28th May, and is said to have been well received.

His movements during the next few months are uncertain, but the news of his landing reached the King at Ludlow, to which he had taken the Prince of Wales. He at once despatched the new Earl of Essex, and other nobles to deal with the invader, but wherever Oxford was at the time of their approach, he withdrew to his ships. He cruised off Thanet a few days later, then for some months sailed up and down the Channel, living by virtual piracy, seizing any ships he encountered and robbing them of their goods and cash.

As the year waned and golden October drew near, Oxford, needing winter quarters, emboldened by his successes and enriched by his depredations, made a daring and victorious seaborne attack on St. Michael's Mount in Cornwall, capturing and occupying the Castle. With him was a force of about eighty men, and as lieutenants he had his brothers George and Thomas, and Viscount Beaumont.

He now sent raiding parties into Cornwall, being well-treated by the common people. This alarmed the King, who feared the insurrection might spread. Orders went to his local commander, Bodrigan, to besiege the castle, considered impregnable, while three ships were told to keep vigil off the shore in case Oxford sought to escape by sea. Bodrigan gathered together a considerable body of men, but secretly favoured his adversary. Day after day, it is said, the castle garrison came out of the fortress gates to fraternize with the besiegers, and when their stocks ran low, they were even allowed to replenish them.

When the King discovered what was going on, he dismissed Bodrigan, and sent Richard Fortescue, one of his personal attendants and Sheriff of the County, with 900 men in four ships, to take his place. During an affray, Oxford was struck in the face by an arrow, for fraternization had now given place to daily skirmishes, but even after this, the siege was conducted with scant resolution. Pauses of some days in the fighting were granted for the burial of the dead and care of the wounded, and during these lulls, friendly talk was exchanged.

The King of France sent two more ships with provisions and supplies during October, but these never reached the rock. One was nearly swamped in a storm, and the frightened skipper tossed his cargo over the side, letting himself be blown back to France. The other was either intercepted by the King's ships or, failing to make harbour in time, was lost.

Both the King and his Council suspected that Clarence had had some part in this rash adventure, but of this there is no certainty.

Soon it was realized that the local soldiery could not be trusted. Consequently, Edward tempted Oxford's men with pardons and much reward, secret messengers urging them to come over to him. So many then deserted that finally only a handful remained. Oxford surrendered, throwing himself on the King's mercy to prevent himself from being kidnapped by his own soldiers. He, his brothers and Beaumont were imprisoned, and when Fortescue entered the castle, he found there food enough to have fed the garrison for four more months.

Attainted early in 1475, Oxford was imprisoned at Hamme, his wife having to sew for her living and accept help from friends. After three years Oxford was found up to his neck in water in a dyke outside the castle, but whether he was escaping or trying to drown himself is uncertain. He was eventually released, lived to fight at Bosworth for Henry Tudor, and died in 1513.

Clarence wished to marry Mary of Burgundy, but Edward refused permission, and when the Queen sought to bring about a match between her and Earl Rivers, the King forbade this, too, on the pretext of inequality in birth.

TWENTY

1473 - 1475

[1]

LEAVING LUDLOW, THE King revisited in turn Coventry, of which he was always fond, Kenilworth, Leicester, Nottingham, Stamford and Fotheringay, where, on the 17th June, the Queen bore a second son, Richard. By way of Lichfield he reached Burton-on-Trent in early September, winding up this royal progress with a return visit to Nottingham and Leicester. These wanderings were probably designed to show off his fine presence, win affection and esteem, and display his power, but they were also necessary to prevent the food shortage experienced whenever the royal establishment remained too long in one place.

To Ludlow Castle had come, like his father before him, the young Prince of Wales. John Alcock, Bishop of Rochester, was instructed to give him "virtuous guiding" here. In military command of the Castle was Earl Rivers. Neither of these high officials was free to follow his own educational ideas. The Prince had had a strict regimen laid down for him by his parents.

Rising at a convenient hour, according to his age, he attended matins in his own room, and when dressed, went to Mass in his private chapel. After breaking his fast he studied, and at dinner "noble stories" were read to him. The afternoon was for sport, exercise and learning military arts. Evensong was followed by supper, after which the child was allowed to amuse himself as he wished, but his choice had to be seemly. His attendants were instructed to "make him merry and joyous towards his bed", to which, at 8 p.m. he retired; his curtains were drawn together, and he was guarded all night long, medical men being on call at all times.

264

None dared swear or jest lewdly in his presence, and no servant known to be foul-mouthed, aggressive, slanderous, a gambler or adulterer, was employed about him. In all this his mother's hand is plainly visible.

The Prince wore usually a doublet of purple or black velvet, lined with black or green satin, and over it a long gown of velvet or satin of the same colours, or sometimes of cloth of gold on damask. His cap was of purple or black velvet, satin-lined. After he had safely reached the age of two, Avice Welles, his nurse, was allowed a tun or two pipes of wine every year, and at a later date was presented with a beautiful rich gown, costing nearly £10.

[2 [

The grants from Parliament proving insufficient for so great a military expedition to France, the money was soon spent. Afraid of imposing further heavy burdens on his subjects, Edward invented an original and ingenious method of raising funds, asking for *voluntary* contributions towards his military expenses. In effect he passed round the royal hat, inviting all and sundry to give what they could or would as a token of goodwill to King and country. On occasion he even invited subscriptions in person from those he believed could afford them. Many gave willingly, and others, though resenting the challenge to their pockets, paid up nevertheless, hoping to recoup themselves from the pickings of victory. London's Mayor, John Tate, a mercer, gave £350, and much money came from the King's original creditors, whose previous loans had all been honourably repaid.

One widowed lady of means gave the King £20, a large sum for those days, and with his habitual gallantry, he kissed her to show gratitude. Carried away by this token of royal favour, the widow promptly doubled her subscription.

The King "plucked the feathers out of his magpies without making them cry out". Those he approached, though at first giving with long faces, went away smiling, so charmed that they no longer deplored the exaction. If offered a sum he considered inadequate the King murmured to himself, but aloud: "Lord . . . gave me £ . . ." The hint was taken. Knights, ecclesiastics, farmers and traders were all invited to give, and few refused. These exactions came to be known as "benevolences".

The country at large was becoming increasingly fonder of the King because he paid what he owed, did not keep burdening them with new taxes, but drew what he needed from those they believed could well afford it. Moreover, he was going to beat the French, and teach them a long-needed lesson.

Edward had now fresh occasion to be suspicious of the Duke of Clarence. In November, sending for his armour, he complained that this conceited, stupid brother of his was puffing himself up with pride and continually quarrelling with Gloucester. He had no desire to become embroiled in a dispute between his brothers, and his words were meant to show that he was more powerful than either, and would not hesitate to use his power if they continued to give trouble.

[3]

Preparations for the invasion of France began slowly. The King was not so foolish as to imagine he could beat Louis single-handed, and looked round for the ally he sorely needed. He had little faith in Charles of Burgundy, ever inconsistent in policy and fickle in character, but knew he was the likeliest to join in a powerful assault on the French. Charles, however, when invited, would not commit himself, blowing now hot, now cold. On the 20th January, 1474, Parliament was told that for this reason the invasion would have to be delayed.

In February of that year the King took an important economic decision. Far-seeing enough to appreciate that an island country must live by trade, he granted the Hanseatic merchants the right to erect wharves and warehouses in Thames Street, at a point in Dowgate Ward known as the Steelyard or Styleyard. Here these German merchants brought and stored their wheat and other grains, cables, ropes, masts, pitch, tar, flax, hemp, linen cloth, wax, steel and many other commodities. For this privilege they paid £70 3s. 4d. a year, being entitled to follow their own customs without needing to conform to the decrees of London's governors. Though this decision was obnoxious to the English merchants, Edward ignored their protests, convinced that in the long run it was to the national and his own advantage. The Hanseatic League would not now interfere with his ships when they set sail for France.

He had always encouraged imports when he could. For example, in 1470, ships from abroad regularly brought in such goods as figs, raisins, oil, sugar, oranges, copper, fans, soap, spectacles and even parrots. From Italy came dyes, wines, timber, alum, wax, writing paper, armour, seeds, etc. From all such exchanges and importations the King drew a good profit, which made it easier for him to live within his income. It is of some significance that during his reign the Drapers Company first began to keep its books, and other trading companies were founded.

Charles of Burgundy at last screwed up his courage and agreed to take part in the attack on France. His ambassadors at the English court undertook in his name to provide a Burgundian army and to give financial support. He and the King signed a joint treaty acknowledging the King of England as King of France, and allotting to the Duke the territories of Champagne, Bar, Nivernais, Tournai and other lands, all of which adjoined his own possessions. For his part, Edward promised to put at least 10,000 men in the field, command them in person, and land them in France before the 1st July, 1475.

The King had been in London towards the end of 1474. He now came to Norwich to prepare for the invasion. His armourers had been busy casting new guns at the rate of one a day. (It had been a year of poor harvests and much sickness. Malt was being sold at Maltby for 1s. 1d., wheat for 2s to 2s 2d. and oats for 1s.) The English foot-soldiers and cavalry assembled on Barham Downs, near Canterbury, the guns at St. Katherine's Wharf, London.

As the English army needed vast amounts of food, the export of such items as malt, wheat, barley, rye, beans, peas, cattle and horses, was now prohibited. The King marched his men out of Canterbury on the 20th June, made his will, and before setting out from Dover in the frail craft of the period, declared war on the King of France, which declaration took three weeks to reach Louis. It was so gracefully written that Comines, the historian, present at the French Court, doubted if it was the work of an Englishman.

The Prince of Wales was made Lieutenant and Governor of the country during Edward's absence. The soldiers disembarked at Calais on the 4th July, 1475. To Edward's disgust, Charles and his proffered army were not there. They were away besieging Neuss in Germany on the banks of the Rhine. The King had mustered 11,000 men, 9,000 of them archers, and 1,200 spearmen, with ample supplies of arrows, bows, food and drink. There were big guns, one of which needed fifty horses to draw it, small and medium-sized guns, cranes and other appliances to lift and manœuvre them, gunpowder, brimstone, saltpetre, stone cannon balls, iron hooks to haul down drawbridges, ladders for assaults on fortress walls, leather boats, entrenching tools, blacksmiths' tools, gun carriages, nails, and a mass of minor stores. In addition, fifteen surgeons accompanied the army.

The daily wages paid to the fighting men were as follows: 13s. 4d. for a Duke, 6s. 8d. for an Earl, 4s. for a baron, 2s. for a knight, 1s. for ordinary soldiers, plus sixpence for conspicuous gallantry. Archers also received an extra sixpence. All these men had been paid one quarter's wages in advance on the 31st January.

Edward had already sent a small detachment under Lord Stanley and Sir William Parr to help Charles. They had departed in the spring, but many never returned, having fallen before Neuss. With the King as his lieutenants were both Clarence and Glouces-ter, Norfolk, Suffolk, Dorset, Northumberland, Pembroke (Her-bert), Rivers, and other peers and barons. No such army had ever before landed in France from the shores of England. Even Henry V had not had half that number.

Finding no Burgundians at hand to receive him, the King sat down to await news of Charles. Learning presently that the French were mustering in overwhelming numbers against him on the Somme, he determined not to throw this magnificent army of his away, and urgently demanded the promised help from his ally. Charles himself with a handful of officers and staff rushed post-haste from Neuss to confer with him. The Duke was in a shocking temper. Completely ignoring the difficulties of transporting so huge a force in tiny ships over a comparatively long sea route, he railed at Edward for landing at Calais instead of Honfleur. The English, he suggested, must advance towards Lorraine, where he would reinforce them with men taken from the army investing Neuss.

Edward and his advisers regarded this as bad tactics. It had always been and still is considered essential that an invading force should maintain a firm footing on the invaded coast so that if disaster comes, a way will lie open for the troops to withdraw to their own shores. To abandon a secure and fortified harbour and march into the depths of the continental land mass was not attractive to the King. Given a port on the sea coast strongly held, Normandy was accessible. So was Paris. But Lorraine . . .

However, he listened to the Duke, who did not linger, but hurried off to Luxembourg. To show willing, Edward with great reluctance struck camp and took the road eastwards to Péronne. He reached Lihons en Santerre by the 12th August, and came next to St. Quentin, fief of the Count of St. Pol, a Burgundian. He had been told that this city would open its gates to him without quibble, but on his arrival, permission to enter was refused, and he was even fired on from the walls. The Count may have been suspicious of so formidable an army presenting itself at his doors.

Edward at once arrested his advance, pitching camp at a point near Nesle. Strongly suspecting treachery on the part of Charles, he would go no farther. That shining weapon, his army, stood idle, glinting in the warm sunshine.

[4]

Before Edward's army had sailed, Louis of France, shrewd and tortuous, had at last received the King's courteous declaration of war, brought to him by an English herald, to whom, when he appeared, Louis conveyed, with his customary subtlety and calm, his belief that the King of England would never attack France unless driven to it by his advisers and his people, or by the Duke of Burgundy. The Duke, a false and perfidious ally, would prove of little use to him. Edward would be wise, therefore to consider carefully a proposal the English herald would take back with him.

The herald replied that his master would listen to no suggestions, because the entire country expected him to sail. The time to propose discussions would be after, not before, the army landed.

When that army came to a halt outside St. Quentin, the King of France saw his opportunity. His envoys, cunningly dressed up as heralds, came secretly into the English camp and obtained an audience. To Edward they offered terms of peace which the baffled monarch found extremely attractive. His men were already turbulent, chafing at their inaction, quarrelling with the local inhabitants, and openly doubting whether their so-called ally would or could defeat the French.

Louis always preferred to buy off rather than make war on his enemies. His ambassadors in London had doubtless told him of Edward's financial difficulties and his growing love of money. Moreover, he was greatly alarmed by the immensely powerful English army at his throat. He now proposed that if the King would withdraw and make a treaty of peace, he would, when all was signed and sealed, pay him an immediate £15,000, appreciating, he said, that to ship back and disperse his men would cost the King much money. Over and above this, he would grant him a yearly pension of £50,000, while his son, the Dauphin, would ask the hand of Elizabeth, Edward's eldest daughter, in marriage. If she were agreeable, she would be given a regular grant of money until the nuptials were celebrated and she had taken up residence in France.

On the other hand, Louis made it perfectly clear that he would not yield up the smallest fraction of his territory, and if this was what England most desired, she would have to pay in blood for every inch she took.

Such handsome offers compared to the recriminations and unreasonable attitude of Charles appealed to the King. He and his Council deliberated with the envoys for some days. Burgundian spies must have got wind of these secret negotiations, for on the 19th August Charles himself came once more storming back into the camp. Without more ado he vented his rage on the King, whom he accused of treachery. It was never good policy to rail at Edward, who sat silent and glowering while the excitable Burgundian Duke poured out his wrath. Then, quietly but bluntly, he reminded Charles that their alliance assumed equal military participation in the war against France, and remarked that he preferred peace accompanied by generous gifts to a single-handed war against a powerful King. The Duke would be well-advised to sign a similar treaty while Louis was in the mood to listen.

Seeing that his hopes of territorial expansion at the expense of the French were about to vanish completely, the Duke lost his head. Furiously berating the King, he vowed he would never speak to or see him again. He and his companions, mounting their horses, left the English camp and took the road to Cambrai.

Stunned by his abrupt departure and this open breach with the potentate on whom they had relied, Edward's Council were divided in their opinions. Gloucester and his party considered that Charles had been shabbily treated, and said so, but the Duke's hot words had greatly offended the King, who refused to have him called back or to budge from his decision to accept Louis's offer, which appealed to his cupidity. Further discussions with the French emissaries took place, and it was agreed that the two kings should meet on the bridge of Picquigny on the Somme, near Amiens, to ratify the proposed treaty. Meantime, a truce would be declared.

Fortunately, we have a record of this encounter, giving a vivid picture of a meeting between medieval monarchs, and of the soldiers of England. Comines, one of the French party at the English camp, found the English men younger than he expected, but considered their riding ragged. Before the meeting, the French king sent in 300 cartloads of the finest wines, using almost as many carts, in fact, as Edward had brought for his entire army.

TWENTY-ONE

1475 - 1477

[1]

THE MOMENT THE truce was declared, the English rushed into Amiens to enjoy themselves, in such numbers of all ranks that if Louis had been so minded and prepared, he could have massacred the flower of Edward's army. To ensure that they did not cause trouble through any failure of the townsfolk to meet their needs, the French King had caused two long tables to be set up at the town gate. These ran down both sides of the street, and were loaded with strong drink and meat, many waiters being in attendance to serve the English. In token of friendship and hospitality, stout men of good family were there ready to welcome, eat and drink with them.

As the Englishmen neared the gate, they saw this magnificent spread awaiting them. French grooms, taking charge of their horses, led them to the tables. When they had eaten and drunk and gone into the town in quest of enjoyment, they found that everything they desired was free. At least nine inns had been supplied at Louis's expense with everything necessary to entertain the visitors. The soldiers remained in Amiens for three or four days, sending back word to their camp of the marvellous time they were having. By the third day, 9,000 Englishmen were reeling and roaring in the streets of the town, where they behaved badly, bringing discredit on themselves and their country.

The French feared serious trouble. When the French King heard of the continuous uproar, he deputed Comines to speak to English officers of his acquaintance, but it was too late. No sooner was one man sent back to the camp than twenty more came hurrying in. At length Louis himself with the Marshal of France entered Amiens to see what was going on, and entering a tavern at 9 a.m. found it full of soldiers either bawling their ribald choruses in well-lubricated, husky voices; lying on the floor fast asleep; or fuddled with drink and shouting noisily. The Marshal concluded that these men were harmless, and the two men withdrew, but Louis was less optimistic than his adviser. Quietly he ordered 2,000 to 3,000 men to arm themselves in their officers' quarters, while others stood guard at the gate by which the English were pouring in.

Louis had his own dinner brought into the gatekeeper's lodge, inviting some English officers to dine with him. By now Edward himself had been informed of the growing drunkenness and de-bauchery in the streets of the town, and promptly despatched a messenger to Louis asking him to shut the town gate and forbid further entry to his troops. Louis feared, however, that if he did this, the thwarted soldiery might batter down the gate and come to blows with his outraged people, so that all the good work of his negotiators would be destroyed. He declined, therefore, offering instead to let the King of England post his own men at the gate to admit those only whom they thought fit.

Edward saw the sense of this. Not only did his men take over, but many of his soldiers in Amiens were ordered back to camp. Thus by reasonable behaviour on both sides a dangerous situation was avoided.

[2]

On the 29th August the two kings came to Picquigny, which stands where the Somme runs through a leafy valley. The river here was narrow and about six feet deep. On each side stretched a fair and level countryside. In those days the bridge over the river was reached only by a long causeway over a marsh. Had they been treacherously attacked as they came along this, the English would have been in great danger, for they were inevitably confined to the path.

The bridge at Picquigny was broad, strong, and rested on tethered boats, having been specially prepared for this great occasion by French workmen. In the very middle stood a lattice-like grating resembling a lion's cage, the bars of which were just far enough part for a man to pass his arm through without difficulty. The bridge was roofed over with boards for a distance long enough for ten men on each side to shelter from the rain, for the weather was exceedingly bad. No unauthorized person could cross the bridge, being prevented by the grating, nor could an enemy approach by way of the river, for only one ferry boat manned by two trusted men was available to take passengers across. The reason for these exceptional precautions was that on a previous occasion men attached to the Dauphin of France had killed a Duke of Burgundy on just such a bridge.

Such a meeting, neither casual nor companionable, was bound to be formal, aloof, and its secret interchanges private. The King of France, attended by about 800 men, reached the bridge gate first. On the opposite bank Edward had drawn up his men, sober now and under strict discipline, in order of battle, both horse and foot. The two Kings had agreed to advance across the bridge from their respective sides with but a dozen of their principal advisers and friends. To guard against treachery, four English were included in the French party, and four French in the English.

In his most magnificent robes, Edward with his huge frame strode forward, Clarence, Northumberland and Hastings beside him, followed by the others, including Lord Scrope and the Frenchmen. Gloucester was not with them, having been left in command of the army on the river bank in case of treachery. Comines opined it was also because he opposed the treaty and would have no part in it.

The King was arrayed in cloth of gold, only the three peers with him wearing similar material. Advancing to within five feet of the grating and removing his cap of state, he bowed so low that his forehead was within six inches of the ground. Obviously he was not yet greatly hampered by his growing obesity. Louis, leaning against the grating, now straightened himself, responding with courtesy and dignity. Each monarch then approached the other, Edward towering above Louis, who, insignificant in appearance and poorly dressed, as was his miserly custom, cut a much less impressive figure. Before Edward embraced him, the French King made another low bow, whereupon they formally embraced, welcoming one another in grandiloquent language.

The Bishop of Ely now recited a pompous rhetorical address to the effect that peace was about to be declared between the two kingdoms, Louis's letter stating his terms was opened, and the Bishop inquired whether the contents were as the French monarch had proposed. The King of France replied that they were. Edward's corresponding letter was now opened, and Louis formally accepted the terms therein suggested.

A missal was brought and opened. Each king laid his right hand on this, and his left on the cross, swearing to keep the peace and conform to his promises for a period of nine years.

This ceremony over, the monarchs chatted agreeably, and Louis pressed Edward to visit Paris, where, he said, he would find many lovely ladies willing to please him. If after thus amusing himself he should feel guilt, he would give him the Cardinal of Bourbon as his confessor, who would readily absolve him. The King, much taken with this suggestion, replied, laughing, that he knew the Cardinal to be a good fellow.

After further exchanges, Louis, to show he both trusted Edward and had full authority over his own men, ordered those with him back to the river bank, saying he wished to speak privately to the King of England. Edward did the same, and both sets of partisans withdrew. After a secret talk with his royal guest, Louis sent for Comines, introducing him to Edward, who recognized him as having once been in Calais, and treated him in friendly fashion.

Louis then asked what he was to do if Burgundy refused to acknowledge the treaty they had just signed. Edward answered that each of them must do as he thought best. What about the Duke of Brittany? Louis inquired. Edward advised him not to try conclusions with the Duke in question, whom he had always found a loyal friend in adversity—a plain hint that he might come to Brittany's aid if the French attacked him.

This ended their meeting. Eloquent parting speeches were made. Simultaneously both kings left the bridge and mounted their horses. Louis went back to Amiens, and Edward to his camp, aided by lights and torches supplied by the French, who had also sent in plentiful supplies of food and drink for their refreshment. Gloucester resigned himself to the peace, and came by invitation into Amiens. The French King made the Duke handsome gifts of silver plate and some admirable horses, fully equipped. He also presented sums of money to Hastings, Howard and the Chancellor.

Although he had invited Edward to Paris, Louis revealed to Comines that he hoped he would not come. Some pretty Parisienne there might flatter and ensnare him so that he would wish to come again. His forbears had stayed too long in Paris and Normandy, and France had suffered for it. He himself had no desire to see this happen a second time. As long as the King of England stayed in his own country, his fellow-monarch could regard him as a good friend and brother, but he did not want him on their side of the Channel. Disappointed by Edward's warning not to go to war with Brittany, Louis made a second attempt to win his consent to an attack, but Edward said bluntly that whoever attacked Brittany would find an English army cross the Channel to defend him. Accordingly the matter was dropped.

[3]

As Louis expected, Edward's imagination had been kindled by the suggested trip to Paris. He sent a few of his nobles into Amiens to sound the French king further on this point, in case it could be arranged. Louis feigned delight at Edward's willingness to accept his invitation, but murmured privately to Comines while washing himself that what he feared most might after all happen. He and the English nobles discussed the matter further at supper that same day, but evidently by great tact Louis warded off the visit. Edward covered up his chagrin with the excuse that he could not go to Paris owing to the necessity of preparing his army to defend themselves against the Burgundians on their homeward march.

The following day many Englishmen, coming once more into Amiens, declared that the peace was the will of the Holy Ghost, for they had seen a white pigeon perch on their King's pavilion, and none could drive it away. Comines, sceptical, like so many of his countrymen, explained that the pigeon had naturally chosen the tallest of the pavilions on which to dry itself after the heavy rain, and probably could not have flown till its plumage was ready to carry it.

The King now received the promised ready money from Louis,

as provided by the treaty, but afraid of being trapped between his present position and the sea by the infuriated Duke of Burgundy, gathered his men together and marched as fast as he could to Calais, which he reached unhindered on the 4th September, having suffered no losses apart from a few stragglers cut off by the Burgundians. These were never heard of again.

As a token of good faith, he left behind with Louis, as hostages, Lord Howard, his Master of Horse, Sir John Cheyne, and two other nobles, who were to be sent home as soon as the English were safely back in England.

His soldiers embarked and sailed without delay, but Edward remained in Calais till the 18th, still hoping, perhaps, for a renewal of the invitation to the French capital, but it was not forthcoming. Some time after the 18th he departed. Bound now by treaty not to re-invade France, he promptly dispersed his many and costly battalions. His countrymen in general were astonished and annoyed, the streets buzzing with murmurs of protest. They could not understand why so bold and brave a warrior should have come home without a victory to his credit, and without even having fought a battle.

Nevertheless, the city of London at least was glad, for now there would be no more appeals to their pockets, and they would get some of their money back, if not all. When Edward came to Blackheath on the 28th, the Mayor, Robert Basset, a drysalter, and over 600 men of the guilds came out to meet him, the city fathers dressed in scarlet and the lesser ranks as usual in "murrey"—dark purple or brownish red. To the sound of many trumpets, and with great cheering, he was led in state to Westminster.

This was the King's last military adventure. His heart had never been in this invasion, into which he had largely been coerced by the desire to regain popularity through victorious generalship, his sneaking desire to win back the territory once possessed by his forebears in France, and his own desperate need of ready money. He was growing stout, and was no longer so active and physically fit as he had been in 1471, when he was, in every sense of the word, a leader of men. One chronicler says that malaria he picked up in France troubled him in later life, but this is conjecture rather than ascertained fact.

He had taken to France with him some of the richest men of the city of London and other towns who had been chiefly instrumental in financing and equipping his forces. He saw to it that when in the field these men were given the most comfortable tents, but being totally unaccustomed to camp life, they hated it. When it was seen there was no likelihood of battle, the King, who had found them a nuisance, frightened them away. In fact, only three days of hardship were required to persuade them that home was the better place. These same men, glad to see him return, now did their best to silence the popular complaints.

The expedition had not won military glory, but it had brought great advantages. Not only had the lives of thousands of English soldiers been saved, and further French raids on English ports prevented, but the King had solved his monetary problems for at least nine years to come, while he might soon marry his eldest daughter to the son of a powerful European sovereign. His brothers and some of his nobles had returned richer than before. Norfolk, for example, had won a pension of 24,000 crowns as well as some plate. Hastings had received 10,000 marks and 2,000 gold crowns (for which he would not give a receipt), and the Chancellor had accepted 16,000 crowns. Cheyne and Thomas Montgomery, too, had not gone unrewarded. The King had good reason to feel satisfied.

[4]

1475 drew to a close with scandalous rumours. The licentious ways of the King were well known and caused much comment, but the rumour that he had seduced an old flame, Lady Eleanor Butler, daughter of the late Earl of Shrewsbury, set tongues wagging in earnest. Another of his mistresses, by whom he had a son and daughter, was Lady Elizabeth Lucy, later married to one of the Lumleys.

Though in his private life sensual, dissolute and fond of good living, Edward governed his country with a firm hand. On the 2nd November the Queen bore him yet another legitimate daughter, Anne. Meantime, he was most disturbed by the unsafe condition of the highways and roads, which were going from bad to worse. It was becoming increasingly difficult for men to go about their business, whether commercial or religious, without being set upon by bands of robbers and plundered of their goods and money. People on pilgrimage to the cathedrals and holy places were halted and forced to hand over the gifts they were taking. Lancashire, Cheshire, Yorkshire, the border counties and the north of Wales, were the worst areas, but even nearer the capital similar conditions obtained.

In consequence, Edward journeyed into Hampshire and Wiltshire to ensure that the law was upheld and to reinforce the local justiciary with a show of power. Early in 1476 he was at Windsor, and later moved to Westminster and Greenwich. There was renewed trouble in Yorkshire, so that in March his brother Gloucester and the Earl of Northumberland, with some thousands of men, were sent to quell the disturbances. During this month the King paid, according to Paston, a flying visit to France, but was back in London on the 30th May, being met by forty members of the Drapers' Company on horseback, which cost that Company £20. Did he after all make his trip to Paris?

His sound business instincts were soon at work again. He was determined not to displease his subjects by wheedling more money out of them, but to live instead within his now greatly improved income. This being so, he felt little need to summon Parliament, since he could enjoy himself, as well as govern the country by firmness, justice and good humour, without interference. Meantime, he went on making money as a royal trader, his own merchant vessels carrying his own goods, particularly wool, tin and lead, to be sold abroad. In his excellent, privileged position, he could obtain good prices for his commodities by offering in return secret benefits to the merchants of whatever country sought to sell its wares in English markets.

An additional source of income, to which none could object, was the heavier fines inflicted on lawbreakers, and as these fines were his perquisite, he saw to it that all his magistrates did their work properly, suppressing disturbers of the peace, kidnappers, thieves, gang warfare and other crimes and criminals. Thus, while gradually restoring law and order, from which the entire country benefited, he at the same time lined his own pockets. As a result he soon became the richest man or one of the richest men in the kingdom, and presently entered the field of usury. When his courtiers needed ready cash, they could draw on him—paying handsomely for the privilege, as was only to be expected.

In July smallpox raged in London. Edward, who was there on the 24th, travelled to Pontefract in Yorkshire. The corpses of his father and brother were now removed from their temporary tomb, and throughout that day the image of the Duke of York, robed in a gown trimmed with ermine and wearing a simple cap of maintenance, also of ermine, lay in state in Pontefract church. Here candles in large numbers cast their flickering golden rays around them, while the vivid hues of banners and standards warmed the cold stone walls. An angel of silver with a golden crown was placed in an erect position beside the bodies as a symbol that the Duke, had he lived, would have succeeded to the throne of England.

The following day a solemn four-day journey was begun to the final resting-place of the bodies at Fotheringay Castle, where they were to be reinterred. The entire party wore funeral dress. The candle-lit hearse drawn by six horses was covered with black cloths showing the arms of England and France. A knight carrying the Duke's banner rode before the hearse. Slowly the cortège travelled, first to Doncaster, where they rested for the night, then through Grantham and Stamford to their destination. Wherever they went crowds garbed in the black of mourning watched them pass, and as they went into Fotheringay church, mass was sung. By the King's order all who joined in the honour paid to his dead were to be given a penny.

The members of the College had gathered to greet the royal party with proper solemnity. Edward, wearing a robe of blue and a cap of mourning, trimmed with miniver, stood at the churchyard gate with his brother George, Duke of Clarence, Earl Rivers, Hastings, Dorset and other friends. When the coffins on their carriage appeared, the King, visibly weeping, kissed the effigy of his father, and then moved into the church, all those present following. In the church two hearses stood; one, for the Duke, was placed in the choir; the other, for the Earl of Rutland, was placed in the lady chapel.

The King now withdrew into a private chamber. The hearses were encircled by peers and officers of the guard. Masses were sung and the respective chamberlains of the King and Queen offered on their behalf five yard-lengths of cloth of gold.

On the 30th, three masses were sung, and the Bishop of Lincoln delivered an eloquent sermon. More offerings of cloth of gold were made. In reverence the bodies were then removed to their final resting-places in the vault built under the chancel. The common people were not allowed into the church till all was over. The King and Queen and two royal princesses themselves then distributed the mass pennies to those present. It is said that 5,000 of them gathered at the door to receive their reward, but this seems an exaggeration.

The funeral baked meats were served in the Castle, either in the royal tent or in pavilions specially built. Here some 20,000 folk, according to the extravagant estimate of the chronicles, sat down to consume fat capons, cygnets, herons and rabbits, with lashings of cream and butter. The total cost of this repast was given as £300, or about 3½d. each if 20,000 were there, which amount is obviously absurd, even for those days.

[5]

The King had long been suspicious of Clarence, and had never allowed his brother to go far from his sight, either in battle or in peace. It is said that both he and the Queen were influenced by a soothsayer, who prophesied that the King would be succeeded by one whose name began with the letter G. Since Clarence's name was George, it was reasonable to wonder if he were this future king. The Duke was, as ever, pompous, garrulous and dictatorial. He was indeed so satisfied with himself that he never understood why his two betrayals, first of Edward, then of Warwick, led all to regard him as untrustworthy. Edward had never forgotten, indeed, that, during the restoration of Henry, Parliament had been compelled to nominate Clarence as potential successor to the Lancastrian heir to the throne, the young Prince Edward, Margaret of Anjou's son.

Clarence now gave his brother fresh cause for annoyance. On the 12th April, 1477, two of his paid bravoes at the head of eighty men forced their way into the house of a young widow in Somerset called Ankarette Twyninghoe, formerly a servant of the Duchess of Clarence, once Isobel Neville, in Warwick Castle. When Isobel died in childbirth in 1476, Clarence accused this former maid of hers of having given her a venomous drink of ale mixed with poison. Without any royal warrant, the poor woman was seized, carried back to Warwick, thrown into a cell, and charged before a body of hastily summoned magistrates.

The accused protested her innocence, and it was argued on her behalf that Isobel was in Tewkesbury, where Clarence had a house—still standing—on the day the poison was said to have been administered. Nevertheless, she was convicted, drawn on a sledge through the town, and hanged on the gallows. Clarence also accused John Thursby of having poisoned his infant son, and hinted that the Queen had instigated his wife's death.

By royal prerogative, both these persons should have been dealt with by the King's judges, not by local justices, and when Edward learned of these impending trials, he at once ordered that the accused should be brought to London, but was too late. They were already dead. Edward was incensed, and his anger was reinforced by Clarence's attempt, through his sister, Margaret, Duchess of Burgundy, to marry Mary, the late Duke Charles's only daughter, Charles having died in battle at Nancy on the 5th June. He had previously forbidden this marriage, and now repeated his opposition. The result was that later Mary married Maximilian of Austria.

At this juncture, a student of the heavens, John Stacy, more learned than some of his fellows in Oxford, being a clerk and chaplain, was commonly believed by the ignorant and superstitious to study the stars with the sole and nefarious purpose of calculating the date of the King's death. It was also alleged against him that he had made leaden images which he slowly melted down, so that by sorcery he was bringing about his sovereign's end. This he was said to have done at the request of Lady Beauchamp, an adulteress, possibly vengeful because cast off. Arrested about a month after the hanging of Ankarette, he was charged with his astrological crime, necromancy, and spreading treasonable reports and verses.

Examined by the barbarous methods of the time, the clerk "confessed", and after his confession one of Clarence's servants, Thomas Burdett of Arrow, accused of being associated with him, was arrested and himself "put to the question". Burdett "confessed" in his turn that Blake, one of Clarence's staff, on whose land at Arrow Park the King had hunted, took great pride in a particular white buck, which he treated as a pet. This the King slew, apparently at someone's suggestion, not knowing the value placed upon it by its owner. Infurated by his loss of a prize beast, the owner exclaimed either to Burdett himself or in his hearing that "he wished the buck's head in his belly that moved the king to kill it". This, it was claimed, showed that he desired his sovereign's death. Blake was arrested, and with the other two, removed to the Tower.

Stacy and Burdett were condemned, and hanged at Tyburn on the 20th May, 1477, but Blake found a friend in the Bishop of Norwich, who secured a pardon for him. During these proceedings the King was at Windsor. Clarence, with the stupidity and insolence habitual to him, burst in upon a meeting of the Privy Council at Westminster, compelling them to listen to his protest against these executions and his own declaration of innocence. Direct approach to the Council not being his prerogative it was promptly reported to the King that he had intruded, and another black mark was set against his name in his brother's memory.

TWENTY-TWO

1477 - 1482

[I]

CLARENCE, THWARTED IN his attempt to marry Mary of Burgundy, now intrigued for a marriage with Margaret, sister of the King of Scotland. Any alliance between the Duke and the Scots was more than the King could stomach, and would, he thought, be as dangerous for him as an alliance between his brother and Burgundy. Once more putting his foot down, he stopped it. A minor insurrection now broke out in the counties of Cambridge and Huntingdon, led by a man passing himself off as the Earl of Oxford. It was speedily quelled, but there was reason to believe that the offender had been aided and abetted by Clarence. At all events Edward assumed this.

Returning at once from Windsor, he summoned Clarence to the Palace at Westminster, and before the Mayor, now Richard Gardener, a mercer, and the aldermen, charged his brother with offences against the constitutional laws of England and of wantonly bringing pressure to bear on magistrates and juries. The Duke, arrested, was thrown into the Tower.

It has been asserted that Clarence was the victim of the Queen and Gloucester, who urged Edward to prevent his brother from doing him more harm, but there is no direct evidence to this effect. By his own acts the Duke of Clarence had already lost his brother's confidence and affection. Parliament was called to hear him arraigned, but the two houses did not meet for the purpose until the 16th June, 1478. During the five weeks of their sitting the members did little more than consider this affair.

The trial itself was as unfair as medieval trials often were. The

Chancellor, who had come over from Calais in June and had ridden
with the King to Windsor and back to London, began the session
with the text "He beareth not the sword in vain". A Bill of Attainder against Clarence was introduced, and his misdeeds over the
previous nine years were recited. He was accused of usurping his
sovereign's legal privileges, wrongfully causing his subjects to be
killed, sorcery, and slander—he was also said to have noised abroad
that his mother had borne Edward after an affair with an archer
named Blackburn, based on a fancied resemblance. There was, of
course, no ascertainable truth in this story, but the King resented it
because Charles of Burgundy, after the King had concluded his
treaty of peace with France, had openly called him a bastard. (At a
later date, Richard of Gloucester resurrecting this legend, also used
it to support his claim to the crown.)

This was not all. The Duke was said to have committed treason,
having compelled his liegemen to swear they would fight for him
against any man he indicated, which could be taken to include his
sovereign. He had instigated and prepared armed insurrection,
shown to his supporters the Act of Parliament that nominated
him successor to the dead Henry and his son, and had accused the
King of using witchcraft against his enemies.

Little evidence was produced for all this, and although witnesses
were called, their bias was obvious. Everyone knew what the King
wanted, and believed it would go hard with whomsoever spoke in
the Duke's favour. "No one argued against the Duke except the
King, no one made answer to the King except the Duke".

The King himself did, in fact, storm openly at his brother, hurling epithets at him from his towering height. Clarence, it must be
admitted, had little self-control. Though his life was at stake, he
did not try to pacify his brother, nor did he defend himself with
skill and discretion. Instead, losing his temper, he denied every
accusation, and being no coward, challenged his brother to ordeal
by battle to determine which of them spoke the truth.

The result was never in doubt. The Bill of Attainder was
passed, and the Duke was sentenced to death, the Duke of Buckingham acting as steward. Parliament also formally cancelled the ver-
dict on Ankarette and repealed the Act of Succession of 1470.

The King made no attempt to modify the sentence or to pardon his brother, but was reluctant to have him executed for fear of the public reaction, though the House of Commons through the Speaker urged him to do so for his own safety, as well as that of the Church and the common weal. It has been suggested that Edward's reluctance was feigned, but this is doubtful. For the sake of his mother and of his own reputation he hesitated, if for no other reason.

[2]

The problem was solved for him. On the 18th February Clarence died, possibly in a room of the Bloody Tower. The legend, which has persisted down to the present day, is that he was drowned in a butt of Malmsey, the wine of Malvasia in the Morea of Greece, by a set of assassins. It is almost certainly incorrect. Polydore Vergil, a contemporary historian of these events, tried in vain to get at the truth. The most recent historians consider it more probable that he was drowned while taking a bath, but one writer suggests his Malmsey wine was poisoned. A chronicler sums up: "Whatever was the manner of it, justice was executed upon him".

Clarence lay in state for thirty-five days. It is said that his head was placed on London Bridge. The King took over all his possessions, landed and otherwise, but spared a portion of them for Gloucester and Rivers. The Marquis of Dorset was appointed guardian of his two orphaned children. All Clarence's estates in Norfolk were settled on the King's second son, Richard, a mere child, affianced to Anne Mowbray, daughter of the late Duke of Norfolk. In later years, Edward is said to have regretted bringing about his brother's death, and whenever asked to pardon any criminal, would cry out: "Oh, unfortunate brother, for whose life not one would speak!"

Gloucester has been accused of causing the Duke's death, but this, too, is doubtful. Sir Thomas More, who did not like Richard, admitted reluctantly that Gloucester was against it "somewhat (as men deemed) more faintly than he that were heartily minded to his wealth".

Clarence's portrait, based on accounts by those who remembered him, was painted about the year 1540 by Louis Cornelius. It shows him with fair hair reaching almost to his shoulders. He is wearing plate armour with a gold edging, and a belt encrusted with jewels. Around his helmet is a coronet rich with gems. His vault in Tewkesbury Abbey measures 9 ft. by 8 ft., 4 ft. 6 in. high at the sides, and in it his remains are contained in a glass case elevated to prevent flood waters from reaching them after heavy rains. His wife had died on the 12th December, 1476.

[3]

Edward's reign, though he did not suspect it, was now approaching its end. Free from fear for his life and his throne, he embarked upon a course that entitles us to consider him the greatest English monarch since Edward III. He was no ignorant baboon. As the guest of de Gruthuyse in Bruges he took pleasure in his host's magnificent library, and on his restoration to the throne added many manuscript volumes to his own collection, some of them beautifully illuminated by the scribes of Bruges. Examples of these are to be seen in the British Museum.

He took great interest in the production of new books, and visited the works of William Caxton, the printer, in his shop at the sign of the Red Pole in Westminster. Caxton presented one of his books to the King, who gave him in return the sum of £20.

When an enforced member of the household of the Archbishop of York, he studied Greek under a secretary, John Sherwood, a Greek scholar of great distinction, who eventually became Bishop of Durham. He had great respect for learning, and can be regarded as the sponsor of a new culture. In 1478 he presented vestments and other clothing to the College at Fotheringay, and made handsome gifts of money to King's College Chapel. But probably his most ambitious project was the reconstruction of the Chapel of St. George at his castle of Windsor. This made such demands on the country's supply of stonemasons that all the most skilled were soon busily employed on this work, depriving the rest of England of their services. William Waynflete, Bishop of Salisbury, begged him to spare a few for work on Magdalen College. Edward also began to get together a library for this Chapel, which he filled with richly decorative objects.

He continued to promote the welfare of his country and its

prosperity, strengthening her fleet and so giving badly-needed work to the craftsmen who built her warships. He introduced the novel practice of allowing a new merchant ship to sail on her maiden voyage unburdened by customs duties or taxes. He also reorganized the customs administration and granted incorporation to the Carpenters' Company.

His Court has been described as a "seminary of pleasant vice", but in 1478 a puritanical reaction seems to have set in, possibly instigated by his Queen, for a statute was passed forbidding such innocuous pastimes, or so one would think, as quoits, football, skittles, croquet, dice, bowls and other games.

[4]

1479 was an inauspicious year, for the land was once more devastated by plague. Little royal business was done, and the King kept out of London, where the disease was at its height, as much as possible. He had taken a great fancy to Eltham Palace, which he constantly visited till the day of his death. During this year he also spent much time at Sheen. A papal dispensation allowed him to add meat, eggs, milk and dishes prepared with it, to his Lenten, Sunday and feast day diet, perhaps because of his recurring malarial fevers and his fear of the plague.

In the beginning of this year Eltham saw a sixth daughter, Katharine, added to his family. He still refrained from summoning Parliament, but nobody appeared to mind. The state was well-governed and administered, and the King worked hard to abolish the feudal practices whereby men were bound closer to their liege lords than to their sovereign. Many of his advisers were well-born ecclesiastics of ability, scholarship and energy. He also checked the increasing power and independence of the towns and cities. For instance he took Coventry to task for breaches of the peace, wearing livery without warrant, and taking the law into their own hands. Nevertheless, he made it his business to know the civic leaders and local gentry, often by personal contact.

His own estates were managed to yield the highest possible revenue, his accounts being correctly audited and his properties surveyed. He was particularly opposed to the brutal occupation, by powerful nobles and knights, of lands not their own, without legal justification. Such unlawful possession was severely punished.

[5]

The instincts of the King were what we should call today thoroughly middle class. He was, if anything, fonder of mixing with the jovial burghers of London than with his nobles, finding their wives complaisant, and sharing their amusements. Much of the affection felt for him was won by his ability to memorize and recall the names, features and rank or office of those dignitaries he met, whether civic, aristocratic or ecclesiastical.

Next to dallying with the ladies, his main pleasures were hunting, strong drink, the feast and the spectacle. He loved to wear rich robes and gay apparel and to line his various royal chambers with the finest work of the cabinet makers of his day, and he had also an eye for noble architecture. State processions gave him the chance to show himself off to advantage, and he was not afraid to introduce a little French or Flemish novelty into the style of his clothing.

In short "he was a goodly personage, of heart courageous, politic in council, in adversity nothing abashed, in prosperity rather joyful than proud, in peace just and merciful".

So the year 1480 came over the brow of Time's hill and rolled slowly downwards. The Duchess of Burgundy, Edward's sister, was now seized with a desire to revisit her native land. As soon as he knew she was coming, the King sent two envoys to Flanders to accompany her to Calais, from which port she was to embark. For her reception he allotted the Cold Harbour or Cold Harbrough, a great house in Thames Street, later known as Poultney's Inn, which in 1472 had belonged to the Marquis of Exeter. This was specially prepared for the purpose, and when Margaret was definitely on the way, Edward sent Sir Edward Woodville and Sir James Ratcliffe with some of his own staff, handsomely dressed in new surcoats of purple and blue velvet, to meet her.

Margaret departed from Bruges, sailing eventually from Calais with 500 men-at-arms and 140 sailors. Landing at Dover, she rode with her escort to Gravesend, where she was met and formally

19

greeted by the Prior of St. John's at the head of a body of civic worthies, and conducted to the royal barge, fitted out to take her up river to London. The master of the barge and his two dozen hands wore brand-new coats of blue and murrey, decorated with white roses.

Edward was delighted to see his sister again, showering gifts upon her, among them ten fine horses, as well as documents entitling her to take back to Burgundy free of duty and tax as much wool as she wished to buy. On her departure he presented her with a splendid pillion cushion of blue and purple cloth of gold, fringed with gold of Venice. Together, they rode to Rochester, were entertained by Earl Rivers, and came to Canterbury. The Duchess sailed home on the 22nd September from Dover in the same ship as had brought her.

Edward's policy was now one of non-commitment in Europe. Although his sister had departed with valuable commercial concessions she had not persuaded her brother to abandon his lucrative pact with the French.

In November Queen Elizabeth bore her seventh daughter, Bridget, at Eltham Palace. Christened by the Bishop of Chichester, the girl in later life got her to a nunnery at Dartford.

1480 saw a bad harvest, serious food shortages followed, and grain became so expensive that unrest and civil commotions occurred in the north, put down, however, without much difficulty, the ringleaders being betrayed by a certain Piers Fillow.

Though now in "the prime of life", the King was deteriorating physically. Having no power of self-denial, he had become sluggish and obese from eating, drinking and concupiscence. More and more he was divorcing himself from the tedious duties of state, leaning heavily on his able, loyal, sagacious brother, Richard of Gloucester, who, by comparison, was austere in conduct, earnest in devotion to the Church, and well thought of in the lands he owned. His administration of the kingdom was, moreover, sound.

Early in 1480 the Scots were back at their old tricks, the bonnets coming over the border again into Northumberland, stealing whatever they could lay their hands on, for James III of Scotland had little control over his subjects. Edward, probably persuaded by Gloucester, declared war on Scotland, and renewed his old claim to be overlord of that country. The English town of Berwick was to revert to him.

James sent envoys to explain that the raids were not his doing, and that he had never wished to invade the borderlands, but he was being continually threatened by his powerful nobles, among them his own brother, and could not keep them in check. Edward refused to hold back his army, and to obtain money for this new war, resorted a second time to gentle blackmail of his wealthier subjects for "voluntary contributions". He also claimed "back money", taxes passed by Parliament six years or so before, but never collected.

The King still loved hunting, and during 1481 invited William Hariot, Mayor of London, a favourite of his, to hunt with him in Waltham Forest. Hariot, an extraordinary man, had travelled widely, and came of a Leicestershire family. A draper by trade, he had lent the King a good deal of money. A "pleasant lodge of green boughs" was put up for him, his aldermen, and their wives. A sumptuous meal was served at the close of the morning's hunt, the King refusing to eat until his guests had all they desired. The meat was cooked as well as if it had come from a proper kitchen. Red and white wines and claret (yellow or light red in those days) were served. The party had good sport, chasing red and fallow deer, and at the end of the day, the King sent two harts and six bucks to the Mayoress and the wives of the aldermen, as well as a tun of wine—consumed later at a banquet in Drapers' Hall, St. Swithin's Lane, Cannon Street.

[6]

In Canterbury on the 17th May, the King visited Dover and returned to the Tower on the 23rd. His adolescent daughter, Mary, was dying, and her life ended at Greenwich on the 29th. She was 15. Wrapped in cerecloth, a waxed material, her body was carried in its leaden coffin to St. George's Chapel at Windsor, and buried beneath the flagstones next to her infant brother, George. The chief mourner was the Prince of Wales, Edward having gone north to meet Gloucester and Alexander Stewart, Duke of Albany, born in 1454 and second son of James II and Mary of Gueldres, who, it was proposed, should be made King of Scotland in place of his brother,

James III. After this meeting, Edward hurried back to London and Dover, to give his fleet a royal send-off on the 9th July, 1481, as it moved out of harbour to assail the Scots. Under Lord Howard it cruised along the shores of Lothian and Fife, seizing or sinking cargo ships and raiding Blackness, which they pillaged and burned. Moving but slowly, the army accomplished little more than a few feeble skirmishes in the Merse and Teviotdale.

In the spring of 1482 Albany came to Fotheringay for negotiations. Rivers was present, and a formal treaty, signed and sealed by both parties, bound Albany on becoming King to acknowledge Edward as his suzerain, and to hand back Berwick, Eskdale and Annandale. Edward's 13-year-old daughter, Cecilia, had been designed to marry James III's eldest son. This marriage had, indeed, taken place earlier by proxy, but had been annulled when war broke out. The new treaty promised her to Albany with a dowry of 20,000 marks in three instalments on condition that "he would make himself clear of all other women", which suggests the Duke already had either a wife or a concubine.

On the 17th Albany rejoined Gloucester in York. Gloucester was now commanding levies from the northern districts, numbering about 10,000. He marched out of York on the 15th July.

Berwick town was taken, but the Castle still held out. The dissident Scots under Albany and the Earl of Angus entered Edinburgh in triumph.

Meantime, the Scottish nobles, turning against James III, locked him up in Edinburgh Castle, and though willing to back Albany, distrusted Gloucester. Knowing themselves unwelcome in a hostile city, the English stayed only to see Albany installed as Governor, and to prepare a formal treaty between the two countries. Then they marched out, making again for Berwick, whose castle did not surrender till the 24th. The success of his efforts both as general and politician was largely responsible for Gloucester's later popularity.

The Scots of that period were never trustworthy where their enemies, the English, were concerned, and Gloucester was no sooner out of the way than he was cunningly overreached. Albany listened to secret messengers with tempting offers from supporters of the imprisoned James III. If he abandoned his claim to the throne and pledged loyalty to the King, his lands and titles should be restored and he would be made President of the Council under James himself. The Duke, agreeing, was made Lieutenant of the Kingdom.

Before many weeks had passed, the liberated James resumed his throne, Albany being dubbed Earl of Mar and Garnock. When Gloucester heard of all this he was astounded. As a sop to Cerberus, the Scots undertook to relinquish Berwick permanently and to marry James's son to Cecilia. Seeing no better alternative, Gloucester advised Edward to agree, and his advice was taken.

[7]

The King's willingness to call off his Scottish war was not solely inspired by his brother. His spies had brought news that the perfidious King of France was shuffling out of part, at least, of the Treaty of Picquigny. Having abandoned his intention of marrying the Dauphin to Elizabeth, Edward's daughter, Louis was negotiating his son's betrothal to the Duchess of Burgundy's daughter, the Duchess herself having died on the 27th March of that year. So flagrant a breach of their pact shocked Edward, especially as it followed on Albany's craven surrender. Both his paternal affection and his personal pride were wounded. He was incensed that the young Princess, now sixteen, should be publicly shamed. To Parliament he revealed the bad faith of the French King, and the humiliation of himself and his daughter, declaring he would avenge himself by war. Dutifully, even enthusiastically, the Commons granted money for the purpose. Moreover, the King took back much of the crown property previously given into other hands, but those, such as Gloucester, to whom he was most indebted, were excepted. He also restricted his personal expenditure to the comparatively small sum of £11,000 a year.

TWENTY-THREE

1482 - 1483

[1]

DURING 1481, WHILE his ships were in the north assailing the Scots, the King had spent a fortnight at Woodstock, then visited Oxford to see the new College (Magdalen). It was his intention to move from there to York and himself lead the army against the Scots, but when he reached Nottingham on the 1st October, he remained there for nearly three weeks, perhaps to hold down the country, still in a state of unrest. When all was once more quiet, and then only, he perceived the unwisdom of marching to the Scottish border. He had suffered once before through leaving London and the south unguarded. He decided, therefore, to leave the Scottish war in the capable hands of Gloucester. It is possible, of course, that ill-health played a part in this decision.

Accordingly, turning south again to Fotheringay Castle, he paused there, and finally returned to London. Soon afterwards, in November, the little girl-wife of his second son, Richard, died at Gravesend, her body being conveyed under royal escort to Westminster Abbey, where she was buried with great reverence and pomp in the chapel of St. Erasmus, over £200 being spent on her funeral. Her remains were recently discovered elsewhere, and re-buried. It was during this year that Edward presented the Grey Friars, through Sir William Corbridge, with a chantry and a little chapel of the Holy Cross.

After the funeral, Edward travelled in state to Southampton and Winchester, remaining for some time, until, as Christmas approached, he came back once more to Windsor. Here he exhibited his usual munificence, bestowing a cup of gold, a cross of gold set with diamonds, diamond rings, gilt flagons, gilt bowls, a saltcellar, pots and cups, to his friends and relations.

During the early part of 1482 he surveyed with an experienced eye the fortifications and batteries, the weapons and munitions, of the Tower. He had ordered a large brass gun to be cast, and towards the end of March, when this was ready, it was transported to the fields beyond the city gate at Mile End for firing tests. To his annoyance, the gun burst when fired.

After some hunting in Waltham Forest, he spent Christmas at Westminster Palace, and also at Eltham, where as many as 2,000 people came to be entertained. About this time the wearing of silks made abroad was prohibited, this edict being aimed at the Jews and Saracens, who monopolized this trade. Fulling mills were replacing manual work, and to prevent unemployment arising out of this, it was also forbidden to sell bonnets and caps made in these mills.

The King did his best to please and flatter those subjects whose financial support for the forthcoming war with France he needed and desired, appearing before them in his richest attire, of the late Gothic style, mainly derived from Burgundy. A long gown with padded shoulders and long, wide sleeves, miniver-lined, over his shoulders, covered his now corpulent, but still powerful frame. About him moved his sons and daughters, as well as his numerous relations. The glittering ranks of courtiers included some of every civilized land.

On the 20th January, 1483, he opened a new Parliament at Westminster, and remained in London throughout the sitting. At Westminster on the 11th February, he obtained the signature of Archibald Douglas, 5th Earl of Angus, to a convention acknowledging his overlordship of Scotland, on condition that he again supported the Duke of Albany in his new claim to the Scottish throne. Albany had fallen from power, and badly needed help.

In the second or third week of March, returning to Windsor, the King remained there till the 30th. On that day he was taken ill, and was soon unable to sit up, having to lie on his right side. The journey from Windsor to Westminster appeared to have been too much for him. News of his serious illness swiftly travelled to all parts of the kingdom.

On the 6th April, a report reached York that he was dead, and a dirge was sung in the Minster, but Edward was then still alive. Knowing his end near, however, he changed his will, and calling Hastings and Dorset, who had recently quarrelled, to his bedside, begged them for the good of the realm to become reconciled, to which they agreed.

On the 9th April, 1483, Edward IV died at the age of 41, his son, Edward V, the new King, being then 13, and by Edward's will the boy was placed again in Gloucester's care.

Opinions differ concerning his illness and its cause. Some ascribe it to a surfeit of fruits and vegetables; others to apoplexy; to the results of previous ailments of long standing; to venereal disease; or to pure mortification at the slight to Princess Elizabeth. In all likelihood, however, his death was the combined effect of previous military hardship and sickness, rich living, over-indulgence in sensual delights, and the hardships, exasperations and frustrations inevitable in the life of a medieval English king.

At all events, his death cancelled the secret treaty with Albany, which cancellation soon became known to the Duke's enemies in Scotland, and led to his banishment. He fled to Paris, and died in France by accident in 1485.

[2]

After the King's death, his body was "laid upon a board all naked, saving he was covered from the navel to the knees". In Westminster Palace he lay for twelve hours, a file of priests, nobles, the Mayor, aldermen and dignitaries of all kinds, passing by him in respect and sorrow. His remains, wrapped in waxed cloth, were next day at dawn taken to the Chapel of St. Stephen, where he lay in state, dressed in a full suit of gold armour, for eight days, the outer coffin of silver being ornamented by raised work. Masses were sung throughout this period and offerings made. Guards were posted every night to prevent desecration.

After the lying in state, the corpse, carrying in one wax-like hand the golden orb and in the other the sceptre, was placed on a movable wooden stand, covered by a broad pall of black cloth of gold. The dead King still wore his crown. A canopy over the coffin showed the arms of England and France worked in gold. On the pall was a white cross, also of cloth of gold.

No fewer than ten bishops and two abbots now walked slowly and gravely into the Abbey, followed by Lord Howard carrying Edward's own banner. The rich canopy of scarlet "cloth imperial fringed with blue and gold silk", was held aloft by four knights, and following it came four more holding the banners of the Holy Trinity, the Virgin Mary, St. George and St. Edward. Behind these came a procession of nobles, some of whom reverently touched the bier from time to time.

In the Abbey stood the royal hearse, and also the image of the King—"a personage like to the similitude of the King in habit royal, crowned with the very crown on his head, holding in that one hand a sceptre and in that other hand a ball of silver and gilt with a cross pate" or ornate form of cross. A hymn in Latin was sung by choristers, while rows of monks and black-clad nuns formed two opposing ranks between which the populace moved, to make their exit from the other end of the chapel. Choir and nave were occupied by knights clad in black mail, their visors closed and bare swords in their hands. Priests carried burning candles of black wax several feet in length. Other ecclesiastics in long white robes knelt around the coffin.

Finally, the bier was placed on the hearse, and the funeral cortège left the Abbey for Windsor, the image of the King accompanying his bier. The chariot carrying the body was draped in black velvet. Six fine horses, also with black velvet cloths, hauled it to its destination, each having a rider astride. On both sides were mounted knights and esquires for the body, some of whom were at times called upon to lead the horses or help pull the chariot because of the bad state of the roads and ways.

Lord Howard, wearing a mourning hood and still carrying the royal banner, preceded the "forehorse". Like the rest, his own mount was furnished with black velvet trappings bearing the King's arms. At Charing Cross the cortège halted for the chariot to have incense burned before it, and another stop was made at the nunnery of Sion House, where Anne de la Pole, a niece of the dead King, resided. The body lay under guard in the church choir till the following day, and at Eton was again censed by the Bishops of Lincoln and Ely and inmates of the College. At Windsor the procession was met by the Canon of St. George's Chapel, and a third censing of the body took place, after which it was conducted into the Chapel, impressive even though not yet completed. Here a "marvellous well-wrought hearse" awaited it.

The dead monarch was again guarded throughout the night by peers and titled men. Next day many offerings were brought—a shield, a sword from the Pope, and a helmet. The assembled Bishops sang the Mass, and a requiem was sung by the Archbishop of York, after which an armed knight, encased in steel, bareheaded and carrying an axe head downwards, clattered on horseback to the choir door, dismounted, and was led into the sacred building to make his offering as "the man of arms". The peers then offered their cloths of gold.

Edward's remains were now lifted from the bier and placed in a great marble tomb he had had prepared some time before, on the north side of the altar. Into this the chief men of his household flung staves "in token of being men without a master and out of their offices". The heralds similarly cast in their coats of arms, and were reclothed in other royal coats of arms of England. They at once shouted, "Le roy est vif! Le roy est vif!" Then followed a collective prayer, a paternoster and an ave maria for the dead King. His own gilt suit of armour, surmounted by a cloth of crimson velvet with the arms of England and France embroidered on it in gold, pearls and rubies, was hung above the tomb together with a banner displaying the royal arms. There they remained for nearly 160 years, being finally removed to Westminster by an unknown Cromwellian. A popular ballad after the King's death put into his mouth the words, "I promesse the good Lorde my lyffe to amende, I knowlege me a sinner wrapped in woe". Later, Gloucester came to St. Paul's to pray and show sorrow at his death.

So ended the reign of one of England's most remarkable kings, who had in him more English blood than any monarch since the days of William the Conqueror.

[3]

Edward was a splendid soldier, imaginative, daring to the point of rashness, fighting all his battles on foot. Luck, that indispensable requirement of a general, favoured him in his boldest ventures. He was aided also by a magnificent presence, a handsome face and extraordinary vitality. Well over six feet in height—when his coffin was opened in 1789 at Westminster, the skeleton alone measured 6 ft. 3 in. long—broad in the breast, his limbs proportionate to his frame, he was quick and assured in the field. It was said of him, "At all time of his reign, he was with his people so benign, courteous . . . that no part of his virtue was more esteemed." At the end of his days this quality "marvellously in him grew and increased".

He was always addressed as "Your Grace", the phrase "Your Majesty" not then having become customary. During his reign the Tower was the focus of a rich and festive Court. While sentries paced the walk above the battlements of the inner wall, the King's flag swirled over the Bloody Tower, and the nobles and ladies paraded the courtyard in fine robes of cloth of gold.

Up and down the Thames went the royal barge, brilliantly decorated with gold and fine colours, pennants flying, awnings, gaily patterned, stretching over the passengers.

As a man Edward IV was merciful except when danger or the need of order demanded severity. A brilliant swordsman and good dancer he rode his horse well, and was an excellent judge of wine and food. He could also speak the French language fluently. Mostly honest in his dealings and undeniably brave, he was nevertheless not greatly gifted with foresight, being inclined to put excessive trust in those whom he had pardoned or befriended. Although he claimed the throne of France and the Suzerainty of Scotland, these were inherited national ambitions rather than his own individual hankerings. He was, indeed, too indolent and pleasure-loving to be territorially ambitious.

Throughout his reign he was inclined to leave the strenuous and toilsome work of administration to his Council, and above all, after Warwick's death, to Richard of Gloucester. Nevertheless, he preferred to be loved and admired rather than hated and feared, and this prevented him from being a cruel, oppressive, hated tyrant, despite his authoritarian rule. Like the men of his period he could be harsh, vengeful and unjust when angry or frightened. If firmness was required, he would swiftly assail and crush his adversaries, enforce whatever laws he considered essential, then relax into genial benevolence, satisfied that he had shown the iron hand. His subjects assumed that his severities were for the public good, not merely because he was innately cruel or self-seeking. In contrast to more ascetic and domineering monarchs, he left the common people alone.

The Lollards seemed to him dangerous, and he had one hanged on a scaffold at Tower Hill, for which he paid himself. The man demanded dinner before he died, saying: "I eat now a good and competent dinner, for I shall pass a little sharp shower before I go to supper".

Edward's hand lay heaviest on the barons. Once firmly seated on the throne, he was swift to suppress unrest, holding the local administrators responsible for disturbances. Faction and riot sprang from weakness at the centre, he believed. In course of time he won both the respect and the affection of his people, few kings of the age being so deeply mourned. Believing that Parliaments should be freely and fairly elected, he prevented the election of the unqualified or the parade of force to influence the result of an election. Much of his success was owed to his sound intelligence and to the work of his administrators in reforming the Church.

He is said to have had a remarkable memory, and it was never difficult to approach him. He loved "a good laugh", which increased his popularity, but he was, if anything, too familiar with private persons, so that it was rumoured after his death that he had been poisoned by one of them (a jealous husband?). Other attributes were generosity and gratitude. He rewarded Nurse Cobb for her kindness to the Queen during her term in sanctuary by allowing her £12 a year, a considerable sum in those days. To the butcher who befriended her he gave some of his business, buying from him regularly large quantities of hides and tallow. The Abbot under whose wing she had sheltered was made Bishop of Hereford and a Privy Councillor "for his great civility".

While Edward showed no particular originality in administrative technique, he did his country enormous service by surrounding himself with clever men, allowing them to function without fear as long as they were honest and capable. He governed with little aid from Parliament, which he called as seldom as possible, and in the end the exhausted economy of the country was put back on its feet without it. His first achievement in this direction was when he made himself a good financial risk by honouring his debts. He even paid off the creditors of Henry VI. In consequence, he did not need to burden the common people with heavy taxes, and after six or seven years, succeeded in balancing his household budget, a remarkable feat. Towards the close of his reign he became somewhat grasping and avaricious, but his kingdom prospered and his people were mostly content.

A man of taste, he patronized the arts and letters, and would have in his Council none but men of high birth and/or learning. He might make rich gifts to his favourites, but would not ennoble them unless they had the necessary qualifications of blood, breeding or ability. Although his foreign policy was inconsistent and pragmatical, he tried as far as he could to shape it to the needs of his people, particularly her merchants and exporters, calling them to London to state their views, and even expounding his intentions to them before sending missions overseas. He would invite their representatives to participate in the work of these missions, and would consider their opinions regarding terms of sale for exported cloth, deciding with them the standard rate of exchange.

In short he made the commons as powerful in national administration as the rest. Civic leaders, high-born ecclesiastics and "yeomen gentry" rather than great barons were the architects of his policy. He came to the throne amid the clash of swords and the thunder of cannon. He left it to the sound of coins clinking in counting houses and cargoes thudding into the holds of his merchantmen. His people could see and admire him in all his magnificence of attire without feeling they had toiled and sweated excessively to pay for it.

Edward's red-gold hair reached to his shoulders, being kept in place by scented unguents. His face was singularly smooth for the period and his great stature was matched by the breadth of his shoulders. In maturity he had strong, resolute features.

Henry VII's wife, his daughter, may have taught her thrifty husband the virtues of royal and national economy she had learned from her father, every penny of whose household was accounted for. His enemies and some historians have alleged that he lacked gratitude, was vindictive, ruthless, egotistical and untrustworthy. Certainly he was all these things at times. What medieval King was not? He, too, had been trained from childhood to be ruthless and ambitious. Nevertheless, he was one of the first kings to make England politically and commercially great. He found a people disunited and at war with itself. He left them an island race—the English—united and flourishing. It was not his fault that some of his successors were not of the same stature or temperament.

Much more legitimate is the accusation that he was notoriously a libertine in private life, guilty of innumerable infidelities, his Court licentious. Certainly, in his later years, if ambition hindered pleasure, he surrendered ambition. Lazy, genial, gay, he ate enormously—after all, he had an immense frame—and drank as lustily. Warwick said that he would rather fight fifty battles *for* him than sup once with him. His banquets lasted for hours, and his boon companions, Hastings and Montagu, were the only ones he could not drink under the table.

Loving fine clothes, he was quick to adopt every current mode. Sometimes he wore a long gown reaching to his feet, ermined at the edges and richly embroidered with scarlet blossoms on cloth of gold. Over this came a small ermine cape with two bands hanging in front. His collar was of uncut gems set in fine filigree work of gold wire. Close-fitting hose covered his legs, and the folds of his robe were carefully arranged to hide the codpiece.

His Queen, self-seeking, unlovable, scheming, bore him no fewer than ten children, and was not entirely neglected, but beyond doubt Edward had many mistresses. All this the Queen endured with calm and forbearance, and to the King's credit, none of the women he fondled, most of them having knowledge and intelligence, were allowed to meddle in affairs of state.

[4]

Of all his loves Jane Shore has come down to us the most convincingly. A woman of London, daughter of Thomas Wainstead, a rich goldsmith of Lombard Street, she had been "honestly brought up", and when quite young was married at St. Andrew's Church,

Holborn, by Dr. Gilbert Worthing to a Cheapside mercer, Matthew or William Shore, "of a very fair character both for religion and morals". Not ill-favoured, he was well able to support a wife, but was probably much older than Jane. Mingling with the prosperous men of London, Edward was attracted by the young wife, and promptly made love to her.

Jane cared little for her husband, whose physical demands had revolted the mere child she was at the time of her marriage. Hastings is said to have tried to carry her off with the help of her maid, who afterwards, repenting, betrayed the plot, but Edward was confirmed in his desire for her when he saw her with her father at St. Paul's, or so the tradition goes.

Awed, delighted and thrilled by a royal wooing, Jane saw the prospect of rich attire, gaiety, comfort and money, as well as petticoat influence and ample gratification of her desire for love and passion, opening out before her. Unhesitatingly she deserted William to become the King's mistress. William, by no means the first husband to be cuckolded by a king, could do little. Wisely he made no fuss, and all relations between him and his wife ceased. Jane went eventually to live at Court as a waiting maid of one of the royal Duchesses, possibly the Duchess of Gloucester, at Eltham, then was given her own establishment in Tottenham Court Road. Her husband, it is said, went abroad or died after her imprisonment.

Edward always called her the merriest of his concubines, saying he had three mistresses "one the merriest, one the wiliest and one the holiest harlot in the realm". She certainly charmed and endeared herself to him, being the only one who could influence him. She is said to have saved by her persuasive powers Eton and King's College, Cambridge, Henry VI's foundations, from having their revenues forfeited to the King. Sir Thomas More wrote: "She never abused her power to any man's hurt, but to many a man's comfort and relief." It was also said of her: "No empress in the world had ever possessed so lovely and merry a waiting maid."

A portrait of her existed up to the days of Elizabeth I, but disappeared long ago. Drayton, who saw it, says the picture showed her rising from her bed in "a mantle cast under one arm over her shoulder, and sitting on a chair on which her naked arm did lie".

Of medium height, she had rich golden hair, grey eyes, and a round full face. Admirably proportioned, she inclined to plumpness, but her complexion and skin were pale. Her face and disposition were cheerful. When still in favour she wore a white kirtle over which was a bodice of purple velvet decorated by embroidery in silks of various colours.

After the King's death she mediated between the Queen and her *bête noir*, Hastings, then became the mistress of the Marquis of Dorset, the Queen's son by her first husband. Dorset is said to have loved her greatly during Edward's lifetime, but was forced to suppress his feelings. When the sombre Richard of Gloucester came to the throne, he accused her of witchcraft, saying she had been encouraged in this by the Queen and Hastings. Her possessions were seized and she was sent to the Tower in June, 1483. Gloucester ordered her to do penance in St. Paul's Churchyard, "no man relieving her."

So one Sunday poor Jane, walking barefoot before the cross and a lighted taper in her hand, headed a solemn procession. Tradition has it that the stones were bloodied by her lacerated feet. After walking from the Palace of the Bishop of London to St. Paul's, she heard herself denounced by Dr. Shaw, the officiating priest, and was left to wander in the fields of Whitechapel, then entirely open country, except for a mansion here, a monastery and its garden there.

More has left behind a charming description of Jane on this day: "She went in countenance and face demure, so womanly and albeit she was out of all array, save her kirtle only. Yet went she so fair and lovely . . . while the wondering of her people cast a comely red in her cheeks (of which before she had most miss), that her great shame was her much praise among those who were more amorous of her body than curious of her soul, and many good folk, also, who hated her living, and were glad to see her corrected, yet pitied they more her penance than rejoiced therein, when they considered that the Protector procured it more of a corrupt intent than any virtuous intention.

"Proper she was, and fair. . . . This say they who knew her in her youth, albeit some who now see her (for yet she liveth) deem her never to have been so well-visaged; whose judgment seemeth to me as though men should guess the beauty of one long departed by her scalp taken out of the charnel-house. For now she is old, lean, withered, and dried-up—nothing left but shrivelled skin and hard bone. And yet, being even such, whoso will advise her visage, might guess and devise which parts, how filled, would make it a fair face.

"Yet delighted men not so much in her beauty as in her pleasant behaviour. For a proper wit she had, and could both read well and write, merry in company, ready and quick of answer, neither mute nor full of babble, sometimes taunting without displeasure, and not without disport."

Few women but would give much for such a record left by a great man.

Jane was eventually taken to Ludgate prison, where the royal prosecutor and King's Solicitor, Thomas Lynon, who had fallen in love with her, entered into a contract of marriage with the unfortunate woman, applying to Richard III for leave to fulfil it. Richard regarded this as an absurd infatuation, but without forbidding the marriage, deferred it till he was next in London. Then, if adequate bail were forthcoming, Jane could leave her prison cell and pass into the safe keeping of her father or whoever the Chancellor, John Russell, Bishop of Lincoln, might consider suitable. For some reason the marriage never took place, Lynon being perhaps dissuaded by friends and relations.

Jane lived till 1527, her last days in poverty such that she "had to beg a living of many that had begged if she had not been". It is said she scattered flowers at the funeral of Henry VII.

[5]

Edward's Queen, once Elizabeth Woodville, lived till Henry VII came to the throne, and was presently imprisoned and thrust into Bermondsey Abbey. She made a will shortly before her death in which she recorded her cruel neglect by Henry VII, husband of her daughter, Elizabeth. The Abbey monks left her name out altogether when they sang for an anniversary service on the 6th February. She lived to learn of the cruel death of her two sons, murdered in the Tower, and in 1492 died in poverty in the very abbey where the anniversary service was performed. Yet the House of Commons had praised her "womanly behaviour and great constancy" during her royal husband's enforced sojourn abroad, and in 1472 she and the King had been welcomed with an oration by the Chancellor of Oxford University.

Her mother-in-law, Cicely, Duchess of York, was still alive when Elizabeth died, but died herself on the 31st May, 1495, being buried, as her will directed, in the Chancel of the Collegiate of Fotheringay Castle, where her husband's remains lay. During the Reformation, this church was destroyed, and the bodies of both Duke and Duchess were exposed once more to view. A Mr. Creuso who saw them wrote: "The bodies appeared very plainly. The Duchess Cecily had about her neck, hanging on a ribbon, a pardon from Rome, which, penned in a fine hand, was as fair and fresh to be seen as if it had been written the day before."

Queen Elizabeth I ordered these remains to be carefully reburied with suitable solemnity.

[6]

Some historians have described Edward IV as a tyrant because he did not govern through Parliament, but although in theory this is arguable, he was in himself too indolent and amiable to be tyrannical. It is fair to say that during his reign from 1461 onwards peasant and commoner were more lightly taxed and oppressed than for many decades. By the time of his death piratical raids on the Channel ports had ceased. There was no more sacking, burning and plundering of property, no more forced requisitions, no more ravaging of the countryside by barbarous troopers. Trade was flourishing, shipbuilding had been stimulated, the fishing industry was developing fast, cloth poured from English weavers' looms and from the manufacturer's fulling mills. Raw wool was finding a ready sale abroad, agriculture thriving and independent yeoman farmers were rapidly replacing serf-like villeins.

Not only this, precious labour was going not into great castles built for rapacious nobles engaged in internecine warfare, but into fine manorial dwellings, churches and cathedrals. True, the Lollards had been put down, but otherwise the Government was tolerant, and the leaders of the church had become competent administrators rather than ecclesiastics with great ambition and a thirst for power; yet few ordinary churchmen were great scholars. The monasteries had largely ceased to produce the historical chronicles on which so much knowledge of medieval England depends. Generally, the intellectual quality of the clergy was bad.

So many heads of aristocratic families had been lost during the civil wars that inevitably the great houses were inherited and ruled by "second-raters". On the other hand, there was a badly-needed revival of interest in the peaceful arts and crafts, while letters, stimulated by the Woodvilles and by the printing press of William Caxton, flourished.

Edward did not, like that petulant "heroic" warrior, Henry V, carve out a new empire for himself from the chaos in Europe. He gave his people a spell of peace and prosperity that was worth all the military glory, and strengthened the foundation of their coming greatness. The Victorian history-writers were sometimes too shocked by his sexual lapses to do him justice.

[7]

The household of Edward was organized down to the last detail. Each member had the privileges of his rank and no others. Thus, a duke could have a chaplain, four esquires and three valets—no more, no less—who ate in the hall. In his chambers he could have but twenty-one liveried men. Even his food was rationed, so that in the night his bedside carried only two "breads" and one pitcher containing two gallons of wine. Furthermore, no member of the Court could keep more children, dogs or ferrets than his form of appointment allowed.

The King's "doctor of physic" advised him on his diet, indicating "the best foods according to their kind and method of preparation". This doctor conferred with the royal chamberlain or chief officer of the King's chamber; the steward—who at meals supervised the table arrangements; and the master cook, to decide the royal menu, which had to conform to the recommended diet. The doctor was always at the King's table and concocted all his medicines.

In the banqueting hall stood a cupboard—a side table or dresser on which cups and other drinking vessels were set out—from which liquid refreshment was served. The meat was usually salted or pickled, there being no other means of preserving it in wintertime. Much barley beer was brewed and drunk.

Whenever the King left London he was preceded by his "harbiger" or harbinger, who arranged suitable lodging for the royal party. The royal palaces were virtually medieval hotels, embodying a laundry, a chandlery for the making and storage of candles, a great spicery, a buttery, cellars for storing and keeping in good order wines and ales, a cup house, a confectionery for the preparation of sugars and sweets, a napery for keeping and supervising cloths and linen for the table, and an ewery for large water jugs. There were also a bakery or "bakehouse", wafery and pantry. In majestic fashion the chief butler patrolled his domain, and the buyer of the royal wines stalked the cellars with dignity, relaxing at times into joviality, and ending up, perhaps, with an erratic stagger through the royal "offices".

Times change. A genial, amorous, luxury-loving, but shrewd and tolerant king was presently replaced by a more austere, efficient and dubious monarch, whose character is still the subject of hot dispute. Over the shoulder of English history the Plantagenet sun was setting, and the dawn flush of the Tudors was yet to come.

BIBLIOGRAPHY

BASIC MATERIAL

Archaeologia Brit. XXVI 275-384, XXIX.

Basin, T. *Histoire de Charles VII et Louis XI.*

Boke of Nobless, ed. Nichols. (1860.)

Calendar of Documents relating to Scotland (1888).

Calendar of State Papers: "Venetian Papers". 1864.

Chastellain, G. *Chronique,* (1868).

Chronicle of the Grey Friars of London, ed. Nichols. Camden Soc. (1852).

Chronicle of London, ed. J. Gairdner. Camden Soc. (1876).

Chronicle of London, 1089-1483, ed. Nicholas. (1827).

Chronicle of the Lincolnshire Rebellion, Vol. I.

Chronicle, Westminster, Caxton. *See Cottonius.*

Chronicles, R. Holmsted. 1577, ed. Dent. (1959).

Chronicles of the White Rose of York. (1845).

Comines, P. *Mémoires.*

Concilia Magna Britannicae. Watkins. (1737).

Cottonius Vitellius M.S. XV. Chronicle. (1450-53).

Daires. *York Records.* (1843).

Davies. *Municipal Records of the City of York.*

Devon, F. *Issue Rolls.* (1837).

Duclerc, *Memoires de.* (1448-67).

Ellis, Sir H. *Original Letters.* (1825-46).

English Chronicle, ed. Davies, Camden Soc. (1856).

Enrolled Customs a/cs. Henry VI and Edward IV.

Excerpta Historica, ed. Nicholas (1831).

Exchequer Accounts. Foreign Merchants.

Exchequer Rolls of Scotland. (1878).

Fabyan, Robert. *New Chronicles,* ed. H. Ellis. Camden Soc. (1844).

Fortescue, Sir J. *Governance of England,* ed. Plummer. (1926).

Grafton, *Chronicle* (ed. 1809).

Gregory, Wm. *Chronicle.* (1451-52).

Habington, Thomas. *Historie of Edward IV.* (1640).

Hall, G. *Chronicle.* (ed. 1809).

Halliwell. *Letters of the Kings of England,* I. (1846).

Hardyng, J. *Chronicle.* ed. (1809).

Harley M.S.

Historia Croylandensis. Vol. I. ed. W. Fulman (1684).

Historical M.S.S. Commission, 12th Report Appendix Pt. IV. Belvoir Castle Vol. (1888).

Historie of the Arrivall of Edward IV in England. ed. J. Bruce, Camden Soc. (1838).

Holinshed Chronicles, 1577.

Household Accounts.

Incerti Scriptores Chronicon II.

Leland, *Itinerary,* ed. T. Hearne. (1460–83). 1774.

Letters of Kings of England, ed. Halliwell. (1846).

Letters of Margaret of Anjou.

Lords' Report, App. iv. 1829.

Manner and Guiding of the Earl of Warwick at Angers.

Marche, Olivier de la. *Memoires.*

Myers, A. R. *Household of Edward IV.* (1953).

Paston Letters. (ed. 1897).

Privy Council Proceedings, Henry VI.

Rerum Scotiarum Historia, (ed. 1697).

Rymer. *Foedera XI.* (1709).

Statutes of the Realms. Ed. IV. (1810).

Stow, J. *Annals of London* (1615).

—— *Survey of London* (1598).

Stubbs, Wm. *Constitutional History of England, iii.* (1874).

Three Fifteenth Century Chronicles, ed. Gairdner, Camden Soc. (1880).

Vergil, Polydore. *English History,* ed. Ellis, Camden Soc. (1844).

Vetusta Monumenta iii, Plate 7. (1796).

Warkworth. *Chronicle of the First Thirteen Years of Edward IV,* Camden Soc. (1839).

Warrants for Issues. Edward IV.

Wars of York and Lancaster, ed. Thompson. (1882).

Waurin, Comte J. de. *Recueil des Anciennes Chroniques d'Angleterre.* (1859).

Westminster, Chronicle of, Ch. xxvi. (1480–82. 2nd ed.)

Worcester, Wm. of. *Annales Rerum Anglicanum,* ed. Stevenson (1864).

Wright. *Political Poems and Songs.*

Wriothesley, C. *Chronicle,* ed. Hamilton, Camden Soc. (1877).

Writs of Privy Seal.

INDEX